Unsettled Belonging

Unsettled Belonging

Educating Palestinian American
Youth after 9/11

THEA RENDA ABU EL-HAJ

The University of Chicago Press
Chicago and London

Thea Abu El-Haj is associate professor of education and an educational anthropologist at Rutgers University. She is the author of *Elusive Justice: Wrestling with Difference and Educational Equity in Everyday Practice.*

The University of Chicago Press, Chicago 60637

The University of Chicago Press, Ltd., London
© 2015 by The University of Chicago
All rights reserved. Published 2015.
Printed in the United States of America

24 23 22 21 20 19 18 17 16 15   1 2 3 4 5
ISBN-13: 978-0-226-28932-8 (cloth)
ISBN-13: 978-0-226-28946-5 (paper)
ISBN-13: 978-0-226-28963-2 (e-book)
DOI: 10.7208/chicago/9780226289632.001.0001

Library of Congress Cataloging-in-Publication Data

Abu El-Haj, Thea Renda, author.
    Unsettled belonging : educating Palestinian American youth after 9/11 /
Thea Renda Abu El-Haj.
        pages cm
    Includes bibliographical references and index.
    ISBN 978-0-226-28932-8 (cloth : alk. paper) —
    ISBN 978-0-226-28946-5 (paperback : alk. paper) —
    ISBN 978-0-226-28963-2 (ebook) 1. Palestinian Americans—Social conditions.
    2. Palestinian Americans—Ethnic identity. 3. Identity (Psychology) in youth.
    4. Minority students—Social conditions. I. Title. II. Title: Educating Palestinian
    American youth after 9/11.
    E184.P33A28 2015
    305.8992'74073—dc23

                                                        2015013434

♾ This paper meets the requirements of ANSI/NISO Z39.48-1992 (Permanence of Paper).

For my daughters, Reem and Saria Rosenhaj, who "walk the walk"—living comfortably with the complexity of multiple belongings. Your unflagging commitments to creating loving, inclusive, and just communities wherever you are make me hopeful for our future.

And for my husband, Steve Rosenzweig. Your capacity for greeting every person you meet with great compassion has taught me so much about living with integrity and for justice.

Contents

Introduction

For Khalida Saba,[1] September 11, 2001, was no ordinary day. It was the first day of her freshman year at Regional High, a large city public school in the northeastern United States. Although it was not the first day of the new academic year, it had taken a few weeks for her parents to successfully register Khalida and her sister, and as a result the girls were beginning their freshman year a little late. Khalida had just returned from a seven-year sojourn in her family's small village in Palestine. Born in the United States, Khalida, accompanied by her mother and siblings, had moved to the occupied West Bank when she was seven. Her parents had decided to raise their children in their family village so that Khalida and her siblings would develop strong roots in Palestine, Arabic language fluency, and a deep knowledge of cultural, religious, social, and political life in the *bilād*[2] (homeland). This arrangement worked well until the second Palestinian intifada (uprising) against the Israeli military occupation began in 2000. The harsh Israeli response to the intifada destabilized the little normalcy that had existed previously under the routine and pervasive restrictive conditions of military occupation; the increasingly punitive military repression of the uprising led to severe disruptions of economic, social, cultural, and political life. Among these many disruptions to everyday life were frequent school closings, and largely for this reason, Khalida's family decided to return to the United States in order to ensure that the children would be guaranteed an education.

Khalida was familiar with the unsettled emotions that a transition to a

---

1. All names of people and places have been changed to preserve confidentiality.

2. *Bilād* also means country in Arabic, but it is commonly used to invoke the idea of homeland as well.

new school in a different country engendered. She had weathered these feelings of not quite fitting in when she first went to Palestine. She remembered her initial struggles as she learned a new language and was teased by peers who thought she was too "American." She anticipated similar experiences and feelings as she began her journey at Regional High. Unfortunately, Khalida's transition to high school and a new country would unfold in quite unexpected ways, beginning from the very first day that she reentered the US educational system. Nothing could have prepared her for what she would have to face in the coming months and years.

Khalida's story of beginning high school on September 11, 2001, is intimately bound up with another incident that occurred there on that day. As news of the attacks spread, the school district decided to close all the city schools and send students and employees home. Regional High's principal, Jack Moore, was in the midst of juggling the complex task of shutting down one of the largest high schools in the city when a teacher marched into his office. Mr. Moore recounted that the teacher demanded he "round up" all the Palestinian students in the school. The principal was shocked and recalled that he responded, "That's absolutely insane. Why don't you just put a target on their backs?"

I begin with these two stories to illustrate the countervailing politics of belonging and citizenship with which this book is centrally concerned. On the one hand, I focus on how young Palestinian Americans navigated and constructed belonging and citizenship across transnational social fields.[3] At the same time, I examine their encounters with an exclusionary politics of belonging emerging out of the routine practices of everyday US nationalism *inside their schools*—a politics of belonging that was in place well before September 11, 2001, and that remains steadfast to this day. At the heart of these stories—and of this book—rests a question about disjunctures of citizenship. Taking an anthropological perspective on citizenship as lived experience through which people negotiate "the rules and meanings of political and cultural membership" (B. A. U. Levinson 2005, 336; see also Ong 1999; Rosaldo 1994; Yuval-Davis 2011), I analyze a fundamental schism between the ways the Palestinian American youth experienced and constructed transnational citizenship and belonging, and the ways they were positioned as "impossible

---

3. This concept of a transnational social field points to the uneven broader social, political, economic, and cultural processes that shape practices and identifications within these communities, whether or not people actually move, or move back and forth (Basch, Glick Schiller, and Szanton Blanc 1994; Fouron and Glick-Schiller 2002; Levitt and Glick Schiller 2004; Levitt and Waters 2002).

subjects"[4] (Ngai 2004) of the nation, despite their juridical status as citizens. I focus on school as the central site at which this disjuncture unfolds, for it is the primary state institution through which young people from im/migrant[5] communities encounter normative discourses of citizenship and belonging. Tracking this disjuncture as it manifested in the everyday lives of young Palestinian Americans, I have three primary goals in the book. First, illustrating the complex, flexible ways that the Palestinian American youth navigated belonging in transnational social fields, I shift from a focus on youth identities to an account of how these social identities are intimately bound up with questions of citizenship. Second, I aim to deepen our understandings of the processes through which im/migrant youth are racialized, focusing on the specific logics of everyday nationalism. Finally, I raise normative questions about educating for national citizenship in contemporary times when more and more people's lives are shaped within transnational social fields.

As members of a community engaged in an ongoing political project that aspires to independent statehood, the Palestinian American youth (and their families) engaged in myriad everyday practices and long-term strategies that constructed and reinforced a sense of belonging to a Palestinian national community. Khalida's parents' decision to raise their children in Palestine was not unusual for their community. Khalida and many of her peers had spent long stretches of time living in Palestine. Through their experiences there, they developed an affective rootedness to place and people—one that engendered a sense of belonging to the *bilād*. However, all of the youth with whom I worked, even those who resided solely in the United States, were engaged in everyday practices in their families and communities that constructed a sense

4. I borrow this term from Ngai (2004), whose work tracks the history of exclusionary, racialized US immigration policies. Ngai's work illustrates the ways that even after the recision of laws that restricted citizenship along racial lines, many communities continue to be constructed as "impossible subjects"—"alien citizens"—who can never fully be encompassed within the national imaginary.

5. I am following Arzubiaga, Nogeuron, and Sullivan (2009), who use *im/migrant* to denote the variety of people included in the category of immigrant. In the few instances when I use *immigrant*, I do so either to signal the terms a particular individual used or to reference particular theoretical frameworks on the social incorporation of migrants. The young people in this research included those born in the United States who migrated back and forth to and from Palestine, children of refugee-status Palestinians, children of immigrants who had come to the United States from other Middle Eastern countries and had not returned, and 1.5-generation youth. (Definitions of the 1.5 generation vary slightly, referring to persons who are born in one country and migrate to another before adulthood, or in some definitions before they reach the age of twelve.) *Im/migrant* destabilizes the term to show the flexible, changing trajectories of people's lives.

of belonging to Palestine and its people, through economic, social, cultural, and political activities. This Palestinian community, similar to many across the world, was committed to building and maintaining national conscious-ness across the generations (Hammer 2005; Schulz 2003). As such, and as I show in this book, through her experiences in Palestine, Khalida developed a deep sense of being Palestinian, one that informed (and was, in turn, con-structed anew through) everyday practices in the United States.

Khalida and other Palestinian American youth with whom I worked rooted their sense of belonging to Palestine, but they also counted themselves as US citizens, and they valued the power of this rights-bearing citizen-ship. Although, as I show, Khalida did not *feel* American in the same way that she would describe *feeling* or *being* Palestinian, she saw herself as a US citizen. Rather than being a primary source of belonging, for Khalida citizen-ship was a valued asset through which people leverage rights to economic, social, political, and cultural resources across transnational fields (Abu El-Haj 2007; Dyrness 2012; Maira 2009; Ong 1999; Sánchez 2007). US citizenship allowed Khalida and her family to access a range of rights that were lim-ited or unavailable under the Israeli occupation of Palestine. As illustrated by her story, when schools were closed in Palestine, it was her US citizenship that made it possible to continue her education. At the same time, it was her family's economic opportunities in the United States that supported many of her relatives in Palestine who were unable to make a sustainable living there. Citizenship, as lived experience, entails practices through which people act upon the world, negotiating social, cultural, and political membership (Abu El-Haj 2007; García-Sánchez 2013; B. A. U. Levinson 2005, 2011b; Lowe 1996; Lukose 2007; Maira 2009; Mangual Figueroa 2011; Ong 1999; Ríos-Rojas 2014; Sánchez 2007; Tetrault 2013; Yuval-Davis 2011). Critically, for Khalida and other members of her community, this lived experience of citizenship does not signal an opportunistic or instrumentalist view. Rather, these young people's awareness of unjust conditions such as statelessness; the abrogation of basic civil, human, and political rights many Palestinians face; and the heightened surveillance and scrutiny faced by many Muslim communities (and those mistakenly thought to be Muslim)[6] in the United States led many

6. In this book, when I reference *Muslims* or *Muslim communities*, I do not intend to suggest that Muslims experience themselves as a collective (in fact, Muslims represent a wide variety of faith traditions), or that all people perceived to be Muslim actually identify as Muslim. I use *Muslims* and *Muslim communities* to illuminate the ways in which people from a broad range of communities are often discursively conflated in the public imagination. Furthermore, racialized policies and practices often target these groups as if they were one and the same. See below for more detailed discussion of the racialization of these communities.

to be deeply committed to the ideals of equality and justice that they believe should be guaranteed to all people.

Khalida and other Palestinian American youth constructed and negotiated belonging and citizenship across transnational social fields and in relation to different national imaginaries (of which I will say more shortly). As a consequence, the sense of belonging and citizenship that they developed was complex and mutable, responsive to the multiple cultural, social, economic, and political contexts across which their everyday experiences unfolded. Unfortunately, the lived sense of citizenship and belonging that these young people developed was markedly different from the normative view of American citizenship they encountered most directly in their schools.

This normative view of citizenship was rigid and exclusionary, and it positioned their community as dangerous Others. The fact that a teacher at Regional High asked that the Palestinian American students be "rounded up" even before it was clear that the September 11 attacks had anything to do with Arabs or Muslims (and, in fact, had nothing to do with Palestinians) illuminates that Palestinians (and a widely cast net of similarly positioned communities) were *prefigured* as outsiders to, and enemies of, this state (Cainkar 2009; Jamal 2008; Gerges 2003; Suleiman 2002). The post–Cold War ideology through which a central conflict between the West and Islam was constructed (Mamdani 2004) was solidly in place well before the attacks on September 11, 2001, and continues to this day. The teacher's demand indexed an already existing politics of belonging that built boundaries of inclusion and exclusion in relation to the national imaginary.

In speaking of the politics of belonging, I reference the ways that feeling part of a collectivity—particularly a national collectivity—is never given, but instead is actively constructed through political projects (Anderson [1983] 1991; Appadurai 1996; Benei 2008; Bhabha 1990; Billig 1995; Scott 2007; Yuval-Davis 2011). This is as true of the construction of a Palestinian national identity as it is of an American one, and in this book, I track the constructions of both national imaginaries. Following a tradition in anthropology and philosophy, I use the language of an "imaginary" to suggest the ways that our sense of the nation—who belongs, what is shared, the norms and values espoused, and more—are *imagined* and *mutable*, constructed and reconstructed over time through discourse and practice (Anderson [1983] 1991; Appadurai 1996; Bhabha 1990; Calhoun 2007; Taylor 2002). Moreover, as Yuval-Davis reminds us, "The politics of belonging involves not only constructions of boundaries but also the inclusion or exclusion of particular people, social categories, and groupings within these boundaries by those who have power to do this" (2011, 18).

In this book, I center attention on US nationalism as a key mechanism through which an exclusionary politics of belonging is forged in the everyday practices of our schools. I argue that research on the processes of racialization in today's US schools has not paid sufficient attention to everyday nationalism (Benei 2008; Billig 1995; Calhoun 2007)—the discourses and practices through which the nation is imagined and constructed in everyday life—as a key mechanism through which some young people become "impossible subjects" (Ngai 2004) of the nation. Because schools are the central institutions through which youth from im/migrant communities are invited to "become citizens," the everyday discourses and practices through which the boundaries of the national imaginary are expressed, constructed, and contested are central, and underexamined, aspects of contemporary[7] educational research in the United States[8] (for exceptions, see Abu El-Haj 2010; Ghaffar-Kucher 2014; Lee 2005; Olsen 1997). I show how the educational experiences of the Palestinian American youth were inextricably bound up with these everyday negotiations over the boundaries of the US national imaginary (Abu El-Haj 2010). Who belongs to this nation? Who is "self" and "Other"? What kinds of people are viewed as capable of being "American" citizen-subjects? These questions implicitly and explicitly pervaded everyday discourse and practice at Regional High, and deeply affected the educational experiences and opportunities of the youth in this study.

In focusing on nationalism as a key mechanism through which this (and other) im/migrant communities are racialized, I also attend carefully to the relationship between nationalism and the United States' contemporary role as an imperial power. I am aware that invoking the term *imperial* comes with at least two risks. On the one hand, the term can appear too broad—an imprecise, impressionistic term better suited to leftist rhetoric of another era than to academic research. I do not intend to use this word in ways that flatten out complex geopolitical realities, or lay sole blame for contemporary conflicts in the Middle East and South Asia at the feet of a conspiratorial American empire. Nor do I suggest that the contemporary US "empire" is a mirror image of empires of the colonial era with designs on capture and sovereign control of territory, resources, and populations in foreign lands. If one risk in using the word *imperial* is painting a flat picture of a multidi-

7. In the United States, the study of the relationship between nation building and immigrant education is often the provenance of historians (e.g., Fass 1989; Kaestle 1983; Olneck 1989, 2001).

8. The relationship between the everyday practices of schools and the production of national citizenship—as a lived experience—has been studied far more extensively in other state contexts (for examples, see Benei 2008; Hall 2004; García-Sánchez 2013; Jaffe-Walter 2013; B. A. U. Levinson 2001; Ríos-Rojas 2014; Schiffauer et al. 2004).

mensional phenomenon, the other is ignoring the particular and contentious academic debates about the relationship between colonialism, empire, and imperialism, and the United States' particular position in relation to these terms (see, for a few examples, Harvey 2003; Maira 2009; Stoler 2006). However, it is beyond the mission of this book to engage these intellectual disputes. Rather, I use the term *imperial* to refer to the range of strategies of global dominance this nation engages that are characterized by explicit and more invisible forms of power exercised through economic, military, cultural, and political means, and result from a confluence of disparate US interests, influences, and alliances (Boggs 2003; Gregory 2004; R. Khalidi 2004; Maira 2009). I contend that understanding the United States as an imperial power is essential to comprehending the processes of racialization and exclusion to which the Palestinian Americans (and many other minoritized communities) are subject—processes that are not confined to, or bounded by, the borders of the nation-state.

Focusing on the United States as an imperial power reminds us of its ever-present roots as a colonial state, and the role it took on after World War II as the self-proclaimed defender of democracy worldwide (Gregory 2004; Melamed 2006). It is, perhaps, precisely this role that makes the term *imperial* and its companion, *colonial*, uncomfortable ones for many Americans to adopt in relation to this nation. The United States has anchored its national imaginary to the idea that particular democratic values—equality, liberty, diversity, and tolerance—are both fundamental to the fabric of American society and worthy of spreading worldwide. Over the past fifty years, with the legacies of US colonialism, slavery, and conquest fading into the historical background, and de jure racial discrimination erased from the legal code, a fantasy of American exceptionalism has been strengthened. Pease (2009) describes American exceptionalism aptly, as "the lasting belief in America as the fulfillment of the national ideal to which other nations might aspire" (7). It is the widespread belief that the United States has made progress, shedding its racist colonial legacy and fulfilling its promises of equality for all, that makes the term *imperial* seem, to many Americans, a poor fit for describing the contemporary nation. However, it is precisely the fantasy of the United States as an ideal for all nations that reveals how the national imaginary remains also an imperial imaginary.

Unfortunately, the belief that the United States represents an ideal form of government and a universal set of values has become a battering ram of US foreign policy, with detrimental consequences for many people across the world (Brown 2006; Das 2001; Melamed 2006). The spread of "American" values has served as a rallying cry to defend US military incursions and the promotion of the nation's economic and cultural policies in the international arena. In the post–Cold War era, the "Muslim world"[9] has come to occupy a particularly fraught position in relation to the United States and other Western nations. With the development of the ideology of a clash of civilizations (Huntington 1996; B. Lewis 2002), the West in general and the United States in particular have come to stand for modernity, progress, and their attendant values—individualism, equality, democracy, secularism, tolerance, and freedom—while Islam has been characterized in monolithic terms as a backward "culture" that is, at its core, undemocratic, oppressive, intolerant, and violent (Abu-Lughod 2002, 2013; Brown 2006; Mamdani 2004; Melamed 2006; Said 1978, 2001). Both the "Muslim world" and the people who are seen to belong to that world have been constructed as posing a particular kind of "problem" for democracies[10] (Brown 2006; Mamdani 2004), as a result of which they have been subject to a continuum of exclusions and violence. In recent decades, the United States' mission to "make the world safe for democracy"[11] has been felt most directly by people living in those regions where Muslims are a majority, and has also had serious consequences for people living in this nation who have been associated with those places.

This broader discussion of US nationalism, the role this nation plays on the global stage today, and the relationship between this nation and the "Muslim world" are deeply relevant to discussions of public education. As I show in this book, this nation is imagined and constructed—always in relation to Other geographies and Other peoples—not only in broadly circulating public discourses in politics and the media but also in the more intimate, everyday realm of schools. The discursive construction of a national imaginary structured the relationships and experiences of the Palestinian American youth in their schools. Through an analysis of local discourse and practice, I track the ways that everyday nationalism co-constructs kinds of people seen to be capable of being democratic citizens in relation to Others positioned as fundamental outsiders, not only because of a notion of their racial/ethnic difference but also because of the ways this difference is tied to their (puta-

9. I put this term in quotation marks to indicate that this is an imagined construction that glosses diverse countries and regions and peoples in deeply problematic ways (see Abu-Lughod 2013; Grewal 2014).

10. This is true not only in the United States. Political debates are raging about the inclusion of Muslims across European democracies. A full review of these debates is beyond the scope of this book; see, for just two examples, Ewing 2008 and Scott 2007.

11. This oft-quoted phrase was the one President Woodrow Wilson used in his justification for launching the United States into World War I.

tive) "cultural" inability to embody "American" democratic norms and values. Looking carefully at the particular discursive terms along which groups of young people are constructed as capable or incapable subjects of liberal states (Abu El-Haj 2010; Ewing 2008; Jaffe-Walter 2013; Ríos-Rojas 2014; Scott 2007), I deconstruct the specific mechanisms of exclusion through which these young Palestinian Americans were positioned as racialized outsiders in relation to the US national imaginary.

Everyday nationalism runs deeply, and often imperceptibly, through our schools, but it is rarely a focus of contemporary[12] educational research in the United States (for exceptions, see Abu El-Haj 2010; Ghaffar-Kucher 2014; Lee 2005; Olsen 1997). This book's ethnographic portrait illustrates my argument that we must begin to take nationalism and imperialism seriously as lenses for analyses of educational experiences and opportunities in this nation. Everyday nationalism constructs both conscious ideas and embodied feelings about who belongs to the nation, what the nation "stands for," and, importantly, the nation's place in the world. It structures ideas and expectations for citizenship. Understanding everyday nationalism at work in US schools complicates our descriptions of the processes through which im/migrant communities are drawn into the racialized social order of this nation. This book illustrates how newcomers' ability to become full members of US society is related to the ways America imagines itself in the world, and imagines Others in its midst.

The post–September 11, 2001, context offers a key historic moment to explore how everyday nationalism unfolds in schools. However, the issues with which this book is concerned are applicable well beyond times of war. School is centrally implicated in the discursive and institutional processes through which belonging and citizenship rights are created and negotiated for this transnational community, as well as others—and belonging and citizenship are always constructed in relation to national imaginaries. If we are to understand the disjuncture between the ways that many young people, such as Khalida, experience citizenship and belonging across transnational social fields, and the impossible expectations for citizenship and belonging they encountered in their schools, we must look directly at the question of US nationalism. In the conclusion of this book, I argue we must face up to and challenge the pervasive nationalism that—sometimes silently and sometimes belligerently—saturates our school practices and curriculum. We must draw upon the actual ways that many young people, like these Palestinian

12. See n. 7.

American youth, experience belonging and citizenship to shape new educational practices that support them as active citizens across local and global contexts.

The Ethnographic Project

> One of the hardest things for me growing up was to have to fight to be Palestinian. One of the hardest things from my youth was being told Palestine didn't exist and then not being able to find Palestine on a map in school. It was the first time I realized I had a contested identity. (Tamara, Palestinian American youth)

Tamara captures well the unsettling sense of contestation that many Palestinian Americans experience in relation to their identification as a nation without a state. Tamara's feeling of having a contested identity began well before September 11, 2001, transformed the lives of the young Palestinian Americans with whom I worked. In fact, I began conceptualizing this project before September 11, 2001. As the second Palestinian intifada unfolded in 2000, I was curious to investigate how young Palestinian Americans developed a sense of belonging and citizenship in relation to the US and Palestinian national imaginaries. As members of an imagined national community that is actively engaged in an independence movement, many Palestinians spread across the world remain affectively and politically engaged in this cause. Moreover, given that the US government has long favored Israel and its political actions, Palestinians (along with people from other Arab communities) living in the United States often find themselves at odds with US foreign policy in the Middle East (Stockton 2009). At the time when I began planning this research project, I was interested in new challenges that the processes of modern globalization and its attendant patterns of transnational migration were posing to the dominant understandings of the relationship between immigration and education (Lukose 2007; M. M. Suárez-Orozco 2001)—understandings that were largely framed by descriptions of differential processes of social incorporation into the receiving state (Portes and Rumbaut 2001; Portes and Zhou 1993).

At the same time, I was concerned with the absence of any discussion about Arabs as racialized communities in the literature on US education. Although racialized images and discourses about Palestinians (as well as other communities from MENA [the Middle East and North Africa] and South Asia) were entrenched in US cultural politics well before September 11, the literature that addresses US racial formations rarely included these communities in its investigations (Joseph 1999; Samhan 1999). (In fact, even a decade and a half after 9/11, these communities are rarely included in educational discussions of race and racism.) The few references to the experiences of Arab American youth in US schools at the time, for example, employed an ethnicity model that focused on cultural differences (Adeeb and Smith 1995; Banks 1997).

Arab Americans have long occupied an ambiguous position in the racialized landscape of the United States (Abu El-Haj 2002; Cainkar 2008, 2009; Jamal 2008; Joseph 1999; Naber 2000, 2008, 2012; Samhan 1999; Shryock 2008[13]). Officially, Arabs are classified by the federal government as part of the racial category "white," which includes persons of European, Middle Eastern, and North African origin. This designation was the outcome of the legal battles that early Arab immigrants fought and won after initially being deemed ineligible for citizenship because they were not considered white (Joseph 1999). This official designation reflects neither the diverse ways that Arab Americans identify themselves nor the ways that they are, in dominant public consciousness, imagined as distinct from "whites," while not fitting into other racial categories. The federal classification system, based on early twentieth-century residual notions of race as a biological concept rather than as an outcome of mutable sociohistorical processes, positions Arabs invisibly within the boundaries of whiteness and conceals the racialized discourses and practices to which these communities have long been subjected (Abu El-Haj 2002, 2005, 2006; Cainkar 2008, 2009; Jamal 2008; Joseph and D'Harlingue 2008; Naber 2000, 2008; Samhan 1999).

If Arabs occupy an ambiguous position within US racial formations, Muslims are even harder to locate. On the one hand, as a highly racially/ethnically diverse religious group, Muslims have never been considered a "race." Nevertheless, in Western imperial imaginaries, there is a long history through which Muslims have been racialized. They have been discursively constructed, not only as a religious group, but as fundamentally Other—ascribed essentialized characteristics—through processes of racialization (Joseph and D'Harlingue 2008; Naber 2008; Rana 2011; Said 1978).[14]

---

13. Although Shryock (2008) agrees that Arabs are positioned ambiguously within the US racial formations, this leads him to argue they should not be viewed through the framework of racialization. I and other scholars in this field disagree for the reasons I outline above.

14. Recent historical research points to the ways that the relationship between Catholicism and Islam shaped Spanish conquistadores' attitudes toward indigenous people in the New World; and the subsequent racial formations that developed in the Americas informed European colonization of the East centuries later (see Rana 2011). In the post–World War II period, the United States inherited the legacy of European Orientalism in relation to the "Arab" and "Muslim world."

These processes of racialization gloss ethnicity, religion, culture, and national origin, constructing an ill-defined category of Other that sweeps up a widely disparate group of people from MENA and South Asia. Although Muslims in general have been subject to processes of racialization, a particular configuration has emerged in the US political landscape that focuses specific attention on certain Muslim bodies as particularly threatening and Other. (For example, popular political or cultural discourses rarely invoke images of Indonesians or Albanians when referencing Muslims.) In this book, I sometimes use *Arab and Muslim* together. Although this configuration is deeply problematic, I use it (1) purposefully to indicate the ways these disparate and incommensurate groups are lumped together through the processes of racialization, (2) as an admittedly inadequate shorthand for diverse groups of people who have been cast together as problematic Others in the US national imaginary, (3) because the fact that the 9/11 hijackers were all Arabs brought particular focus to the configuration of Arab Muslim, and (4) because the focus of this ethnography is Palestinians who are Arabs, and mostly Muslim. (See also note 6.)

To theorize the racialization of Arabs and Muslims, I draw on Etienne Balibar's analysis of differentialist racism that understands race as a "transnational phenomenon" (1991, 17) tied to colonial legacies. As Joseph and D'Harlingue (2008) explain:

> Theorizing differential racism, which operates through the tools of essentialism, allows us to analyze race beyond discourse of phenotype, while not disregarding moments in which discourses of phenotype still operate. Culture bears the marks of natural essentialism in ways that allow it to do work imagined in the discourse of phenotype. The work of differentialist racism is to construct essential cultural difference; to mark cultural distinctness as homogenous, static, and embedded; to install boundaries between cultures; and to reproduce and represent a hierarchy of cultures based on the essentialization of cultural difference. (232–33)

Thus, to understand the ways that racial formations, at this historic moment, sweep Arabs and Muslims (along with South Asians, Iranians, and many more nonparallel categories) together into one ill-defined group of Others, we must explore how race as a transnational phenomenon takes new forms. There is a long history of imagining these populations not only as coterminous with one another but as *embodying* an ambiguous, shifting set of imagined physical, psychological, behavioral, and cultural characteristics that mark out their essential difference from norms of white Europeans and Americans. One way to recognize the racialized nature of this grouping is to consider the violence that targeted a wide group of people (many of whom were neither Arabs nor Muslims) in the aftermath of September 11, 2001. However ambiguous and shifting this group is, certain *bodies* are imagined to be Arab or Muslim— bodies that are seen to entail particular strange or dangerous behavioral, psychological, and cultural traits. Moreover, as with all racial formations, there are discursive and material consequences to these racializations. Within the public imagination, Arabs and Muslims have occupied unenviable positions as, for example, enemies of the state, opponents of freedom and democracy, and oppressors of women. The material consequences for people perceived to be members of these communities are also long-standing. Violence against people perceived to be of Arab, Iranian, or South Asian origin constitutes an ongoing—although rarely recognized—problem in the United States (Ahmad 2002; Cainkar 2009; Jamal 2008; Naber 2000; Volpp 2002). Legislative, legal, and policing practices have denied Arabs, and Muslim communities, basic civil rights, even before September 11, 2001, and led, in its aftermath, to more routine surveillance, detention, and even extraordinary rendition. Thus, in planning this research, I wanted to track the impact of processes of racialization on Palestinian Americans in their US schools.

In developing this project, I drew not only on my intellectual interests, but also on deep knowledge about these issues that I had developed as a Palestinian American. My experiences growing up in Iran and Lebanon, and spending significant time with my father's family in Jerusalem shaped a sense of belonging and political commitments to a broader Palestinian community. I had good reason to believe that the young people with whom I planned to work might also have forged a sense of belonging to Palestine as an imagined homeland or an actual place. At the same time, although my K–12 education took place in other countries, my experiences in college and later as a teacher and researcher gave me plenty of reason to think that Palestinian American youths' education would be, at least in part, shaped by the dominant frameworks through which the Palestinian-Israeli conflict is understood in this country, and by their position as a racialized community. However, despite our shared identifications as Palestinian Americans, I do not claim any insider status in relation to the young people with whom I eventually worked. Enough separated us in terms of age, education, and life experiences, and I knew I would have to earn their trust before doing this work. I had no knowledge of the particular forms and meanings that belonging and citizenship would take for the local community with whom I worked. As Palestinians living in the Occupied Palestinian Territories renewed the struggle for independence due to frustration with the failed promises of the Oslo Accords, I wanted to understand what this meant for young Palestinians living in the

United States and attending US schools. I wondered how they would develop a sense of belonging and citizenship across these transnational social fields, and I wondered what kinds of racialized discourses about their community they were encountering in their schools.

September 11, 2001, both heightened and reshaped the scope and salience of the project that I was in the process of developing. An investigation of how Palestinian American youth forged a sense of belonging and developed citizenship practices within transnational social fields now had to account for their new position in relation to the United States' rearticulated national imaginary, which brought focus to Muslim and Arab communities. In this book, I highlight the young people's national (Palestinian) over religious identifications because the young people described themselves first and foremost as Palestinians. However, as I describe throughout the book, national and religious identifications often coexist, blend into each other, and shape how other people viewed the young people.

Thus, a research project conceptualized before September 11, 2001, became one I undertook only in its aftermath. And, given the climate that the Palestinian Americans faced in their schools and communities, I shaped the work to follow in the traditions of both critical and action-oriented[15] ethnography (for overviews, see Foley, Levinson, and Hurtig 2001; Foley and Valenzuela 2005). As I learned about the conditions that many Palestinian (as well as other Arab and Muslim) youth were facing, particularly in their schools after 9/11, I felt the need to support them in examining and articulating responses to the challenges they confronted. It was through cofounding an after-school club for youth in one local high school in a large city, and leading a teen video camp at an Arab American community arts organization,[16] that I met most of the participants in this research. Through that work, I was able to build the kinds of connections and relationships necessary to conduct research with a community that found itself vulnerable to the hostility of many members of the general public, and frightened by new levels of scrutiny and surveillance from the state.

15. This book does not focus on the action-oriented aspect of this work. However, in the context of both the Regional High after-school club and a summer teen video camp, I taught and supported young people as they first learned to investigate and then created artistic media to speak back to dominating images of, and oppressive conditions facing, their communities (see Abu El-Haj 2009b).

16. This community arts organization was founded in the summer of 2002 with the explicit goal of providing a place for Arab American children and youth to develop the knowledge and skills to respond to the conditions facing their communities and to reach out to other communities to be educated about Arabs, Arab Americans, and the Arab world.

THE RESEARCH PROCESS

In the wake of 9/11, a local Arab American community organizer, Mazen Khallil, asked me to join him to meet with parents and school personnel at Regional High, the high school that served the largest percentages of Arab American students in the city. Mazen knew from parents in the community that there were conflicts in the school—conflicts that predated 9/11 but had been exacerbated in its wake. In the past, Mazen had been called by the school on several occasions to help calm tensions when there had been fights between Arab youth and other ethnic, im/migrant groups. Mazen had developed a good relationship with the school's principal, Jack Moore, and the school social worker, Robert Malloy, who were both concerned that 9/11 would have repercussions for the Arab American students in the school. Through a series of meetings we had with parents, administrators, and students, I began to develop a picture of a school climate that many of the Arab students experienced as tense and hostile.

As a result of what I was learning, in the fall of 2003, three Arab American colleagues from a local Arab American community arts organization and I joined a concerned activist Regional High social studies teacher, Anne Larson, in forming an after-school club for Arab youth. Although there were some Arab American youth from other Middle Eastern countries in the school, the majority were Palestinian, and it was these students who chose to attend the club and take leadership roles in it. The club created opportunities for the Palestinian Americans to share and collectively analyze their experiences, and, through a variety of media (writing, photography, and video), to develop critical responses to the dominant and dominating images and narratives about Arabs and Muslims. With the resources of the Arab American community arts organization, we were able to bring in a photographer during our first year, and a film educator during our second, to work with the youth to represent their experiences through artistic expression. The students displayed the photographs and other artistic products within the school. The films that these young people produced were disseminated to wider audiences through youth film festivals, local community events, and teacher workshops.

For three years, I facilitated and documented the club's activities, and as I got to know the students, I invited them to participate in the larger research project. I wrote field notes and, whenever possible, digitally recorded[17] the

17. It was not always possible to audiotape our meetings. Although there was a core group of consistent attendees, other students dropped in and out, and they were not always comfortable with digital recording.

after-school meetings. I conducted thirteen in-depth ethnographic individual interviews with members of the youth club, and with relatives and peers attending Regional High to whom the group members introduced me (their ages ranged from fourteen to nineteen). In addition, in the second year of this project, I invited four students (Khalida Saba, Samira Khateeb, Adam Mattar, and Zayd Taher) to be focal participants for this research. I chose these four young people because they were representative of a range of experiences found in the community, including extensive to no residence in Palestine; different levels of fluency in English and Arabic; enrollment in an ESL (English as a second language) or a mainstream academic track; and postgraduate expectations from no plans to pursue higher education to a desire to attend a four-year college. A research assistant and I conducted participant observation with these focal students, shadowing them through their school days, and on occasion in community and family settings. We interviewed each focal student multiple times throughout the shadowing process, and conducted extensive interviews with all but two of these focal students' teachers, as well as the department heads of English, social studies, and the ESL program; the vice-principal responsible for student affairs; the principal; and the school social worker (a total of twelve). I also interviewed the teachers who sponsored our after-school club (Anne Larson and Mira Rubin), and the director of multicultural curriculum development for the school district, May Liu.

Following the period of intensive fieldwork (from 2003 to 2006), in the 2008–9 academic year, another research assistant and I conducted a round of life history interviews with a broader group of twelve Palestinian American youth (ages fifteen to twenty-four), including some who attended Regional High, others who attended area schools with smaller concentrations of Arab youth, and some who were now university students. In addition to providing a wider data set, these interviews offered perspectives on the experiences of young people who had attended different schools in the area, and they allowed me to hear from several youth who, after graduating from Regional High, had matriculated into a four-year state university. (None of my focal students and only one of the girls in the original group had matriculated directly into a four-year college or university.) At this time, I also reconnected with a number of the youth from the after-school club, catching up on their lives, and in the case of one of the focal students, Samira Khateeb, conducting another in-depth interview.

A third source for data collection (through participant observation and formal interviews) was the local Arab American community arts organization, where, for two summers, I cotaught a video workshop for teenagers, and for a third summer I documented, but did not teach, the program (see

Abu El-Haj 2009b). The camp drew young people from diverse backgrounds (Arab as well as non-Arab) living in both the city and its surrounding suburbs, a number of whom were Palestinians. I met four of the young people whose voices are represented in this book (Zayna and Kamal Sha'ban, Musa Baladi, and Lena Deeb) through my work at the camp.

All research has its limitations, and mine is no exception. While I had hoped to include parents' perspectives in this research, multiple factors led me to focus my attention on the youth rather than the families. The demands of a new job that had me commuting several hours from my research site meant that I needed to scale back my ambitions for this project. In addition to the difficulties that ensued from these logistics, however, there were more significant barriers to including parents that were as much a consequence of their busy lives as they were of the broader post-9/11 climate of scrutiny and suspicion that affected their desire to participate in this research. Although I spoke with parents informally in different contexts (community meetings, weddings, in the home) and for different purposes (for example, helping parents find a lawyer to contest a school expulsion), and all but one parent readily agreed to have their children participate in the research, few agreed to be formally interviewed. I do not have enough data from parents to be able to confirm the significance of themes and patterns that emerged from the limited interviews I conducted, and therefore their perspectives are not included in this book. Since my concern has been to understand the perspectives of Palestinian American youth on belonging and citizenship, I have made peace with this research limitation.

THE COMMUNITY AND ITS CONTEXT

Although, as I described above, this research draws on three sources of data (ethnographic data from Regional High, interview data from a broader group of Palestinian youth living in the same city, and ethnographic data from the Arab American community arts organization's summer camp), the focal context was the community of Palestinian students at Regional High. The majority of young people who attended Regional High, and all four of the focal students, are members of a closely knit Palestinian Muslim transnational community residing in a large US city.[18] Most of their families came from the

18. According to the demographic count of the local Arab American community organization, at the time I began my research, there were approximately ten thousand Arabs and Arab Americans living in a city of approximately 1.5 million residents. Palestinians comprised over half of this Arab community. However, the organization's demographic count was significantly

same village, which I call Irdas, in the occupied West Bank near Jerusalem. (Of the four focal students, three [Adam, Khalida, and Samira] were from this village. The fourth, Zayd, was from a different town near Ramallah.) The first member of this community to migrate to the United States did so in 1908; however, beginning in the 1960s, and intensifying throughout the 1980s and 1990s, more families migrated because of the economic and political conditions engendered by the Israeli occupation. Most of the families own small businesses or work as sales clerks and managers in family-owned and local businesses. Many of the families financially supported relatives in Palestine (or other Arab countries) because of the difficult economic and political conditions.

Born in the United States, a majority of these young people, including three of the four focal students, had spent many years living with relatives in Palestine. As I discuss in detail in chapter 1, many parents made the decision to raise their children in their hometowns in the occupied West Bank. Parents wanted their children to benefit from a religious, linguistic, cultural, and political education they could not get in the United States. Typically, mothers took their children to live with their extended relatives in Palestine while the fathers remained in the United States to work. The families were often reunited during summer vacations. However, many of the families that had lived in Palestine in the 1990s returned to the United States after the inception of the second intifada in 2000 made daily life in the West Bank difficult and risky.

Although most of the youth in this research, particularly those who were part of the Regional High community, had lived in or visited Palestine, some had not. Some families felt that the educational opportunities in the United States provided more possibilities for future economic success. Others could not afford the cost of traveling to visit relatives during summer vacation. Still others were members of families displaced and dispossessed in the 1948 and 1967 wars, and these families had ended up living in Jordan, Syria, and Iraq before migrating to the United States. The parents of two of the youth in this research, Zayna and Kamal Sha'aban, were refugee-status Palestinians until first the mother, and then the father, obtained US citizenship. One of the young men, Musa Baladi, was a Palestinian with Israeli citizenship whose

---

higher than that of the US Census Bureau, which listed residents claiming Arab ancestry at 5,119. By 2010, the US census showed a 21 percent growth in the state's population claiming Arab ancestry, with a slightly higher rate of growth for the city (with a total population of just over 8,000) (Arab American Institute Foundation 2011). For a number of reasons, the US census tends to undercount Arab Americans.

parents had moved to the United States when he was five because of the discriminatory employment conditions they had faced. Despite these different migration trajectories, all of the youth identified as Palestinians and considered Palestine their "homeland." In chapters 1 and 2, I discuss in detail the meaning and parameters of Palestinian identity and belonging, and how this sense of identity and belonging evolved from their experiences living in transnational social fields. A majority of these young people lived in close proximity to extended family members and socialized almost exclusively within this network; most spoke Arabic in their families and with their peers; they were exposed to Arab satellite television in their homes; and they were in regular contact with relatives in Palestine and other Middle Eastern countries. As a result, whether they had actually experienced life in Palestine or not, the youth were all connected to the Palestinian national imaginary through transnational practices of everyday life.

REGIONAL HIGH SCHOOL

Although I interviewed Palestinian American youth from many different schools, I conducted my school-based ethnographic work at Regional High, the school at which I established the after-school program and from which most of my participants, and all of my focal students, were recruited. Regional High is one of the largest and most racially/ethnically diverse high schools in its city.[19] The massive two-story building occupies a square city block on a large thoroughfare. In the early morning hours, a long line extends around the block as students wait impatiently to pass through the metal detectors and have their bags scanned. During passing times between classes, the hallways can feel overwhelming, a semiorderly crush of teenagers and adults being directed by the commanding voices of the school's nonteaching assistants and security personnel. Educators talked with pride about the school as a symbolic United Nations in which, at the time of this research, fifty-nine languages were spoken; as one walked the hallways, this international diversity was quite audible.

19. School district statistics for 2003–4 (the year I began intensive fieldwork at the school) listed white students as the largest racial group (1,424 students) and black students as the second largest (1,061 students); Hispanic and Asian / Pacific Islanders comprised the next largest groups (494 and 483, respectively); and the school lists six American Indian students. The district keeps no record of Arab students because, following federal guidelines, they are categorized as white. Administrators and students estimated there were around 100 Arab students enrolled in the school at any given time. I met 40 over the course of this research, most of whom identified as Palestinian.

In a city where many neighborhood high schools suffered from a lack of public confidence, Regional High was a sought-after placement. Despite the routine security screening and the presence of police officers in the school, the school was generally considered a safe place. It was, however, the school's academic options that made it especially attractive to families seeking a good public education for their children. Regional High boasted a magnet program and an advanced placement (AP) track. Numerous sports and clubs enhanced its reputation in a district where many such programs had been cut. Hallways and classrooms were lined with posters encouraging students to be academically successful and seek out a college education. Over the course of my fieldwork, I heard teachers, guidance counselors, and administrators lecture students to think seriously about a future college career.

However, for the students with whom I worked, this college-bound message seemed more rhetoric than reality. The vast majority of the Palestinian American students were housed in the low-track small learning communities, or in the school's English as a second language program, through which they had little access to the types of curricular opportunities that would lead to the "American Dream" that so many of their teachers confidently espoused. As my research assistant and I shadowed students through their school days, we observed classroom after classroom in which students were participating (and not participating) in schoolwork that did not demand deep or critical engagement with the subjects they were studying. Typical activities included entire periods spent copying outlines of textbooks or lists of vocabulary words from the board without guidance from or conversation with teachers; viewing movies that had nothing to do with the subject matter at hand; and cutting and pasting information from the Internet. The seniors' culminating project for their computer class was a PowerPoint presentation of a state report for which students copied and pasted pictures of the state flower, animal, flag, and so forth from the Internet.

I must note that, although these were typical academic experiences for the young people in my research, they cannot be generalized to the experiences of all students in this school. There were strong teachers in the school—two of whom were sponsors of the after-school club—who engaged students in thoughtful, critical reading and research experiences. There were, as I mentioned above, several academic programs that had earned good reputations in the district. However, with the exception of one Palestinian American girl, Sana Shukri (who, unfortunately, did not want to be one of the focal students for this research), none of the youth with whom I worked had access to those programs and teachers. This was partly the luck of the draw. Anne Larson, the social studies teacher who initially sponsored the after-school club, had taught some Palestinian American students in previous years, but none were in her classes during my tenure at the school. In addition, Ms. Larson left the school before I commenced fieldwork with the focal students. However, the academic experiences of the majority of these youth also reflected typical patterns, well documented in the educational literature, by which students from racially minoritized im/migrant communities are often segregated from white peers and/or are exposed to less academically challenging education that leads to fewer opportunities for higher education (for examples, see Lee 2005; Lopez 2003; Olsen 1997; Valenzuela 1999).

This was not a study about students' academic opportunities and out-comes, and as such, I do not want to stretch the credibility of the data to make generalizations about the academic education of the Palestinian American youth. The picture I am able to offer about their academic opportunities and experiences is impressionistic. Had I been more interested in these academic questions, I would have designed a different study and made sure to collect data across the different school tracks. Nevertheless, the data from shadowing offered a view into the young people's daily experiences of sitting in class-rooms that were boring, characterized by rote exercises and a lack of critical engagement. And, of course, these observations allowed for moments when the questions that were at the front of my research agenda came to the fore.

Palestine: A Brief Introduction

For readers unfamiliar with the history of modern Palestine, and the Palestinian-Israeli conflict, I offer a brief sketch of this complex history.[20] I do so, however, with reservation. This is a history that, particularly in the United States, provokes quite heated debate, and it is impossible to do justice to the complexity of the issues, especially in such a short introduction. Although there is no one definitive history to any conflict, there are critical and verifi-able events that occurred, and I aim to convey key junctures that led to the current "facts on the ground" that affect the everyday lives of Palestinians. I offer this history from one (admittedly not the only) Palestinian perspective. Given that this book offers an account of Palestinian American youth, I be-lieve it is critical for readers to have a general understanding of how Palestin-ians make sense of the history and politics of the Palestinian-Israeli conflict, as well as to have some idea of the conditions shaping the lives of Palestinians today.

20. For interested readers, detailed histories of Palestine include R. Khalidi 1997, 2006; Kim-merling and Migdal 2003; and Kramer 2008.

The late 1800s offer a starting point for understanding the source of the current conflict. At that time, Palestine was a part of the Ottoman Empire, a fully inhabited, largely agricultural land in which the majority of residents were Arabs. Although the majority was Muslim, Christian and Jewish communities were an important part of the demographics of the region. In the late 1800s, Palestine became a focal point for leaders of the modern Zionist movement in Europe. (Zionist leaders had considered Uganda and Argentina as possible sites for establishing a Jewish homeland.) This was a nationalist movement seeking a homeland for Jews facing persecution in Europe. Beginning in 1878, Zionists began to purchase, from absentee landowners, small parcels of agricultural land in Palestine, launching a project to build a state that would serve as a homeland for Jews. As Zionist settlers moved to Palestine through the end of the nineteenth and early twentieth centuries, they displaced Arab peasants from the lands they had traditionally tilled, generation after generation, in the established economic system. The colonial nature of the Zionist project is evident in the land settlement policies, displacement of indigenous inhabitants, and political aspirations for the establishment of a Jewish nation-state.

World War I and the dissolution of the Ottoman Empire opened a new historic chapter that would prove disastrous for the Palestinians. The British promised the grand mufti of Mecca that in return for Arab support for an uprising against the Ottoman Empire, they would help establish a unified, independent Arab state after the war. At the same time, with the 1917 Balfour Declaration, the British government stated its support for the establishment in Palestine of a Jewish national homeland. After the war, the victorious European powers divided the Middle East into territories that they would administer. The British occupied Palestine and were awarded a mandate by the League of Nations to administer the territory. The anger and frustration that developed as a consequence of the thwarted promises of Arab independence, and the increasing numbers of Palestinians displaced by the growing population of Zionist settlers, led to the Palestinian revolt from 1936 to 1939 against the British Mandate—a revolt that was crushed and left Palestinians without the leadership needed to face the upcoming challenges to their bids for independence (R. Khalidi 1997, 2006).

In the aftermath of World War II, the British asked the newly hatched United Nations to decide the fate of Palestine. The United Nations—a fledgling institution dominated by Western powers—did not consult the Palestinian population in this process. In 1947, the United Nations passed, by a narrow margin, a plan to partition Palestine into a Jewish and an Arab state, with Jerusalem to be administered as an international city—a plan that was established without the consent of the majority of the inhabitants of the land. Although, at the time, Jews represented 35 percent of the population and held only 13 percent of the land, they were awarded 56 percent of historic Palestine. The war that broke out in 1948 in response to this partition plan resulted in the mass expulsion of Palestinians from their historic homes. As a result of the massacre of Palestinian civilians and a specific plan of forced transfer engaged by Zionist paramilitaries well before the start of the war, and in concert with ordinary people's instincts to flee from violent conflicts, approximately 750,000 Palestinians (more than half the Arab population) were forced to leave Palestine during the war.[21] Despite the United Nations General Assembly's 1948 Resolution 194, which demanded that Palestinians be allowed to return to their homes if they wished and to receive compensation for their property, they were never allowed to return by the newly established Israeli state, nor have they been compensated for lost property. Although the actual numbers continue to be in dispute (R. Khalidi 2006), according to current statistics kept by the United Nations Relief and Works Agency (UNRWA)—the unit created in 1948 to minister to the needs of Palestinian refugees—some five million Palestinians still have refugee status more than sixty years after the establishment of Israel.[22]

Referred to as *al-Nakba* (the catastrophe, in Arabic), memories and stories of 1948 resonate in Palestinian communities everywhere. For many, particularly those who remain to this day living in refugee camps in Lebanon, Jordan, and Syria, the hope that, one day, they might return to their ancestral land is no idle dream. From the perspective of many Palestinians, resolution of the plight of refugee-status Palestinians must be a key component of any negotiated peace accord. For Kamal and Zayna Sha'ban, two of the youth in this study, the history of *al-Nakba* remained highly relevant. Their grandparents were expelled from their village (which was subsequently destroyed by the Israelis), and their parents were born refugee-status Palestinians. The struggle their parents underwent to secure legal citizenship centrally shaped the ways that Kamal and Zayna understood their opportunities in the United States and their political commitments to Palestine.

At the end of the 1948 war, the new state of Israel had expanded the territory assigned to it by the United Nations to 78 percent of historic Palestine. The remaining 22 percent of what would have been an independent Pales-

21. For accounts of what happened to Palestinians during the 1948 war, see Hirst 1977; Flapan 1987; W. Khalidi 2006; Makdisi 2008; Morris 2004; Pappe 2006.
22. United Nations Relief and Works Agency, "Who We Are," accessed December 26, 2014, http://www.unrwa.org/who-we-are?tid=93.

tinian state was placed under Jordanian and Egyptian rule. Jerusalem was divided in half, with Jordan administering the eastern section and Israel taking the western region. The war resulted in all Palestinians, whether they remained on their lands or not, being subject to the political and administrative rule of others. To this day, UNRWA is the primary provider of social and educational services for refugee-status Palestinians living in the West Bank, Gaza Strip, Jordan, Lebanon, and Syria. Different Arab countries took various approaches to dealing with the Palestinians in their midst. For example, in Lebanon, Palestinians continue to be denied citizenship, and this status affects every aspect of their lives, from education to work and political participation. Jordan has had a complex relationship with the Palestinians, who constitute a large portion of the population, posing challenges to Jordanian "national" identity.

Palestinians who remained inside the "Green Line" (the boundaries of the 1949 armistice negotiated at the end of the war) faced further dispossession of lands and denial of rights of citizenship, and the struggle for full equality as citizens of the state of Israel continues to this day. During and even well after the 1948 war, over four hundred Palestinian villages inside the Green Line were destroyed and their Palestinian inhabitants were dispossessed of land (Davis 2011; W. Khalidi 2006; Makdisi 2008). From 1948 to 1966, Palestinians inside the new state of Israel were subject to military law (Jiryis 1976). Through a series of administrative measures, many had their land confiscated and were unable to return to their homes. Some Palestinians continue to fight in the courts to return to their confiscated homes and land (Kimmerling and Migdal 2003), while many Palestinian villages remained "unrecognized," denied basic services, and subject to demolition orders (Makdisi 2008). To this day, Palestinians in Israel face systematic discrimination (Tocci 2010). For Musa Baladi, the only Palestinian Israeli citizen in this study, the military law to which Palestinians had been subject in the early decades of the Israeli state did not feel like distant history. His father's family came from the village of Kufr Qassem; in 1956, Israeli police massacred forty-eight villagers, including one of Musa's great-uncles, as they returned to their homes from work in their fields. It was the systematic discrimination against Palestinians in Israel that pushed Musa's parents to leave their homeland in the late 1990s. Unable to find work commensurate with their advanced degrees, Musa's parents moved to the United States to work at a major university. In making this move, they hoped to offer their children better educational and job opportunities.

Another shock wave for Palestinians came in 1967. At the end of a six-day war between Israel and Syria, Egypt, and Jordan, Israel occupied the West Bank and Gaza Strip—the remaining lands that had been part of the original

British Mandate of Palestine—and the Golan Heights, which was Syrian territory. In violation of international sanctions and law, Israel established a military occupation in the West Bank and Gaza, and laid claim to East Jerusalem,
and the Golan Heights through annexation. The occupation of the West Bank
and Gaza entails severe administrative measures that control all aspects of
Palestinians' lives, including rights of residence, movement, land use, travel,
water, and access to basic services. At the same time, the Israeli government
rolled out a settlement plan that transferred increasing numbers of Israelis
to the Occupied Palestinian Territories—a move that violates international
law's prohibition against changing the demographic composition of land that
is occupied. In developing an extensive network of settlements, Israel has expropriated Palestinian lands and natural resources, built a two-tier segregated
road network in the Occupied Palestinian Territories that Palestinians are
prohibited from using, and facilitated the development of an armed settler
population. Moreover, the military occupation places extreme restrictions on
all aspects of Palestinians' lives, regulating the right of residence, movement,
travel, and livelihood. Israel controls land and water use. Palestinians are subject to indefinite detention without trial and have little recourse to challenge
violations of their civil and human rights (Makdisi 2008).

Palestinians' political resistance to the conditions of colonization and exile
has taken a variety of forms. In the 1960s,[23] the Palestine Liberation Organization (PLO), an independence movement that included armed resistance,
developed out of the experiences of Palestinians living in refugee camps in
Jordan, Syria, and Lebanon. Inside the Occupied Palestinian Territories, the
independence movement took the form of civil resistance, which erupted
in the first intifada (uprising) in 1987. This intifada opposed the occupation through a combination of strikes, mass demonstrations (particularly by
youth), and grassroots civic development. Although initially Palestinian resistance was largely secular in nature, increasingly over the past few decades, an
Islamist opposition has developed and become an important presence in the
nationalist movement. Palestinian resistance to the occupation has included
both violent and nonviolent methods. Some members of the Palestinian resistance have engaged in bombings, particularly suicide bombings, against
both Israeli military personnel and civilians. A discussion of the reasons for
the rise of suicide bombings is well beyond the scope of both this introduction and my area of expertise, but much has been written on this topic in
the popular media as well as in academic venues. As a person who has lived
in a civil war and long been a pacifist, I do not condone the use of violence.

---

23. Yasir 'Arafat established Fatah in 1959.

Unfortunately, too often, especially in popular media in the United States, the Palestinian resistance movement is reduced to a singular view of militant terrorism, while Israeli military violence, which has taken a disproportionately larger toll on Palestinian civilian lives across the region, often remains invisible, and is typically cast as a legitimate form of self-defense. In order to understand the political perspectives that many Palestinians hold about the conflict, it is necessary to acknowledge the severe violence the Israeli army has wrought in its repeated military campaigns in Palestine and in Lebanon, and the routine violence that pervades the harsh occupation, as well as the Palestinians' ongoing unresolved dispossession. At the same time, it is important to highlight the multitude of nonviolent means through which Palestinians continue to resist the occupation.

In 1993, after several years of secret talks, the PLO and Israel signed the Oslo Accords, a declaration of principles upon which peace was to be negotiated at a future date. Although in the West these accords were mostly hailed as a sign that peace would, or could, soon follow, from the perspectives of many Palestinians, including leading members of the Palestinian intelligentsia (see, for example, R. Khalidi 2013; Makdisi 2008; Massad 2006; Said 1994), these accords proved deeply troubling. The PLO recognized Israel's "rights as a state to exist in peace and security"—a position it had taken since 1982, one that conceded to establishing a future state in the West Bank and Gaza.[24] However, Israel made no comparable concession. For its part, it recognized the PLO as the legitimate representative of the Palestinian people and agreed to commence negotiations with the PLO in the context of a Middle East peace process. The Oslo Accords allowed the PLO leadership to return from exile to the West Bank and Gaza and form the Palestinian Authority, which took over, in specified parts of the West Bank and Gaza, some of the administrative functions (municipal and police) that Israel had previously performed as part of its occupation.[25] Oslo left open all of the critical questions for the establishment of a Palestinian state (borders of the state, right of return of refugees, status of Jerusalem), ostensibly to be negotiated at some future time. Israel retained control over the borders, airspace, water and other natural resources, labor, tax collection, and rights of residence. Israel also closed off access to East Jerusalem for Palestinians from the Occupied Palestinian Territories, cutting them off from jobs, markets, and places of worship.

24. The PLO's initial position was to advocate for a democratic, secular state in all of historic Palestine.

25. Israel divided the Occupied Palestinian Territories into a series of areas (A, B, and C), giving control over only some of the areas to the Palestinian Authority.

It was the Oslo Accords that opened the doors for families of the youth with whom I worked to return to live in the West Bank and Gaza (see Hammer 2005). The years following Oslo saw the return of many members of the Palestinian diaspora wishing to participate in the building of a new nation. However, as the decade wore on, little seemed to change for Palestinians living under Israeli occupation. Israel stepped up its settlement development, nearly doubling the number of settlers in East Jerusalem, the West Bank, and Gaza. This meant a large increase in the amount of land expropriated from Palestinians for both settlement development and expansion of the network of segregated roads restricted to Israelis. Moreover, these armed settlers remained largely above the rule of law (Makdisi 2008). Settlers frequently used violence and intimidation against Palestinians, and it was not unusual for them to disrupt the agricultural harvests and uproot trees on Palestinian farmers' lands. Palestinians' lives were increasingly constrained by restrictions on work, travel, use of natural resources, rights of residence, and ongoing land expropriation. The Israeli military routinely used collective punishment measures, such as home demolitions and curfews, against the Palestinian population.

In 2000, Palestinian frustration with the ongoing Israeli occupation, the lack of progress toward an independent state, and the huge increase in settlement activity since the Oslo agreement, erupted into the second intifada. Ignited by Prime Minister Ariel Sharon's visit to the Dome of the Rock compound in Jerusalem accompanied by Israeli soldiers, mass demonstrations broke out across the Occupied Palestinian Territories. Israel responded to these demonstrations with intense violence. At the same time, suicide bombings and rocket attacks on Israeli towns increased. The Israeli response to all forms of resistance comprised severe military campaigns, including air strikes that targeted cities, refugee camps, and individuals. At the same time, the Israelis deployed ever-increasing restrictions that curtailed Palestinians' right of movement throughout the Occupied Palestinian Territories, closed schools, imposed draconian curfews, and detained huge numbers of Palestinians. Since the start of the second intifada, Israel has continued its policy of land expropriation and settlement building at an ever-increasing rate (see Aronson 2013; Makdisi 2008). It was this changing and deteriorating situation in the West Bank that led the families of many of the youth in this study to uproot once again and return to the United States to pursue economic and educational opportunities, and to live with a sense of general safety and security.

Since the time that the families of many of the youth in this research returned to the United States, two other major developments have seriously affected the everyday lives of Palestinians. In recent years, Israel has built a wall that cuts across the West Bank, separating Palestinians from the settlements, but also from one another, and in many cases, from their agricultural lands. This wall has restricted Palestinians' movement even further and has meant another huge land grab by Israel.[26] Land expropriations continue to this day. The second important change is that in 2005, Israel withdrew from the Gaza Strip, and since 2007 Gaza has been under an Israeli blockade that has resulted in an extreme humanitarian crisis there as people are cut off from even the most basic necessities. This humanitarian crisis has been exacerbated with the repeated rounds of Israeli military incursions, most recently in the summer of 2014, that kill large numbers of people, destroy innumerable homes, and severely damage basic infrastructure. Despite endless talk about restarting negotiations, there is no resolution in sight for the Palestinian-Israeli conflict (for a recent discussion of the US role in this process, see R. Khalidi 2013). This reality means that, at least for the foreseeable future, Palestinian communities across the world are likely to remain connected to, and actively engaged with, the politics of Palestine. The young Palestinian Americans in this book, similar to peers across the world, felt tenaciously connected to, and struggled for, a future in which an independent state of Palestine might be realized.

Im/migrant Education in an Era of Globalization and Empire

Questions about how young Palestinian Americans develop a sense of belonging and citizenship at the nexus of multiple national imaginaries are interesting ones to pursue, not only in their own right, but because they shed light on broader issues of im/migrant education in contemporary multicultural states. This book makes a specific contribution to the literatures on youth studies, im/migrant education, and citizenship education. My ability to contribute to these larger fields of research is enhanced by the focus on Palestinian American Muslim youth at this historic juncture. Before September 11, 2001, and the inception of the "war on terror," there was very little research on Arab youth (or youth from Muslim im/migrant communities) in US schools (for an exception, see Sarroub 2001, 2005[27]). Since then, the body of literature about this population is growing (for examples, see Abu El-Haj 2005, 2006, 2009a, 2009b, 2007, 2010; Ajrouch 2004; Bayoumi 2008; Bonet 2011; Ewing

---

26. In one of the many Kafkaesque aspects of the occupation, Israel expropriates Palestinian land if it has been fallow for three years, even as the government has refused to allow farmers access to their land situated on the other side of the wall.

27. Even though Sarroub's book was published after 2001, her research was conducted before then.

and Hoyler 2008; Ghaffar-Kucher 2009, 2012, 2014; Kibria 2007; Maira 2009; Mir 2014; Sarroub, Pernicek, and Sweeney 2007; Sirin and Fine 2008; Wray-Lake, Syversten, and Flanagan 2008); however, most of this research is not focused on documenting the everyday experiences of children and youth *inside US public schools* (for exceptions, see Abu El-Haj 2007, 2010; Ghaffar-Kucher 2009, 2012, 2014; Sarroub, Pernicek, and Sweeney 2007). Thus, one goal of this project is to bring attention to the nearly invisible experiences of Palestinian American Muslim[28] youth—youth who have lived their lives at the crossroads of two major political conflicts. However, it is the ways in which this community is positioned at these crossroads that allows me to analyze larger processes of migration, globalization, nationalism, and political conflict that also frame the lives of many youth from other transnational communities. As such, I am able to make a contribution to the literatures on youth studies, im/migrant education, and citizenship education in two related areas.

BELONGING AND CITIZENSHIP

My research tracks a different set of questions from those that have dominated the debates on US im/migrant education (for recent reviews, see Arzubiaga, Nogeuron, and Sullivan 2009; Gibson and Koyama 2011).[29] In concert with a growing field of scholarship, I call into question the immigration framework, for it implicitly takes the nation-state as the boundary for our investigation (Abu El-Haj 2007, 2009a; DeJaeghere and McCleary 2010;

28. Although all but one of the Palestinian youth in this study identified as Muslims, it is important to remember there is a significant population of Palestinians who identify as Christians. Moreover, some Palestinians identify as secular.

29. An exhaustive review of the vast literature on im/migration and education is beyond the scope of this book, but the difference between approaches that had until recently framed the literature and new approaches is worth noting. Scholars of contemporary US immigrant education have long sought to explain factors that contribute to groups' differential patterns of incorporation into the economy and society and the variability in youths' academic achievement (Portes and Rumbaut 2001; Portes and Zhou 1993; Zhou 1997), focusing on issues such as cultural, national, and religious identities (Lee 1996; Ramos-Zayas 1998; Sarroub 2005); the protective power of ethnic communities (Gibson 1988; Portes and Rumbaut 2001; Valenzuela 1999); sociohistorical trajectories (Ogbu 1987; Ogbu and Simons 1998); and the institutional processes of schooling through which youth come to take their place in the racialized hierarchy of the nation (Lee 2005; Lopez 2003; Olsen 1997; C. Suárez-Orozco, M. M. Suárez-Orozco, and I. Todorova 2008; Valenzuela 1999). Until very recently, research on im/migrant education has largely focused on questions of social incorporation into the host nation, tracking differential pathways by which young people from newcomer communities have made their way through school and into their adopted society.

Lukose 2007; Knight 2011; Maira 2009; Mangual Figueroa 2011; Sánchez 2007; Sánchez and Kasun 2012; M. M. Suárez-Orozco 2001). Shifting from a focus on the category of immigrant, I attend to contemporary processes of globalization and migration that lead many young people to forge a sense of belonging and citizenship across transnational social fields. Contemporary patterns of migration and the technologies of modern life that facilitate movement and communication across borders have raised new questions about the extent to which social incorporation into the new nation-state is to be expected in an age of transnational migration that may engender sustainable forms of diasporic cultural productions (Appadurai 1996; Fouron and Glick-Schiller 2002; Basch, Glick Schiller, and Szanton Blanc 1994; Levitt and Waters 2002; Levitt and Glick Schiller 2004; Ong 1999). The Palestinian American youth in this book offer a rich picture of the multifaceted, creative ways that young people navigate the complexity of living lives in transnational social fields.

Shifting away from a focus on the nation-state as the locus of im/migrant communities' affiliation and activities opens up new pathways for inquiry. Rather than exploring how young people navigate between cultural norms, values, and beliefs they learn in their homes and communities and those they encounter in schools and society (Gibson 1988; Olsen 1997), this framework suggests that, *around the world*, young people are producing multifaceted citizenship practices that creatively respond to the transnational fields across which their lives unfold (see, for example, Abu El-Haj 2007; Abu El-Haj and Bonet 2011; DeJaeghere and McCleary 2010; Dyrness 2012; Ewing and Hoyler 2008; Maira 2009; García-Sánchez 2013; Grewal 2014; Sánchez 2007; Sánchez and Kasun 2012; Knight 2011; Tetrault 2013). Thus, this framework moves us away from talking about youth as negotiating between cultural identities to thinking about how they develop discourses and practices of belonging and citizenship across these transnational social fields.[30] This means understanding young people as political, economic, cultural, and social actors who are

30. There is a vast literature on transnationalism that I do not review in this book. This literature includes debates about the definition and parameters of transnationalism (see Levitt and Glick Schiller 2004; Levitt and Waters 2002; Portes, Guarnizo, and Landolt 1999; Vertovec 1999; Waldinger 2008); descriptions of the kinds of activities in which transnational communities engage (e.g., Basch, Glick Shiller, and Szanton Blanc 1994; Ong 1999); the cognitive and imagined elements of transnationalism (e.g., Fouron and Glick-Schiller 2002; Wolf 2002); and questions about the long-term sustenance of these ties (Rumbaut 2002; Levitt 2002; Waldinger 2008; Waldinger and Fitzgerald, 2004). My focus is on the ways that young people's sense of belonging and their citizenship practices develop in relation to the transnational social fields (see n. 3) that shape these practices and identifications.

creating new citizenship practices that draw on, and in turn contribute to, the transnational fields across which their lives range.

The jury is still out on the question of whether and in what forms im/migrant communities will sustain transnational relationships over the generations (Fouron and Glick-Schiller 2002; Kasinitz et al. 2002; Levitt 2002; Rumbaut 2002; Waldinger forthcoming, 2008). However, the challenges these communities pose to traditional models of social incorporation into receiving states are salient whatever the long-term outcome of these transnational relationships may prove to be (Sánchez and Kasun 2012). In fact, much public political debate about immigration in multicultural democracies centers on the question of new im/migrant communities' willingness to let go of affiliations to their homeland. In the United States and many other Western states, these political anxieties have focused increasingly on Muslims, who are regarded as potentially dangerous to the extent that they do not view themselves as wholly "American" or "British" or "French" and so forth. However, the assumption behind these anxieties is out of step with the facts on the ground as many youth (and adults) across the world increasingly develop complex, transnational practices of belonging and citizenship. Aided by modern technologies and modes of transportation, the spheres of cultural, social, and political practices in which many young people routinely engage are not necessarily bounded by the arbitrary borders of nation-states (see, for example, Abu El-Haj 2007, 2009a; DeJaeghere and McCleary 2010; Dyrness 2012; Grewal 2014; Ewing and Hoyler 2008; Lukose 2009; Maira 2009; Miller 2011; Nabulsi 2014; Sánchez 2007; Tetrault 2013).

Although this research is of general interest in the area of im/migrant youth studies, I am particularly focused on US schools and on questions of democratic citizenship education. I understand democratic citizenship education from an anthropological perspective, which B. A. U. Levinson (2005) has aptly defined as "efforts to educate members of social groups to imagine their social belonging and exercise their participation as democratic citizens" (336). This means that rather than being primarily interested in the formal ways that schools explicitly educate students for citizenship (e.g., civic education, or government and history courses), I am more concerned with the quotidian lessons that young people get—both inside and outside the school walls—about what it means to belong to and participate in society (Baumann 2004; Hall 2002; Jaffe-Walter 2013; B. A. U. Levinson 2001; M. Levinson 2012; Mannitz 2004a, 2004b, 2004c; Mannitz and Schiffauer 2004; Sunier 2004; Ríos-Rojas 2014; Rubin 2007). Documenting the particular ways that these Palestinian American youth are creating practices of political, social, cultural, and economic belonging and citizenship across transnational fields, I raise questions about the normative models of citizenship education they encountered in their schools. Ultimately, I suggest we need new frameworks for citizenship education that better account for the actual ways that many young people negotiate belonging and citizenship in the midst of contemporary processes of globalization, mass migration, and conflict.

EVERYDAY NATIONALISM AND EDUCATION

This book makes a second key contribution to the field of educational research by strengthening our understanding of the central role that everyday nationalism plays in drawing youth from im/migrant communities into the racialized social fabric of this country. Contemporary analyses of this racialization process, and the critical role that schools play in this process, have focused on the differential and discriminatory educational opportunities offered to youth from various communities and the assimilationist frameworks that ask young people to abandon their cultural and linguistic resources (Lee 2005; Lopez 2003; Olsen 1997; C. Suárez-Orozco, M. M. Suárez-Orozco, and I. Todorova 2008; Valenzuela 1999). This literature shows that new im/migrant children and youth get pulled into two different Americas: either moving up the racial hierarchy to become white, or moving down into the racially minoritized black and brown underclass. While acknowledging that "white" and "of color" are socially constructed categories that change and shift over time, these categories are often taken to be self-referential (constructed by who is allowed to belong in one or the other category at a particular time). More difficult to track are the *everyday mechanisms* through which the categories of who can and cannot belong fully to this nation are established in ways that build a complex and uneven map of inequalities (for exceptions, see Abu El-Haj 2010; Ghaffar-Kucher 2014; Lee 2005; Olsen 1997).

The experiences of the Palestinian American youth allow me to explore those specific mechanisms of exclusion. I show how tenacious beliefs about the particular values taken to rest at the heart of the American national imaginary co-construct kinds of people capable of being democratic citizens in relation to Others positioned as fundamental outsiders because of their (putative) "cultural" inability to embody democratic values. I argue that these mechanisms of exclusion reflect cultural politics that create racialized Others—mechanisms that illustrate the ties between this nation's colonial/imperial past and present. My analysis of the relationship between the marginalization of Palestinian American youth and the production of the American national and geopolitical imaginaries (how relations between the United States and other nations are ideologically constructed) focuses on how these cultural politics *find traction in everyday life* in school. I focus attention on the everyday cultural politics through which categories of immigrant/native, outsider/insider are forged within our schools. I also pay attention to the ways that young people take up, respond to, and recreate these categories (see also Hall 2002; Lee 2005; Ghaffar-Kucher 2014; Olsen 1997; Jaffe-Walter 2013; Maira 2009; Ríos-Rojas 2014). I show that to make sense of these cultural politics, it is critical to foreground nationalism in our analyses of the education of young people from im/migrant communities, for at the heart of these cultural politics rest definitions of who can and cannot be part of the national imaginary—definitions that, as I show, many young people are calling into question in word and deed (Abu El-Haj 2007; Hall 2002; Jaffe-Walter 2013; Ríos-Rojas 2014).

Organization of the Book

Part 1 focuses on the ways that Palestinian American youth constructed a sense of belonging and citizenship within transnational fields. I investigate the distinction they made between *being* Palestinian, belonging to a Palestinian national imaginary, and *having* US citizenship, a status that accorded them a range of important rights that many in their community did not possess. Chapter 1 analyzes the ways that the youth and their families forged a sense of belonging to Palestine, its people, and its land. I explore the various long-term strategies and everyday practices through which this sense of belonging developed. I analyze the specific themes that organized the Palestinian American youths' understanding of what it means to *be* Palestinian, illustrating how the embodied feeling of *being* Palestinian is constructed through particular discourses and practices.

If the Palestinian Americans described themselves as first and foremost Palestinian, tied to a culture, people, land, and nation, they also identified as US citizens with attendant rights. Chapter 2 investigates how this identification with citizenship and the powerful rights it confers developed out of myriad experiences they and their families had due to the denial of citizenship rights. It was the contrast between rights-bearing citizenship and the denial of rights (particularly by the state of Israel) that led the youth both to feel appreciative of the guarantees of democratic citizenship and to see the contradictions when rights were not conferred equally on all people. Acknowledging the distinction Palestinian Americans make between belonging and citizenship, I argue against public conservative political discourses on immigration that see this as a problem for democracy; rather, I suggest that this distinction strengthened Palestinian Americans' sense that the rights of democratic citizenship should be due to all.

Part 2 turns attention to the mechanisms of exclusion that positioned the young Palestinian Americans and their community as outsiders to this nation. I argue that this exclusion occurred through normative discourses of liberal multicultural nationalism that saturate both public political discourse, and, equally important, the everyday discourses and practices inside Regional High. Chapter 3 sets the stage with a wide-angle lens, investigating public political discourse after September 11, 2001. I track the circulation of discourses of American liberal multicultural nationalism that simultaneously set up an oppositional relationship between the United States as a beacon to the world for liberal, democratic values and the "Muslim world." Drawing on critical recent scholarly work, I examine how this dominant discourse of liberal multicultural nationalism is intimately bound up with the United States' imperial ambitions. After examining these broadly circulating public discourses, I illustrate how these themes are echoed in school textbooks, in a curriculum controversy that occurred in the school district in which I worked, and in a student newspaper exchange at Regional High.

Chapter 4 takes this discussion of liberal multicultural nationalism right into Regional High, tracing the ways that everyday nationalism informed educators' discourse and practices. It shaped the educators' beliefs about the Palestinian American youth, and about the role that education could and should play in assimilating them to the liberal values of this nation—values that they assumed were inimical to the places and "culture" from which they came. I argue that the narratives through which this nation is imagined—narratives about *American* values of individualism, liberty, diversity, and tolerance—circulate in everyday practice inside our schools, co-constructing boundaries of belonging and rules for participation that excluded the Palestinian American youth from full participation. My goal in this chapter is to parse the specific terms through which the seemingly benign discourses of liberal multicultural nationalism construct the youth as racialized Others, illiberal subjects who belong to places presumptively ruled by violence and oppression (Gregory 2004).

Chapter 5 turns attention to moments when this "benign" liberal multicultural nationalism turns into a more belligerent politics of belonging that often emerges in times of war, silencing critique and dissent, particularly for the Palestinian American youth who were viewed as enemy aliens. I argue that this "hot" nationalism does not simply hatch in the moment of international conflict, and we must understand how it is rooted in the expressions of liberal multicultural nationalism that existed well before September 11,

2001. This chapter also focuses on the ways that the Palestinian American students contested this politics of belonging. I examine their everyday bids for citizenship, by which I mean their ways of making claims for belonging, and of challenging the United States to live up to its stated ideals of equality and justice for all.

In the conclusion, I focus on the disjuncture between the norms and expectations for citizenship education that align with nationalism, and on the practices of transnational citizenship and belonging as lived by the Palestinian American youth with whom I worked. I argue that in educational research and practice, we must focus more attention on everyday nationalism as a key mechanism through which inclusion and exclusion are negotiated in our schools. Ultimately, I argue we must draw lessons from the transnational citizenship practices that young people are constructing in order to reshape citizenship education that supports young people in attending to both the local and global contexts across which their lives range.

PART ONE

Belonging and Citizenship

1

"Trying to Have an Identity without a Place in the World"

To me to be a Palestinian, or, or just, not, not to be a Palestinian, but the idea of me being a Palestinian means that in some way or other I have to fight for the freedom of Palestine and the freedom of Palestinians. So, and oftentimes I have, I have socialist leanings. And so oftentimes these two things come into conflict with being an American. So when, when these two are in conflict I am a Palestinian, not an American. But at other times when you ask me about Barack Obama, when you ask me about, about [city] public schools, when you ask me about these, these types of things I am wholly an American. So it's, I'm, I'm, my identity's sort of flipping between these two constantly.

—KAMAL SHA'BAN

Kamal was a nineteen-year-old sophomore at a state university when I first interviewed him. Inspired by the early life of Che Guevara, Kamal aspired to become a physician and to dedicate his life to delivering medicine to Palestinians living in refugee camps. As the child of refugee-status Palestinian parents, Kamal had been fundamentally influenced by his parents' struggle to gain citizenship, and he well understood the power that legal US citizenship affords to those who have it. His father grew up as a refugee-status Palestinian in Syria. His mother, Amira, held Jordanian citizenship, but as a woman, she was unable to pass it on to her children. In her early twenties, Amira was fortunate to gain a US green card through her sister, who had managed to immigrate to the United States. In order to guarantee that her children would also have legal citizenship, Amira made sure that Kamal and his older sister, Zayna, were both born in the United States. Soon after each delivery, Amira had to return to Iraq to reunite with her husband, who, as a Palestinian with no state's citizenship, was unable to travel. As a result of their family's move to Iraq, in their early years Kamal and Zayna directly experienced the effects of violent conflict. When the war landed in their backyard in the form of an American bomb,[1] Amira and her children returned to the United States, living for many years without their father, until finally their attempts to secure him a green card succeeded.

---

1. The bombing was from US military actions to enforce the UN sanctions imposed against Iraq during Saddam Hussein's regime.

Kamal's life was intimately bound up with the unresolved historic and political conflicts that shaped his life and the lives of other Palestinian American families residing in the United States. These conflicts influenced the trajectory of Kamal's growing identification with the struggle for Palestinian national self-determination. When he first returned to the United States as a young child, Kamal recalled crying constantly at school because he could not speak English. The teachers often tried to help him by bringing in his older cousin to spend time with him. Once he gained English fluency, however, Kamal threw himself into being "just another American kid." This changed in middle school because of September 11, 2001. Initially, Kamal decided to hide behind the fiction that "I was American. I was Spanish, whatever." He told me, "I completely understood how alienated I might be, right, if I told people I was Arab." Kamal had been scared by experiences with people in his neighborhood who harassed his family because his mother's hijab made it evident that they were Muslims. However, slowly, as he moved through his later years in middle school and on to high school, Kamal began to embrace his Palestinian identity and speak out politically about Palestine. He described the change, saying, "I held up a [Palestinian] flag." Kamal began actively teaching himself about Palestine, not only through reading and alternative media, but by asking his parents and family members to tell him their stories. Through these stories, Kamal learned about his family's life in Palestine, their expulsion from their village in 1948, and his parents' history as activists working on behalf of Palestinian refugees in Syria. The more Kamal learned, the more he began to educate others about Palestine, and to plan a future dedicated to service on behalf of the Palestinians.

As Kamal described, this commitment to the Palestinian cause occasioned some conflict with his sense of himself as an American. For Kamal and the other youth in this study, the United States' close alliance with Israel and its foreign policy in the Middle East and South Asia created tensions about what it meant to be "American." At times, Kamal saw himself as "wholly American," particularly in relation to the promises of US democratic equality, such as the election of an African American president and the educational opportunities afforded by public schools and universities. Kamal identified with the equal rights that US democracy aspires to confer on its citizens. However, he also understood, not only intellectually but intimately, the powerful role that the United States played in the Middle East—one that supported the Israeli occupation of Palestine, had bombed his family's backyard in Iraq, and had launched the recent invasions of Afghanistan and Iraq. As Kamal's life story unfolded across several countries, and in relation to two national imaginaries, he developed a multifaceted, sometimes conflicted, sense of who he was and where he belonged. This complex, fluid, "flipping" sense of belonging led Kamal to develop social, cultural, and political commitments and to enact active citizenship practices in relation to both the United States and Palestine.

This chapter and the following one take up the question of how Palestinian American youth carve out a sense of belonging and citizenship within and across the imagined and actual landscapes of Palestine and the United States. Similar to youth from many im/migrant communities in the United States (Gibson 1988; Lee 2005; Maira 2002; Olsen 1997; Sarroub 2005), these young people often spoke of struggling to figure out where they belonged in relation to the differences they perceived between American and Palestinian cultural practices. However, for this community, these questions about cultural belonging were far overshadowed by—and, in fact, inextricably interwoven with—the politics of belonging raised by the Palestinian nationalist movement, the ongoing Israeli occupation of Palestine, the quest for the rights of citizenship, and the political context of the US "war on terror" (which I take up in part 2 of this book).

In this chapter and the next, I explore these questions of the politics of belonging. As I argued in the introduction, I aim to complicate the existing literature that addresses the social incorporation of youth from im/migrant communities living in the United States, exploring what we can learn by focusing on the experiences of youth growing up in transnational fields (Abu El-Haj 2007; DeJaeghere and McCleary 2010; Dyrness 2012; Ewing and Hoyler 2008; Maira 2009; Sánchez 2007; Knight 2011; Louie 2002; Wolf 2002). The stories of Kamal and the other Palestinian American youth challenge us to reconsider what can appear, at first glance, to represent conflicts between "home" and "host" cultures, or between family and school values and expectations. Instead, these stories suggest a need to analyze culture as the terrain upon which larger political conflicts about belonging and citizenship are played out (Abu El-Haj 2007; Abu El-Haj and Bonet 2011; Hall 2002; Lukose 2009). These young people's sense of belonging to a Palestinian national community calls into question the normative assumption that one-way social incorporation into the United States (or other receiving nations) is, *or should be*, the goal for youth from transnational communities (see also Abu El-Haj 2007, 2009a, 2010; Fouron and Glick-Schiller 2002; Lukose 2007; Maira 2009; Sánchez and Kasun 2012)—an assumption that invisibly structures not only research but also educational policies and practices. The disjunctive political experiences that these Palestinian American youth and their families had in relation to various nation-states shaped a different sense of belonging and citizenship for this community.

In addition, recent research with Muslim youth from im/migrant com-

munities living in the United States and other Western democracies has
sought to understand how these young people negotiate their religious and/
or ethnic identities in relation to their mainstream identities given the post-
9/11 political context (Ewing and Hoyler 2008; Ghaffar-Kucher 2009; Mir
2014; Mondal 2008; Sirin and Fine 2008; Zine 2001, 2006). Sirin and Fine,
for example, have documented multiple pathways of identity formation (hyphenated, parallel, or conflicted) these youth take. Ewing and Hoyler noted
that even as the middle-class South Asian Muslim youth in their study described feeling American by citizenship and culture, they were increasingly
aware of and connected to their religious identifications, and this tied them
to a worldwide community of Muslims. Mir explores the multidimensional
identities that young Muslim women forge as they "become themselves"
in relation to their Muslim communities and the mainstream community
(2014, 4). On the whole, this research has shown that the majority of Muslim youth are not alienated from the societies in which they reside, despite
often feeling religious or cultural disconnections from the dominant society
and experiencing prejudice and discrimination from the mainstream (see, for
exceptions, Ghaffar-Kucher 2009; Grewal 2014; Kibria 2007). This research
has been valuable in providing data that contradict the popular belief that
Muslim youth, and their communities, are generally hostile to the countries
in which they live, and thus potentially suspect. However, to some extent,
much of this recent focus on Muslim youth has been premised on a model
of immigrant acculturation that presumes the receiving nation is, and should
be, the primary locus of social and political engagement. The two chapters
in part 1 interrogate this model of citizenship and belonging, examining how
their experiences growing up in transnational fields educate young Palestinian Americans into other forms of citizenship and belonging.

Migration has not been a one-way ticket for many in this Palestinian community. For a majority of the youth, experiences living in the United States
and in the Middle East fundamentally shaped the meaning and affective
dimensions of belonging. Moreover, these young people are members of a
community that has worked for over a century to build and sustain national
consciousness in the face of ongoing political struggle for a state (Hammer
2005; R. Khalidi 1997; Said 1979). To do so, Palestinians living across the world
develop strategies through which they can continue to maintain a connection
to Palestine, even as they integrate into the countries in which they live (Abu
El-Haj 2007; Hammer 2005; Schulz 2003). This situation is not unique to
Palestinians. I argue that the assumption that integration should be the goal
for im/migrant communities fails to describe the meaning and parameters
of citizenship in modern times. The case of Palestinian Americans, then, il-

lustrates why debates over citizenship—on the ground, and in the academic literature—cannot be limited to questions about the extent to which modern democratic states can accommodate a multitude of linguistic, cultural, and religious affiliations. Citizenship and belonging for these young people involves civic and political practices shaped in transnational fields that are not, and cannot be, restricted to the borders of any one nation.

The Palestinian case represents a particular diasporic configuration because of Palestinians' unrealized nationalist aspirations and the role that the United States has consistently played in thwarting these aspirations (R. Khalidi 2013). However, the issues raised in this chapter and the next are relevant to youth from many communities that have migrated to the United States and other Western states due to ongoing and historic political conflicts, as well as the economic disjunctures wrought by those conflicts. Moreover, even in the absence of political conflict, more and more young people's lives are shaped in the crucible of modern globalization, with its attendant mass migration, dislocation of culture, and technological advances that allow people to remain connected to multiple places (Appadurai 1996; Basch, Glick Schiller and Szanton Blanc 1994; Levitt and Glick Schiller 2004; Ong 1999). Given this context, it is critical to understand how youth construct and negotiate belonging and citizenship through everyday practices in their homes, schools, and communities to reflect their ongoing (cultural, economic, social, and political) engagement with more than one nation-state—engagement that may or may not entail actual physical movement across borders (Abu El-Haj 2007; DeJaeghere and McCleary 2010; Dyrness 2012; Ewing and Hoyler 2008; Maira 2009; Sánchez 2007; Knight 2011).[2] These everyday practices constitute an implicit citizenship education—one that was at odds with the models of citizenship they would encounter in their schools. By listening carefully to the way that young Palestinian Americans imagine belonging and citizenship, I explore how youth from this and other transnational communities are reshaping the meanings and practices of citizenship and belonging in this era of globalization and mass migration (see Abu El-Haj 2007; Dyrness 2012; Fouron and Glick-Schiller 2002; Maira 2009; Sánchez 2007; Sánchez and Kasun 2012; Seif 2011). Understanding the complexity of belonging and citizenship for young people who grow up in transnational fields holds implications for education in modern multicultural democracies, a subject to which I return in the conclusion of this book.

2. Grewal's (2014) study of Muslim Americans seeking to find and define authentic Islamic identities through travel to, and study in, Muslim-majority countries complicates even further the portrait of transnational fields, entailing religious, not necessarily national, imaginaries.

In this chapter and the next, respectively, I take up two related questions raised by Kamal and his family's story, and echoed throughout the lives of the young people with whom I worked: that of belonging and that of citizenship. Palestinian American youth forged a strong sense of belonging in relation to the ongoing nationalist struggle for an independent Palestinian state. In this context, the affective sense of *being* Palestinian trumped other affiliations and often left them feeling tentative about their connections to their "American" identities. However, despite this hesitancy about claiming fully an American national identity, these young people identified strongly as US citizens. The encounters that they and their families had with the state of Israel and its military occupation, or with exile and statelessness, left them with an appreciation for, and commitment to, their status as US citizens and the rights it entails. Thus, for these young people, national identification and citizenship were not necessarily tightly interwoven categories. The lived experiences of these Palestinian American youth offer a window through which to reconsider basic assumptions of what it means to *feel* and *enact* "citizenship."

In the rest of this chapter, I examine how the sense of being Palestinian and belonging to a national community was continually produced through everyday practices that unfolded across transnational social fields. That is, these young people's sense of being Palestinian cannot be understood as an essential condition—a cultural residue—of the Palestinian diaspora. It reflects ongoing, everyday *work* that produces the nation and individuals' connections to this national imaginary. Thus, everyday practices in families and communities constitute an informal citizenship education through which their sense of national belonging was continually constructed. The Palestinian youth and their parents in this study engaged in everyday practices, and long-term migration strategies, that reflected the broader movement to maintain national consciousness in the face of ongoing statelessness. Many im/migrant families seek ways to maintain their children's linguistic and cultural connections to their "homeland" (see, for example, Gibson 1988; Hall 2002; Kibria 2002; Louie 2002; Sánchez 2007; Sarroub 2005). In recent times, these practices have been aided by modern technologies that facilitate the construction of transnational identifications, creating more opportunities for imaginative and actual experiences with the places from which family members have migrated. For Palestinians, these identifications are bound up with an independence movement, simultaneously constructing a sense of self, and a notion of "a people," and in doing so, constituting a relationship with an imagined national community.

In what follows, I first examine how these young people describe themselves in relation to a national identity. Next, I explore the various strategies and everyday practices through which this transnational community continually produced itself as a part of the Palestinian national imaginary. Finally, I turn to consider how the meaning and parameters of this imagined community were constructed in relation to three key themes that I explore in further detail: a connection to a particular land that is experienced as an intimate, moral space; a notion of cultural authenticity (albeit a contested one); and a sense of Palestinian identity as inextricably linked with suffering, struggle, and sacrifice.

Being Palestinian

Adam Mattar described himself by stating, "I'm an Arab, *Falasṭīni* (Palestinian) Arab. I got an American citizen[ship]. I was born here, but my home, it's not here." Adam was born in the United States, but he had spent seven of his seventeen years living in his family's village near Jerusalem in the occupied West Bank. Back in the United States, Adam passed most of his school days in the company of his cousins and Palestinian peers; his dominant language was Arabic; and he worked after school in his father's store, alongside his brothers. The distinction that Adam made between *being* Palestinian and *having* US citizenship followed seamlessly from the experiences he had growing up in Palestine and only recently returning to the United States, where his daily life remained grounded in a kind of extended Palestinian village.

Khalida Saba—the young woman whose first day at Regional High was September 11, 2001—was also born in the United States, and lived in the occupied West Bank for seven years before returning to the United States as a teenager. Like Adam, she spent most of her time hanging out with Palestinian friends and family members, but she seemed more comfortably bicultural than Adam, perhaps as a consequence of her bilingual fluency. Speaking of how she identified herself, Khalida stated:

> I don't think of myself as both. I only think of myself as Arab—a Palestinian, actually. Most people ask me, "You're a Palestinian American?" I told them, "No, just Palestinian." Then they start getting stupid about it: "And then how do you know English?" I'm like, "No, I'm American Palestinian. I just want to be a Palestinian."

Unlike Adam, whose sense of identification as a Palestinian seemed unequivocal, Khalida's words—her hesitancies and clarifications—indicate the complexity that many young people express as they forge identities at the nexus of multiple, intermingling systems (Abu El-Haj 2007; Bhatia 2002; Hall 2002; Maira 2009; Mir 2014; Sánchez 2007). Khalida simultaneously acknowledged

("I'm American Palestinian") and rejected an identity that is *both* American and Palestinian. Her words suggest the ways that, for some youth, being Palestinian American was fraught with tensions and sometimes involved a fractured rather than a hybrid or even hyphenated sense of identity.

Ali Bitar was another young man who had spent his childhood and early adolescence living in Palestine. He described himself as follows:

> I identify myself as Palestinian. And then, born in America. But I won't say like oh an American Palestinian, 'cause I was raised there. You know what I mean? I was born here, that's true, but I think you are where you're raised at and where you speak the language and what you know more about. And as you come from there you're still connected to Palestine. It's where you're from. You can't deny it. And then you're American by your passport, where you was born at, can't, can't deny that. So it's kind of in between.

For Ali, then, the experiences of being raised in Palestine and speaking Arabic were formative and led him to identify himself as Palestinian. However, Ali acknowledged his connections to being "American" by virtue of his citizenship, referencing the in-between status that these two identifications entailed. And, like Adam and many of their peers, he made the distinction between being Palestinian—by virtue of connection to the land, culture, and language—and his citizenship status. This distinction was crucial to the ways that many of these young people understood belonging and citizenship.

Even Adam, who of all the students with whom I worked was most unqualified about his Palestinian Arab identity, wrestled with the dual status that he had living in the United States:

> I know that I'm a *'arabī* (Arab). I won't consider myself that I'm a[3] American. But I'm already here. What I'm doing here if I'm not American? That's how you get it. But I'm here, working, go to school, and doing my job. That's what I, but I could be American, but I won't like to be. I don't want to be American. But now we are, because we're here. But for me, I'm a *'arabī*. I'll stay *'arabī*.

As Adam pondered the meaning of living and working in the United States, he again suggested a distinction between his fundamental sense of himself as an Arab and a Palestinian, and the knowledge that he was, to some extent, an American by virtue of his citizenship. For Adam, "American" was about citizenship status; "you get it" (implying citizenship, and a passport). Citizen-

---

3. Interviews were transcribed verbatim. I neither change nor note moments when the participant's language does not conform to standard English grammatical constructions. English translations of Arabic words are provided in parentheses.

ship allowed one to participate in the rights and opportunities (education and work) afforded by living in the United States. In chapter 2, I take up the ways that, for these young people, "American" signified the rights guaranteed by US citizenship. However, Adam was clear that he did not choose to identify himself as an American. In a statement of ultimate belonging to Palestine, Adam insisted that his *'azā'* (the mourning ceremony for Muslims) would take place "back home."

Zena Khalili was one of the few young people in this study who had grown up entirely in the United States. In describing herself, however, she was emphatic: "I always say Palestinian no matter what." Musa Baladi, a Palestinian with Israeli citizenship, moved with his family to the United States when he was five. His parents, both scientists with advanced degrees, decided to move to the United States because of the educational and job discrimination they had faced as Palestinians in Israel. At seventeen, Musa described the reasons for the strong emotional connection to Palestinian identity:

> [Being Palestinian] means that you are, that it's kind of like you know who you are but nobody else really does. And it's more like it's just *trying to have an identity without a place in the world*—to have that identity because it's such a conflict always to even exist over there and over here. So that being Palestinian is kind of a tricky thing like to ask 'cause people can't understand—people outside your own—your situation can't understand why you're so passionate about your identity and your country. (emphasis added)

Living in a world *without a place* strengthened the emotional commitment these young people had to their identities as Palestinians and to the *bilād* (homeland). These young people's identifications with their parents' or grandparents' country of origin may be commonplace among some 1.5-, second-, and even third-generation youth; however, for this community, the strength of this affective identification with Palestine must be understood in the context of the history of Palestine and the politics of the Palestinian nationalist movement, described briefly in the introduction. The community's ongoing statelessness and its struggle for an independent nation-state heightened the salience of producing and sustaining national consciousness. Whether they had migrated to the United States from Palestine or other parts of the Middle East, or had grown up solely in the United States, these young people identified first and foremost as Palestinians—members of a diasporic national imaginary. The strength of this identification grew directly from a positive political commitment and aspiration for a free and independent Palestine rather than, as many of their teachers supposed, a simple rejection of an American identity.

Transnational Migration: Building Connections with the *Bilād*

This strong sense of being Palestinian was forged and maintained in the context of transnational migration through multiple familial strategies and everyday practices. For a majority of the young people with whom I worked—particularly those at Regional High—the robust connection to the *bilād* was an outcome of the years they had lived "back home." Many of the youth had moved back to Palestine with their mothers during childhood in order to live among their relatives and attend school there.[4] Rather than the more common reverse pattern of im/migrant youth visiting relatives in the summer (see Kibria 2002; Sánchez 2007), these young people spent the academic year in Palestine, often returning to the United States for school vacations. The families' decision to move to Palestine marked a historic moment when, after the signing of the Oslo Accords, some members of the Palestinian community were granted permission to return and reside in the Occupied Palestinian Territories (see Hammer 2005; Schulz 2003). However, the second intifada drove many families back to the United States due to deteriorating economic and political conditions, and perhaps most important, because of the difficulties of getting to and from school and contending with routine school closures. Once they returned to the United States, a more typical pattern followed, with summers spent in Palestine when families could afford it, or when the conditions permitted travel. However, even though the trend after the intifada was migration back to the United States, at least one family I knew decided that the mother would move back to Palestine with the children to complete their precollegiate schooling there.

While this pattern of reverse migration signifies the strength of this community's ties to extended family, it also serves a political purpose in the context of the Palestinian nationalist movement. Despite the fact that educational and economic opportunities were much greater in the United States, parents made the decision to take their children back to the *bilād*. Parents wanted their children to be fully conversant in the language and customs of Palestine, and, as members of a Muslim community, they desired a deeper religious

---

4. This pattern of purposefully seeking out education for one's children "back home" is less typical than the general trend to move to the United States at least in some part for its educational opportunities. Kasinitz, Waters, Mollenkopf, and Anil (2002) found that an unexpected number of West Indian and Latino parents sent teenagers home for schooling to help them avoid the perceived dangers of the New York streets. Moreover, there is evidence that global migration trends lead many children to move back and forth between sending and receiving states for education, even if this isn't necessarily a purposeful strategy for maintaining their linguistic, cultural, and social connections (Zuñiga and Hamann 2009).

education than their children could get in the United States. As members of a nation without a state, parents strategically maintained the linguistic, cultural, and religious resources of their children while also forging their strong affective connection to Palestine—to both a place and an aspiration.

Khalida Saba moved to Palestine at the age of seven. She described how this move came about:

> It was 1993 when we went back, and my parents decided to take us back there. They told us—actually they tricked us into going because they told us it was just for vacation. And my grandparents, my dad's dad and my mom's dad were still alive, and they said we were going to go visit them and come back. And after like a year, I said, this is no vacation. I just realized. And they were like, "We just brought you guys here for your own good to learn Arabic and religion and culture and get to know all your cousins and family." And after seven years, we just finally came back. The vacation was over.

Khalida's parents moved the children in order to foster deep family relationships, and to engender knowledge of and facility with Palestinian culture, Islam, and Arabic. Khalida's sister Leila spoke of the reasons for their seven-year sojourn in similar terms:

> We were there for a long time. My parents wanted us to stay so we could learn the language, how people are treated there, how Islam is there, to read the Qur'an, to know right from wrong, how Palestinians, the difference between America and Palestine. They wanted us to see both different [cultures] and they wanted us to put them together and to be one. Now we know two languages. We know English is our primary language and now we know Arabic. That's what they wanted us to know. They support people, like our relatives in Palestine. We don't have that many relatives, but . . . the money that comes to Palestine, it comes from America. It comes from our parents; it comes from people that donate [to charities].

Leila also acknowledged her family's goals for their children to become conversant with the cultural, linguistic, and religious resources of their Palestinian heritage. Interestingly, she noted their commitment to having their children be comfortably bicultural—to know both cultures fluently in order to "put them together and to be one." In addition, Leila suggested that another important motivation her parents had was to develop their children's commitment to economically support family members living in Palestine.

Ali Bitar spoke of learning about the rich cultural heritage of Palestine during his childhood and early adolescence living there:

> We went to like Jericho, Nablus, like all around Ramallah, West Bank. That's all like villages and every village has its own people and customs and ways of

living, which is beautiful. It's good. I'm connected to it by living there so it's like I don't have problems with like wherever you go you just kind of fit in 'cause of the language and probably the mentality or the things you know and learn.

Cultural, linguistic, and religious knowledge, and affective ties to family members grounded young people such as Ali, Leila, and Khalida to Palestine, imbuing them with a strong sense of belonging to the land and its people.

Adam Mattar described his family's decision to have the children and his mother move back to Palestine as a necessary sacrifice on the part of his father. Recalling the reasons for their return, Adam said:

> Yeah, it's different if I lived here. Like, let's say that I was here. I was born here from one month, from one day to, say, to now, I won't speak Arabic. I won't be able to say, "*Al-salām 'alaykum*." It's gonna be hard for me. But when I was seven, my dad said, "That's it. We have to take him back home." And I started thinking, like he's going to be here working and sending money and come for visit for three months. Like he stays away from my mom like for nine months. Like it's hard. But my dad and my mom, they want us to be—like, my dad is always telling me, I want you to be better than me. Look at me, I'm working in the store, I'm working in the deli, I want you to go to college. I don't want you to come and be like me. That's why I want to send you back home. I want you to learn. I want you to do everything great. I don't want you to do nothing wrong.

Adam's story suggests the emotional sacrifices that families made in order to attain different goals (C. Suárez-Orozco, H. J. Bang, and H. Y. Kim 2011). For Adam's parents, the goal of having the children learn the language and customs "back home" outweighed the difficulty of separating the family for nine months of the year. Implied here in his father's words ("I don't want you to do nothing wrong"), Adam's narrative also points to a view of Palestinian village life expressed by many youth I interviewed: Palestine was represented as a safer environment, one more likely to inculcate values that would keep him away from the implicit lures of life in a major US city. At the same time, Adam's father believed that the United States would ultimately offer his children greater possibilities for social mobility through a college education—a possibility that, unfortunately, Adam and many of his peers did not realize.

For Adam, Khalida, Leila, Ali, and others who had spent much of their childhood and early adolescence in Palestine, "back home" was a salient space resonant with emotionally charged memories. However, even life in the United States provided opportunities for these young people to construct and maintain a relationship to Palestine. For the youth at Regional High who were living in a close-knit community that was mostly related by birth or marriage, the practices of everyday life in the United States sustained and reinforced the strong sense of belonging to a cohesive society. These young people spent their in-school and out-of-school hours in one another's company, rarely interacting intimately with peers or adults who were not family members. Recent im/migrants spoke almost exclusively in Arabic, and those who were completely comfortable speaking English shifted seamlessly between the two languages. Late spring marked the start of wedding season, and weekends were often taken up with many nights of festivities that included up to one thousand relatives and friends. One afternoon during wedding season, Khalida, Dina, and Zena schooled my research assistant in the etiquette of delivering wedding invitations. They drew out maps of each house in the neighborhood to which an invitation to Khalida and Leila's sister's wedding had to be—as they explained—hand-delivered. This process of walking around and visiting neighbors while hand-delivering wedding invitations felt resonant with small village life in Irdas. In many ways, these young people felt they were part of an extended village. Even before Skype and Facebook were commonplace, these families were in constant contact with relatives "back home"; the girls in our after-school club, for example, often remarked how quickly news of their activities, especially rumors about impending engagements, reached their relatives in the *bilād*.

The connection to Palestine was as deeply political as it was social and cultural. The Palestinian American students structured many of our after-school club activities around the politics of Palestine. As our group was beginning to break up one late March evening in the spring of 2003, Sana clapped her hands and asked for our attention for a few more minutes. She then proceeded to read us a powerful poem she had written about the everyday struggles that Palestinians experienced living under occupation—struggles that seemed all but invisible in the US media. At one of our first fall meetings in 2004, Khalida, who had been elected cochair of the group, arrived flushed with impatience to share the quiz show about Palestinian history that she had organized for our session. At first, her peers refused to settle into her planned activity because they were upset about a fight they feared was brewing between some of the Palestinian boys and boys at another nearby high school. However, Khalida refused to give up, and after we had defused the crisis, she set herself up as MC of the game show. Interestingly, as she quizzed her peers about major events in Palestinian history, it became clear that many were shaky on the details of the early history, such as when the first Zionists had arrived. The answers to questions about more recent events, such as the assassination of one of the leaders of Hamas, and the formation of the

PLO, were more readily on the tip of their tongues. Over the years I spent at Regional High, I witnessed these young people strive to integrate their connection to Palestine into their school life. From the topics they chose for their senior projects (for example, Adam's exploration of marriage customs in Palestine, or Khalida's timeline of the history of the *Nakba*), to the projects they undertook in art class (for example, Zayd's scratch painting of the Palestinian flag), to the tight-knit social and linguistic community they formed inside Regional High, the Palestinian Americans at Regional High continually constructed their relationship to Palestine.

The fact that the Palestinian youth who attended Regional High lived in a concentrated community made sustaining these connections to Palestine fairly seamless. However, the families that did not live in a concentrated Palestinian community found other ways to create and sustain a relationship to Palestinian and Arab linguistic and cultural practices. They actively sought out other Arab families in their neighborhoods. Some, such as Musa Baladi and Kamal and Zayna Sha'ban, participated on weekends and in the summer in a local Arab American community arts organization. Musa joined an Arabic percussion group, becoming highly skilled in the musical traditions of the region. As an adolescent, Zayna was a founding member of a Palestinian *debke* (folk dance) troupe that performed to raise money for Palestinian children living in refugee camps. Parents spoke with their children in Arabic to maintain their linguistic skills. For some, religious school at a local mosque provided connection to religious practice and the Arabic language, and although religious and cultural identities were not one and the same, they were deeply interwoven for many of these young people.

Whether they were actually moving back and forth to and from Palestine or not, the young people's lives unfolded within transnational fields. They were living in cultural, linguistic, political, and economic spheres that sustained relationships between Palestine and the United States. For many Palestinian American families, creating these spaces to maintain connections to Palestine is a critical strategy given the condition of statelessness.[5] The ongoing struggle for an independent Palestinian state has been sustained by the ability of Palestinians to forge a national consciousness across communities spread around the world. Palestinians have maintained this sense of national belonging despite the inability of many to visit the historic land

5. Unlike Ong's (1999) study of flexible citizenship that links the practices of transnationalism to the logics of contemporary global capital, Palestinians are also creatively responding to the logics of colonization.

from which their families were expelled in 1948 and 1967; the destruction of a majority of Palestinian villages inside the Green Line;[6] the more than forty years of military occupation of East Jerusalem, the West Bank, and Gaza;[7] and the continued Israeli settlement of the Occupied Palestinian Territories. The experiences of these Palestinian American youth illustrate a politics of belonging (Yuval-Davis 2011)—the ways that, through everyday practices and across transnational social fields (Basch, Glick Schiller, and Szanton Blanc 1994; Fouron and Glick-Schiller 2002; Levitt and Glick Schiller 2004; Maira 2009; Ong 1999), Palestinians construct a sense of belonging to a place and an aspiration. This process of constructing a sense of transnational belonging is one experienced by more and more youth in today's world (see, for example, Abu El-Haj 2007; DeJaeghere and McCleary 2010; Dyrness 2012; Fouron and Glick-Schiller 2002; Maira 2009; Sánchez 2007). As I explore in the remainder of this chapter, the sense of *being* Palestinian was constructed in relation to three particular themes resonant in the Palestinian national imaginary: land, culture, and suffering and sacrifice.

The Land of Palestine as an Intimate and Moral Space

Palestinian national identity is firmly anchored to the land of historic Palestine—one that is often imagined as an intimate and moral space (for similar observations on Mexico, see Dick 2010). A majority of these young people expressed a desire to return to live in Palestine at some future time. Because of the ongoing independence struggle, this anchoring to land is qualitatively different from the connections that many youth from im/migrant communities maintain with their families' "home" country. Since 1948, in the face of dislocation, exile, and occupation, Palestinians have constructed a sense of rootedness to the land of historic Palestine, and to specific places within that land (Abu-Lughod and Sa'di 2007; Hammer 2005; Schulz 2003). Through stories told and retold, arts and literature, and saved objects (such as keys and deeds to family homes), Palestinians have kept alive the memory of a land lost, and the aspiration for justice realized (see, for example, Abu-Lughod and Sa'di 2007; Hammer 2005; Schulz 2003). The Palestinian

6. As noted in the introduction, the Green Line refers to the 1949 armistice line demarcating the borders at the end of the 1948 war.

7. As noted in the introduction, the Israelis withdrew settlers from Gaza in 2005; however, they continue to maintain strong economic and military control over the region through their control of the borders, blockade, and intermittent invasions.

American youth with whom I worked described their connections to the land
of Palestine in ways that resonate across the literature on the construction of
Palestinian national identity.

The youth described ancestral descent, "blood," and land as key aspects
that grounded their sense of belonging to Palestine (for similar observations
about other communities, see Fouron and Glick-Schiller 2002; Kibria 2002).
Zena Khalili, a seventeen-year-old senior who had lived her entire life in the
United States, explained, "I always say I'm Palestinian no matter what because
that's where my mom and dad and all our ancestors are from. And I'm proud
to be a Palestinian." Maryam Suleiman, who grew up in Jordan before coming
to the United States, said her Palestinian identity was "in my blood." Samira
Khateeb, who had also lived only in the United States, referenced ancestry
and land as the foundation of her Palestinian identity:

> My ancestors grew up there; my grandparents grew up there; my father has
> land there. And my father's land sooner or later is going to become my broth-
> er's land.

In a similar vein, Adam spoke of the importance of patrimonial descent, recit-
ing the line of men who all conferred upon him, his siblings, and his cousins a
Palestinian identity symbolized through the shared family names.

This tethering of identity to the land was immediately visible upon meeting many of the youth. They carried the land and its attendant nationalist
iconography with them, displaying symbols of Palestinian national identity
(such as the flag, the map of historic Palestine, or the Dome of the Rock[8])
on their clothes, backpacks, key chains, and jewelry. In the first activity we
undertook in the after-school club, we asked each participant to decorate a
tile to represent herself or himself. These tiles, which drew on a traditional
geometric Islamic art form, were then assembled into a mosaic that, upon
completion, was bursting with the Palestinian flag, and *Palestine*, written in
Arabic calligraphy. These young people frequently wore the black-and-white
checkered headscarves (kafiyyeh) on their heads or across their shoulders.
The kafiyyeh symbolizes the dual figure of the fellah (peasant farmer) and
the feday (resistance fighter), both key images of the Palestinian resistance
movement. All of these symbols locate Palestinian identity in a particular
land and place.

Folk arts provided another medium for constructing relationships with

8. The Dome of the Rock is the golden-domed mosque in Jerusalem that houses the rock
from which Muslims believe the Prophet Muhammad ascended to heaven.

Palestine. Zayna Sha'ban, Kamal's sister, curated an exhibition of Palestinian embroidery, *taṭrīz*, at a small local arts education center. At the exhibition's opening event, the women artists demonstrated their craft, and those of us in attendance spoke of how the various designs came from different villages, many of which had been destroyed during the *Nakba*. For Zayna, and her fellow artists, *taṭrīz* not only keeps alive particular artistic traditions but also serves as a larger national reclamation project. This local exhibition is but one manifestation of the ways that *taṭrīz* has created historical memory within the intimacies of Palestinian families (including my own), in formal museum exhibitions and their attendant catalogs, and in wider public women's collectives that I have visited in Palestine and Lebanon (see also Abourahme 2010). Another example of the ways that artistic expression was intimately intertwined with the larger nationalist project was the *debke* troupe mentioned earlier. As a teenager, Zayna and a small group of her Palestinian peers started this traditional dance troupe in order to perform benefit concerts to aid Palestinian children living in refugee camps. Thus, these practices that might appear at first glance to fit into the well-worn groove of US multiculturalism, engender other meanings as they construct young people's ongoing relationship with the Palestinian national imaginary.

For some of the youth with whom I worked, the land to which they anchored their Palestinian identity was imagined through stories told and retold within families. These stories and the images they create play an important role in maintaining connections to Palestine in the face of the political barriers to many Palestinians' return. Zayna Sha'ban kept alive the memory of her family's village outside of Haifa—among those destroyed by the Israelis after 1948—through stories that she had learned and then retold. She recalled her family's situation before 1948: "They were peasant villagers, farmers. They had communal olive trees, you know our family had groves." Zayna spoke of the village well where her grandparents would meet in secret. Her recollection of how her parents met in the 1970s illustrates the ways that Palestinian families maintain connections to their village communities decades after their expulsion from, and in many cases the subsequent destruction of, those villages:

> My dad's dad and my mom's dad were friends in [the village]. They were distant relatives and my dad's dad was like older and he was like really good looking and, you know the women loved him. So my mom's dad was younger and would hang out with him 'cause he was cool. And that's how they knew each other. So, when my dad's brothers knew that my mom was in Damascus—his older brothers knew my grandfather, my mom's dad—so when they knew that Abu Hani's daughter was in Damascus they told my dad to go visit her and

meet her and you know take care of her and, and my grandparents—I mean
her parents—also told her like this is you know someone from your village and
take care of him and all of this stuff, so that's how they met.

Zayna's story reflects the ways that Palestinians often maintain connections
to particular places and communities across generations (Abu-Lughod 2007;
Davis 2007, 2011). For Palestinians—especially those who, like Zayna, have
family members who remain stateless more than sixty years after the *Nakba*—
stories that sustain a relationship with the particular village or city from which
they were expelled serve a private and a public role. Stories shape individuals'
inner landscapes of belonging while also asserting public claims for justice
and restitution (Abu-Lughod and Sa'di 2007). Moreover, it is not only those
families living in exile who work to sustain their rootedness to specific places.
For example, the youth from Irdas married almost exclusively within their
extended families, strengthening connections to their particular village. There
is a long history of marriage within extended Palestinian families, as in many
other societies; and this contemporary practice reflects this well-established
tradition. However, the practice also serves other purposes, such as deepen-
ing ties to the land for those who live outside Palestine while simultaneously
securing the powerful rights attendant on US citizenship for those who marry
US citizens. Rootedness to specific villages is one key aspect of maintaining
community relationships across generations in the face of dispersal and exile,
and sustaining a sense of connection to a Palestinian national imaginary.

For many of the youth with whom I worked, though, the sense of being
Palestinian was rooted to a place they actually knew. Adam Mattar often
spoke longingly of life in the *bilād*, which evoked vivid memories of strong
familial relationships. For example, speaking of himself as a person who likes
to "help others," Adam recalled:

> Back home when I was back home I used to work with my uncle. He has a little
> store. I used to work with him. I didn't take money from him. I just worked
> with him. I used to help my grandfather who was eighty-five years old. He was
> sick for four years before he died. He couldn't walk. And later on he couldn't
> see. So we have to take [care of] him. I used to always help him.

Adam's memories reflect the intimacies of life in a large extended family.
However, Adam often spoke of having to remain in the United States—despite
a deep desire to return home—in order to support his family in Palestine. In
this context, Adam's recollections of working with his uncle without "tak[ing]
money from him" and caring for his ailing grandfather suggest the ways
that Palestine was imagined as an intimate, moral space—one in which filial
bonds, not economic ones, connected people (see also Dick 2010).

Adam was not alone in speaking of his time in Palestine in relation to deep ties to a small community village life. Ali Bitar had also spent his childhood and early adolescence in Palestine before attending Regional High and matriculating to a four-year state college. He recalled the reasons for moving to Palestine in terms of the support of close familial relationships:

> My family's—we got family living in Palestine too, so, so it's kind of like half of us here half of us there. So that's why when we, when we were young it's easier for us to go there and just go to school and have support, I mean when we come here my dad is here so we came here, went to school, started working, and went to college. [But] I mean there when you have uncles, family, it's easier to go around, travel. Let's say you need help in something or to get stuff. So makes it easier, especially the, the town when we're, we used to live in didn't have too much problems. It's just the way [in the village].

Ali remembered his time in the village as easy and free from major problems. Without denying that his overall experience in Palestine was a positive one, the fact that Ali was talking about life under Israeli occupation suggests that, at least in part, he was evoking an idealized imagination of Palestine as safe and intimate. Ali glossed over the more troubling aspects of his experiences in Palestine that he had described in his interview—for example, the checkpoints he mentioned having to pass through each day to get to school, even before the outbreak of the second intifada—in favor of a memory of a life made easy by familial connections.

Khalida described similar ties when she explained what she missed about living in Palestine:

> Knowing everybody there. It's just the, we live in a small village where everybody knows everybody. There's no, you would walk in the street and everybody would just say hi to you, you know everybody. It's not like here, you go somewhere and you don't know nobody. I've been in a lot of situations where I go someplace and I do not know one person, and that can be really uncomfortable.

Life in this small village seemed safe and comfortable; unlike the big US city, it was a place where one could be known. Khalida often spoke of missing her relatives in Palestine:

> I do miss Palestine because I have a lot of relatives there. And my aunt— actually she's my grandfather's aunt. She raised my mom. She's kind of old and stuff. I used to like staying near her. I wanted to stay near her and not come here [back to the United States] but my mom wouldn't let me. She said you got to go see your sisters and your nephews. So I just decided to come and when my mom told me we were going back [for a visit to the United States], I was

really looking forward to going back. I didn't really want to stay, but I had no other choice. My family is here. I have to stay.

Built into the migration to and from Palestine was an inevitable sense of loss; family members sacrificed both to live apart and to stay together. Khalida contrasted life in Palestine favorably with the anonymity of the big city to which she returned.

As young people described their time in Palestine, and spoke nostalgically of a wish to return to the loving fold of their families, there were often echoes of an idealized sense of place. Hania Nabulsi, who had lived for two years in Palestine, described her life there:

> You don't have to be afraid for anything, nobody's gonna steal there no nothing. *Al ummahaat* (the mothers) *mijir'een* (they're brave), ya'nī (I mean)[9] they're tough, the mothers. They're tough over there, and it was beautiful. Now [after the second intifada] everything is closed but when I went there we went to Bir Zeit and the, the, I don't know what you call it, the *sila* (basket) in the air, I don't know what it's called, it's like you go on this basket thing and it goes across to this mountain and they have this resort there, it was beautiful, and the *arḍ* (land), the air, everything like. Like here you breathe in and it's all fat, and oil, pollution and, and dirtiness, and attitude. Everything, there is like, like, organically and naturally. Everything's bad here. As for there, it's—it's clean, it's healthy.

Similar to Adam, Ali, and Khalida, Hania's description, in part, reflected the contrast between US city life and the more rustic environment in Palestine. However, the superlative quality of her memory also suggests a theme resonant in the collective memory of Palestine—of a land uncorrupted by the evils of modernity, occupation, and exile (Hammer 2005; Schulz 2003; Abu-Lughod and Sa'di 2007). Thus, through her recollections, Hania constructed an ideal nation, one in which everything—the land, the air—reflected organic beauty and healthy living.

Much has been written about the ways in which Palestinians have created a nationalist consciousness articulated through memories of, and longing for, an idyllic land—one blessed with the simplicity of the agricultural life of the fellaheen (peasants); the beauty of the land and its olive, fig, orange, and lemon trees; and the fragrance of orange blossoms and thyme. These images of Palestine are threaded throughout Palestinian arts and literature. They are

9. Language was another key way that these young people maintained their connection to Palestine. As noted earlier, they often spoke with one another in Arabic. However, it was also not unusual for young people—even those who were completely fluent in English—to use Arabic words and phrases in their English as Hania did here.

kept alive in stories told by those living in exile (Sa'di and Abu-Lughod 2007; Schulz 2003). And they echoed throughout the narratives and images constructed by the Palestinian American youth in my research.

This inextricable weaving together of an idyllic land and the struggle for Palestinian independence is visible in a poem that Lena Deeb, a fourteen-year-old Palestinian American, wrote about her grandfather during a youth filmmaking workshop I cotaught for the community arts organization. That summer our three-week workshop was organized around the theme of migration, specifically exploring experiences of power and exclusion. Lena's grandparents had migrated to the United States from Jerusalem, and she had visited her relatives in Jerusalem many times. Lena narrated this story in a film the teens produced that summer, voicing the poem over alternating images of her walking under a flowering tree and pictures of the wall Israel has built around many parts of the occupied West Bank.

> How could they define him as an enemy of the state?
> I was so confused.
> How could my grandfather not be allowed back to his home in Jerusalem?
>   Picking figs from the trees:
> Is that an enemy of the state?
> Smoking an *arghile*[10] and sitting with his brothers:
> Is that an enemy of the state?
> Milking the goats in the backyard:
> Is that an enemy of the state?
> They divided our land and built this monster of a wall.
> How could the world have let it gone this far?

This poem challenged Israel's decision to deny Lena's grandfather the right to visit his home in Jerusalem. Through words and images, she connected this specific story about the exclusion of one person to broader political questions about the partition of Palestine and the contemporary construction of a physical wall around the Occupied Palestinian Territories. In making this political challenge, the narrative centered around reframing the images of her grandfather (and, implicitly, Palestinians) as "enemies of the state" (or "terrorists"), shifting to portray him as a gentle fellah and family man: one who picks figs and milks goats and shares a relaxing moment with his brothers.

Palestinian American youth root their identities in a land that is, for many, a tangible place, but that also symbolizes for their community a much larger idea—a longing for return to a homeland torn apart by war, expulsion, and

10. *Arghile* is a colloquial Arabic word for a water pipe, also referred to as a *narghila* or *shisha*.

occupation. For the Palestinian American youth who had spent time in Palestine, their stay in the *bilād* only strengthened their nostalgia for a land they described as a space of safety, intimacy, and beauty. This nostalgia for the beauty of the land and the simplicity of life echoes images commonly found in Palestinian arts and historiography, suggesting that this sense of longing reflects a politics of belonging.

Producing Cultural Authenticity

The Palestinian American youth described being Palestinian as a simple fact of their heritage—their connection to a land and its people. However, they explained what it meant to be *truly* Palestinian in reference to an ideal of Palestinian identity rooted to cultural, linguistic, religious, and gendered practices they believed represented *authentic* ways of being Palestinian. That is, the sense of being Palestinian, and belonging to this national community, was made and remade in everyday life, and this work was done largely through producing notions of cultural authenticity (see also Hall 2002; Naber 2012; and Grewal 2014 on producing religious authenticity). The parameters defining this cultural authenticity, however, were a source of constant debate among the youth, and through the process of negotiating these parameters, they produced ideas of "Palestinianness." This process of constructing a relationship to the "homeland" by adopting, adapting, and resisting cultural practices resonates across the experiences of youth from many im/migrant communities, pointing to a politics of belonging through which young people negotiate inclusion and exclusion across transnational fields (Hall 2002; Maira 2002, 2009; Naber 2012).

Zayd Taher spent most of his life in the United States. However, he lived in Palestine for two years as a young adolescent. For Zayd, what makes one Palestinian seemed clear:

> To be a Palestinian, you're an Arabic speaker. You follow the customs. You go up to the Friday prayer. It's either that or you go to the coffee shop. It's one of the two. You go do prayer. You go to the coffee shop. You just do the customs.

Zayd described Palestinian identity in relation to a set of givens: you speak the language and you "do the customs." For Zayd, these ossified customs inextricably intertwined cultural, religious, and gendered practices. Friday prayer (as well as other religious practices such as fasting during Ramadan and strict guidelines for relations between males and females) offered key markers of Palestinian identity. Although many Palestinians are not Muslims,

Zayd and a majority of his peers at Regional High seamlessly linked Palestinian national identity with their religious identities as Muslims. In addition, Zayd's reference to the coffee shop—generally a segregated space in which Arab men gather to discuss everything from business to families to politics—also highlighted gender distinctions in everyday practices as another source of Palestinian identity.

Explanations of what it means to be Palestinian revolved, in large part, around distinctions that the youth perceived between "Palestinian" and "American" practices. Not unlike youth from other im/migrant communities (see, for example, Hall 2002; Lee 2005; Maira 2002; Olsen 1997; Sarroub 2005), these young people often defined Palestinian identity by drawing sharp contrasts between the values and behaviors of Palestinians (and other Arabs and Muslims, in general) and Americans. For many, establishing an authentic cultural identity entailed distinguishing carefully between "Palestinian" and "American" cultural practices, and committing not to be "Americanized." For example, Khalida Saba distinguished herself and her peers from "Americans" by pointing to perceived differences in "lifestyle":

> Well, I only consider Americans are people that live the American lifestyle, which is like, for instance, American girls, they go out, they are sometimes like at bars and things like that, that's like American lifestyle.

Zayd spoke even more explicitly about the contrast between "Americans" and Palestinians as he described what makes someone an American:

> You don't have to be a citizen. To be an American is to do the things they do here. You see something on TV and you do like them. You become, as they say, Americanized. Most of [the Palestinian girls in the after-school club] they're from a new age, not like the old age where they don't go to school. I'm saying there's no problem with going to school. But I'm saying they have it in their head where they're not cooking for their man. They're not doing this, not doing that, and "I'm going to do this if they want it or not" and that's—their thinking is Americanized. It's not like that in our background, our culture and stuff.

For Zayd, *being* American, rather than indicating simply a citizenship status, reflected both everyday practices (for example, women not cooking for men) and ways of thinking that assert independence, particularly for the girls and women in the community.

Following a familiar pattern among many im/migrant communities, the regulation of female bodies and sexuality offered the most obvious site for producing a "culturally authentic" identity for many of these youth and their families (for examples, see Ajrouch 2004; Gibson 1988; Hall 2002; Lee 2005; Maira 2002; Naber 2012; Olsen 1997; Sarroub 2005; Yuval-Davis, Anthias, and Kofman 2005; Wolf 2002).

The production of notions of cultural authenticity often proves problematic in that these ideas tend to reinforce dominant gender regimes and heteronormativity (Naber 2012). However, these claims to culturally "authentic" forms of gendered identity do not go uncontested. Girls and boys at Regional High continually debated what it meant to *be* Palestinian. This debate is evident in the very words Zayd used to describe what it means to be Americanized. His criticism of the Palestinian girls whom he saw as straying from "our culture" illustrates the processes of cultural production[11] at work. Members of his community were not simply adopting or rejecting static cultural traditions from "home"; rather, different members of the community were constructing variable ways of being Palestinians in their everyday lives—some of which did not suit Zayd's notions of genuine "Palestinianness."

The girls of whom he spoke—girls such as Khalida and Leila Saba and Samira Khateeb—described themselves as fully and genuinely Palestinian, and they refused to be constrained by the parameters he and some of the other boys established. It was the boys at Regional High who often supported restrictive roles for girls in public spaces as markers of culturally appropriate behaviors. For example, in February of 2004, there was a heated debate in our after-school club as the students were organizing for the school's annual multicultural fair. Adam and several of the other boys were threatening to withdraw from performing at the multicultural fair if the girls also insisted on dancing in public. Khalida, Samira, Lamia, and Sana were furious, demanding to know who the boys thought they were to tell them what they could and could not do in public. This argument went on for a few months, and in the end the girls decided not to dance—but not, they claimed, because they had come to agree with Adam and his peers. Although the boys at Regional High seemed, in general, to hold restrictive ideas about girls' public behaviors and dress, among the girls, there was much more disagreement about appropriate gender roles. Some girls defended their right to dance in public while others vociferously disagreed, viewing public performances as unacceptable for both cultural and religious reasons.

As noted above, for a majority in this community, religious practices were deeply entwined with cultural practices in the definition of what made one a

11. B. A. U. Levinson (2011a) offers a useful definition of cultural production as "the making of meanings and identities by knowledgeable social actors in contexts of structure power" (115). For a full discussion of the construct, see B. A. U. Levinson and D. Holland 1996.

Palestinian. The hijab provided a particularly hot topic of contention for the students at Regional High as they debated what behaviors they deemed appropriate for themselves as Palestinian Muslims. Most of the male students believed that wearing a *mandīl* (the word for hijab in their Palestinian dialect) was a requirement of Islam. However, while some of the girls believed that Muslim women were obliged to wear a *mandīl*, others did not. The Palestinian American girls made different choices about whether to cover their hair, and these decisions often changed over time as girls adopted or removed their headscarves as they progressed through adolescence and early adulthood.

The sisters Khalida and Leila Saba had gone back and forth between wearing and not wearing a *mandīl*. On numerous occasions, the sisters discussed the fact that wearing or not wearing a *mandīl* did not make one more or less faithful. In their words, being "true" to oneself, and "respecting" oneself—rather than wearing or not wearing a scarf—were the sign of real faith. This philosophy had led both of them to go against the preference of their parents and take off their headscarves in the months following September 11, 2001. Their friend Samira Khateeb made a different decision. After a summer she spent living with one of her sisters in another city, and attending the local religious school there, Samira decided to wear a *mandīl* to make her faith publicly visible. For Samira, Leila, and Khalida, it was essential that girls themselves made choices about whether or not to wear a *mandīl*. Moreover, they felt that following practices of Islam did not necessarily require covering one's hair, while it did require honesty and respect in one's everyday practices. Leila (who no longer covered her hair by the time I met her when she was a high school junior) explained her reasons for having worn the *mandīl* in the past:

> The thing is the *mandīl* is a big thing. But if you don't respect yourself with others, at least have the dignity and the, like, just honor yourself, respect who you are. Be pure to yourself. I didn't wear the *mandīl* because somebody said, "Oh, this girl doesn't wear a *mandīl*." I wore it because it's part of the religion and I wore it because God wanted me to wear it. Not like some of these girls in this school, they just wear 'cause they either want to get married or something.

These girls also reserved their highest condemnation for parents they perceived as forcing their girls to wear the hijab. Unlike many of the boys at Regional High who were quick to criticize girls who did not wear a *mandīl*, the girls acknowledged the different decisions about religious dress that they made, and they all defended the choices they made as being compatible with their commitments to their religious faith. Although the *mandīl* is clearly a marker of religious, rather than cultural or national, affiliation, for these youth the two were inextricably linked as they constructed their Palestinian national identities.

Although the boys at Regional High expressed the view that Muslim girls should cover their hair, it is important to note that this was not the position of all Palestinian American boys. There were other young men, such as Musa Baladi, who knew that Muslim women made different kinds of choices about whether or not to express their faith in that way. Musa chafed against representations of the hijab as a sign of oppression, and Islam as essentially repressive to women, reflecting that while some women, such as his mother, chose not to cover their hair, others, such as one of his high school friends, wore a hijab in order to, as he reported, "take gender out of" the interactions she had with others. From Musa's perspective, Islam allowed women to make various decisions about their dress. Thus, even though there was lively debate about what the requirements of Islam were, all the students saw their position as reflective of honest engagement with the faith, and in their own ways, they constructed notions of appropriate religious practices for their community.

The *mandīl* was only one arena for the ongoing debates about what constituted authentic, appropriate, gendered behavior for their community. Over the years, I was privy to myriad conversations about public interactions between unrelated males and females. There appeared to be general agreement among the youth at Regional High that interactions between unrelated boys and girls were culturally inappropriate and cause for unleashing the gossiping tongues of relatives here and in Palestine. However, there were hot discussions about what kinds of interactions constituted real violations of culturally appropriate behavior. On one occasion, when I asked several of the girls to walk me through what was considered appropriate behavior, Leila responded:

> I'm not trying to say don't talk to a boy. He's a classmate. It's just a innocent and friendly conversation. There's a difference between walking with a boy in the hallway and talking to him in the classroom as a classmate. Some of the people here—take classmates—it's not appropriate for a *'arabī* (Arab), especially from Irdas [her village], to walk with a boy in the hallway. To others and to us I think like if it's, "Hi, Bye," you know a kid from your class, there's nothing wrong with it. To me, there's nothing wrong with it. Because you know deep inside yourself that you're not intending or thinking anything inappropriate.

In her explanation to me, Leila illustrated that the parameters of what was and was not appropriate for Palestinians and Arabs were nuanced and debated within the community. In the same discussion, Leila and Samira insisted that although the restrictions on interactions between unrelated boys and girls were supposed to apply equally to both parties, in reality there was a double standard—one at which they chafed. However, in weighing the consequences of acting outside the appropriate boundaries, the girls lamented:

LEILA: [If you're a boy], your past goes away. But if you're a girl, you're—
SAMIRA: Your past stays.
LEILA: It's really, really important. It's like a shattered glass. You can't put it back together.

These lively discussions among the youth about the practices that defined what it meant to be Palestinian Muslims indicate that cultural and religious claims, in fact, reflect actively negotiated and contested practices. Moreover, these negotiations and contestations illustrate processes of cultural production in transnational fields. These young people were actively figuring out what it meant to create and maintain a sense of being Palestinian in the midst of "American" public spaces.

However, it is critical to remember that the process of negotiating and enacting these variable gendered practices is not restricted to the context of migration. That is, there is not a set of static, authentic Palestinian practices that people engage in "back home." Plurality and cultural contestation are the norm, not the exception. Samira pointed, for example, to the differences between villages in Palestine:

> It's just [my father's village]. I have cousins from different villages. They don't think nothing like how we think. For me, my parents, they give me freedom. They allow me to go out; they allow me to do things that other parents wouldn't allow their kids to do. But when I take a look at my aunts—my mom's from a different village—but when I take a look at her sisters, which are my aunts and their kids, it's so different. I thought that all their daughters are going to be in the *mandīl*, and trapped at home, because they live in the *bilād* or whatever, but when I, I never went there, I never visited them, but when I asked my mom and I took a look at a wedding that they, one of their son's weddings, it's so different. They go out and dress the way I dress. They do the things I do, and even more, you know. It's just to the point where their parents trust them, because their parents trust them and they trust what they do. And their brothers trust them and their uncles trust them, you know. So that village there's so much more freedom than in [my father's village] for girls.

Moreover, even within the same village, there were differences in what families deemed culturally appropriate. In several hot debates, the girls from Irdas argued vociferously about where they enjoyed more freedom—in the United States or Palestine. What became clear during these arguments was that even within the same extended family living in the same village, the parameters defining culturally appropriate behaviors were widely variable. Thus, even as the youth argued that there are "Palestinian" versus "American" ways, the boundaries of cultural practices were, in reality, highly variable and mutable even in Palestine.

Despite the mutability of cultural practices, in a pattern that these young people shared with other adolescents from other im/migrant communities, claims for cultural authenticity were often positioned as incompatible with "American" practices (Hall 2002; Lee 2005; Naber 2012; Olsen 1997; Sarroub 2005). As such, for some youth, the contrast between "Palestinian" and "American" cultural practices became grounds for generational conflict with parents, relatives, and older siblings (Hall 2002; Lee 2005; Naber 2012; Sarroub 2005). This was especially the case for the girls at Regional High who had to constantly negotiate with parents and the prying eyes of other family members over whether or not they might go to the mall with friends, stay late after school, or walk home on their own. Zena, for example, described her struggle to be allowed to go to the prom:

> I was gonna go to prom, and then everybody's telling us, like, in less than a day, everybody knew. And everybody started talking about it because no Arabic girls are going but me. Everybody started talking about it. And my mom, because you know, my mom's so protective. She wouldn't let me go. And all my cousins and everybody got into it and said, "Why are you gonna let her go? Don't let her go. No, that's not for us, that's for [Americans]." Like I think it's important, because it's my last year and I want to go, and I just tell them, "I don't want to go dance and I don't want to do anything. I just want to take that picture. Take the picture so it could be memories forever." And everybody's like, "No, you don't have to go."

If this prototypical "American" rite of passage seemed beyond the realm of possibility for a young Palestinian girl, Zena's willingness to fight for her right to attend the prom marked the typical ways that the children of im/migrants often press to adapt to new norms.

Although it was more typical of girls to have to fight for the right to participate in normative "American" teen activities, boys were not immune to these conflicts with their parents. Musa Baladi lived in a nearby suburban community that did not have a large concentration of other Palestinians or Arabs. Unlike the Regional High students, Musa moved between worlds, becoming an accomplished Arabic music percussionist, participating in youth video workshops that sought to educate others about anti-Arab racism and the plight of Palestinians, while also throwing himself into quintessentially

"American" activities such as football. He spoke of the conflicts he had with his parents as a teenager:

> Well you know my friends are allowed to do things. My friends are allowed to do things that I can't even ask to be allowed to do. My parents still get really angry if I try to sleep over somebody else's house. And I've witnessed my other friends, even if their parents say they're strict, I've witnessed their phone calls at like 12:30 at night being like I'm just gonna sleep out tonight and their parents like OK. So they have a lot more freedom and my parents are living in the Arab system and I'm living somewhere in between, where I want the freedom and at the same time obviously like feel guilty when I, when I ask for things that I know my parents aren't gonna approve of, and that's where we conflict 'cause I want the, I want the American way so that I can do more things. My parents want me to do what they want.

Whether young people, like Zena and Musa, were asking their parents to be allowed to behave in more "American" ways or, like Zayd, were trying to maintain what they perceived to be appropriate Palestinian behaviors and resist "Americanization," the youth described Palestinian/Arab cultural norms and American ones as different and often at odds with each other.

The complex conversations that young people had about what constituted Palestinian identity revealed that, although most of the Palestinian students described the existence of an authentic Palestinian cultural identity, the parameters of that identity reflected the processes of cultural production (for similar observations, see Hall 2002; Maira 2002). These youth are constructing variable ways of *being* Palestinian that draw upon their everyday experiences living within and across multiple communities and national spaces. This attention to the complexity of cultural production is of critical importance to understanding the politics of culture—the ways that discourse about culture does political work—which I discuss further in part 2. The notion of fundamental differences *between* cultures can work to produce a sense of national cohesion, particularly in the context of diaspora, but it can also construct boundaries of inclusion and exclusion—boundaries that become rigid and impassable in particular contexts.

Palestine as a Site of Suffering, Struggle, and Sacrifice

If the parameters of what it means to *be* Palestinian were defined in relation to notions of cultural authenticity, they were just as strongly tethered to the suffering of a nation that was not yet free, and the sacrifice of its people to realize an independent state. Interestingly, the youth usually kept the images of Palestinian suffering and sacrifice separate from recollections of their own life in

Palestine, which reverberated with a sense of emotional intimacy and security. Research has shown that Palestinian national identity is often anchored to a state of suffering and sacrifice (Schulz 2003). Khalida Saba, explaining why she identified as Palestinian rather than Palestinian American said:

> Most of the reasons I feel that way is because Palestinians suffered a lot. And they're still suffering actually. And most Palestinians that died, so many Palestinians that died are known as heroes. And there's just something about that that makes me proud of being Palestinian. Not ashamed.

Although Khalida spoke of her own life in Palestine in terms of safe, intimate, loving relationships, she described feeling connected to Palestinian suffering and struggle for an independent state as a source of pride.

For Samira Khateeb, suffering also seemed to be at the heart of the definition of Palestinian identity:

> The people in Palestine, when I think about the people in Palestine and I see on the TV what happens, you know, to all these Palestinians and kids are dying and everybody, I don't know, when I think about them, I feel so sorry for them that I just want to become a Palestinian so bad, and even though I am, I don't consider myself to be as one of those Palestinians who's sitting there throwing rocks at the Israelis, trying to fight back for the country.

Samira's words here complicate her definition of what it means to be Palestinian. Positioning suffering and resistance for the cause of Palestinian independence as fundamental to Palestinian identity, Samira equivocated about her own place in the national community. And she wondered what would happen if she were living in Palestine. Speaking of the Palestinian adolescents who were resisting the occupation, she continued:

> They're fighting for our land. They're fighting for my father's land, where my grandparents' house was built. So that makes me a Palestinian right there. Sometimes I wish I could be the one throwing the rocks back at them, but you can't, you know, just because, you just can't. If I was there, I think that if there was an Israeli pointing a gun at me or pointing a gun at a child right in front of me, I think that I would do something like throw a rock at him.

Samira, like her peers, felt pulled by the nationalist movement. Wondering aloud what she would do in the face of an Israeli soldier's gun, she tried to imagine a place for herself in that struggle.

In fact, the question of how "Palestinian" one could be living in the United States with the privileges of US citizenship was a recurrent theme in discussions we had in the after-school club. On a chilly December afternoon in 2004 just before the winter holidays, we met to say good-bye to a young Egyptian

American lawyer who had been one of the adult mentors of our group for the past year. Dima Al-Fadl was leaving to take a job in a big law firm in New York City. Khalida had organized a party for Dima, complete with snacks and a cake. Thinking it would be fun to watch a movie together, Khalida had asked an older cousin of one of the Regional High students, Nadia Khabbaz, to orchestrate a viewing and discussion of *Gaza Strip*, a 2002 documentary film by American James Longley. The film explores everyday life in the Gaza Strip in the early months of the second intifada, focusing on a thirteen-year-old boy whom Longley had met at weekly protests by children and youth at one of the key checkpoints in the northern Gaza Strip. This film follows the young boy while also illustrating the everyday lives and perspectives of many other Palestinians living in the Gaza Strip.

At our December meeting, we watched about twenty minutes of the documentary. Students seemed alternately engaged by the movie and distracted by the festivities, and Dima decided to stop the film early to begin a discussion about the devastation we were seeing. Dima offered background on the movie, telling the group that it was made by an American director who had planned to spend a week in Gaza but found the situation so compelling that he decided to stay for three months. Dima directed the group's attention to the decision that the director had made to focus on Palestinians telling their own stories rather than offer his own narration of the events. She encouraged them to think about how, "one day, you too could bring something like this to an American audience." With one exception, none of the students had ever been to Gaza. The one boy who had, confessed that it had only been to enjoy the beaches, before the inception of the second intifada.

Nadia then launched into a passionate and provocative speech admonishing her peers on the importance, as Palestinians and Arabs, of knowing "what is really going on—what is really happening." She then threw down a gauntlet of sorts, stating, "Those are the real Palestinians. We are not Palestinians." Nadia argued that as Americans living privileged lives in the United States, no one in the room (including herself) was really a Palestinian. She talked about her guilt for not living in Palestine, for "choosing" to live in the United States, and for spending outrageous amounts of money shopping for shoes and clothes at the mall. As the students from Regional High digested her moral challenge, a vigorous and spirited debate ensued. One young man, Kareem, agreed with her, stating that "Palestinians there are fighting the occupation, while in America we are doing nothing." Hamid and Na'ima (both of whom had lived in Palestine) vociferously disagreed. Hamid reminded her that as Palestinians in the United States, they were working for the national cause by supporting those living in Palestine economically and politically.

Na'ima seemed close to tears, saying, "I love my country. I'm a Palestinian."
This debate centered on the critical question of whether personal suffering
and sacrifice were necessary for claiming an *authentically* Palestinian identity. No matter which side of the disagreement they fell on, all of the youth
oriented their sense of being Palestinian to notions of sacrifice, struggle, and
suffering for the nation. Even those who felt guilty for living the relative ease
of life in the United States expressed an aspiration to do more, to be part of
the suffering of—and sacrifice for—the nation.

Many of the young people identified strongly as Palestinians because of
their intimate knowledge about what was happening to family members living under military occupation. Hasan Hamadi grew up in the United States
and had spent a few summers in Palestine. His sense of himself as a Palestinian grew over time as he became more intimately connected to Palestinian
peers in the United States and to the stories of his family in Palestine. Hasan
attended an elementary school that he described as majority white, and there
were no Arab students he could befriend. As this was before 2001, the only
occasion in which his Palestinian Muslim heritage stood out was during Ramadan, when he was required to go to the lunchroom despite fasting, and
other students often baited him to eat. However, as Hasan's knowledge of
Arabic and of Palestinian politics and culture strengthened with each summer visit to his father's home village, and as he moved on to more diverse
schools, he grew more comfortable seeking out friendships with other Palestinian students at his middle school and at Regional High. By high school,
Hasan visibly sought to identify as Palestinian, wearing a necklace with a map
of historic Palestine, donning a kafiyyeh across his shoulders, and speaking
in Arabic with his peers. Wearing the land around his neck, and the symbolic
scarf of both the fellah (peasant) and the feday (resistance fighter) across his
shoulders, Hasan's developing Palestinian identity was visibly linked to his
emerging political consciousness about the situation on the ground in Palestine. Describing how he came to identify strongly with being Palestinian,
Hasan spoke of his growing awareness of what his family members endured
living under the Israeli occupation:

> I view myself as being Palestinian only because I could, I guess I could kind of
> relate to the, to the Palestinian people, 'cause of what's going on. I'm not over
> there. It's happening to my family. It's happening to real members of my family.
> I recall one event that happened to my cousin. My second cousin was—in my
> town the soldiers actually would take, would take like a, like a boy and just
> like just beat him, like tie him up, like, like tie him up, bag him and drag him
> in their car and just drive to the town. This, this happened to a couple kids in

our town, and this happened to one kid in particular where, and then they, they would drive them and just leave them in the street there for a night, like tied up, and you would have to, you would have to leave in the night you would have to find a way to get yourself freed and just leave. Because they would come back in the morning, if you're still there they would beat you again. . . . And this happened to my cousin who, like afterwards was just like, was forever changed, forever changed. . . . Because beforehand I would say, I would view it as, as a war and I knew it was wrong that it was happening. I knew what was happening like essentially, but I didn't know the details of anything. It wasn't until I heard that that I kind of really looked into it. And then, that was, that was before my trip that was when I was still in high school. And then, and then after that like just things like that just like led me to say that I'm Palestinian.

It was intimate knowledge of the suffering wrought by the occupation and the struggle for independence that strengthened Hasan's identification with being Palestinian. By the time Hasan was at the university, he had become a student activist working with a group promoting a just and peaceful solution to the Palestinian-Israeli conflict. Hasan and other Palestinian American youth developed commitments to the Palestinian nationalist movement through direct experience, stories of their relatives, and stories about the conflict in both Arabic- and English-language media.

Moreover, these young Palestinian Americans' tenacious sense of being part of the Palestinian national project led many to imagine their lives in relation to a collective political purpose. Speaking of why she longed to return to Palestine, Khalida said:

Well, there's a difference between, if I lived here, I would have a big fear of dying. But if I was in Palestine, I wouldn't. I'd never for one minute fear dying, because I knew if I die, I'll be dying for something at least and I'll be dead and buried somewhere I loved being.

Khalida cast her desire to die in Palestine in terms of "dying for something," imagining herself as part of a larger cause—one that would permanently connect her with the land through her burial. On more than one occasion, I heard young people speak of a willingness to die for Palestine. When pressed further, it was clear that this was an adolescent fantasy that had more to do with the guilt of living in relative safety in the United States. In their discussions about Palestine, young people often expressed a desire to dedicate their lives to working on behalf of Palestinians and supporting the realization of an independent nation-state. Constructing a sense of belonging to the suffering

of Palestinians led these young people to develop political commitments that
were not bounded by the country in which they now lived.

Being and Belonging

Being Palestinian—the deep sense that these young people shared that they
belonged to a Palestinian national community—entailed much more than an
attempt on the part of an im/migrant community to maintain its cultural,
linguistic, and religious practices in the context of immigration, and against
a dominant pressure toward assimilation into the United States (Gibson 1988;
Portes and Rumbaut 2001, 2014; Portes and Zhou 1993). The ways in which
these young Palestinian Americans constructed and negotiated their sense of
being and belonging within these transnational social fields suggest the ways
that modern globalization and migration are changing many young people's
experiences of belonging in relation to nation-states. The transnational sense
of belonging they developed offers a more complex picture of the relationship
between "home" and "host" cultures in today's world, suggesting that traditional frameworks for understanding the processes and various trajectories
of im/migrant social incorporation into the United States (see Gibson 1988;
Ogbu 1987; Portes and Rumbaut 2001; Portes and Zhou 1993) may no longer
be sufficient to describe the facts on today's ground. The sense of belonging that these Palestinian Americans were constructing and negotiating suggests a different model—one in which youth from im/migrant communities
do not simply integrate (to varying degrees depending on their position in
this nation's racial hierarchy) into the ethnic fabric of the United States but
rather construct deep transnational connections and commitments (see Abu
El-Haj 2007; DeJaeghere and McCleary 2010; Grewal 2014; Maira 2009; Sánchez 2007; Sánchez and Kasun 2012). This shift from an immigration frame
to a transnational frame has, as I argue in the conclusion of this book, serious implications for understanding youth belonging and citizenship, and for
shaping models of citizenship education.

The everyday practices and long-term strategies through which this community created strong ties to their "homeland" illustrate the ways that these
young Palestinian Americans and their families, similar to other im/migrant
communities in today's context of globalization and mass migration, have
enduring affective ties and political, economic, and social commitments that
span more than one nation-state. Moreover, the strength of their sense of
being Palestinian, and belonging to a Palestinian national community, cannot be explained as primarily a rejection of the United States or a reaction to
the post-9/11 racialized, exclusionary context that these young people experi-

enced in their schools and communities. Certainly, as I illustrate in part 2 of this book, the climate in the United States after September 11, 2001, heightened young people's sense of belonging to a Palestinian national community. However, their sense of being and belonging developed from the everyday practices (embedded across transnational social fields) through which they collectively created and sustained a Palestinian national imaginary and its political project. These everyday experiences must be understood to be fundamentally educative, constituting transnational forms of belonging.

At the same time, as I show in the next chapter, these young people developed their sense of being and belonging not only in the context of everyday discourses and practices within their communities. In fact, it was often through the intersection of their experiences with citizenship and their encounters with the state (particularly the state of Israel) that they developed and articulated dual identities as Palestinian nationals *and* as US citizens.

2

"We Are Stateless, but We Still Have Rights"

Zayd Taher was in seventh grade when his mother took him for a two-year sojourn to a small village near Ramallah. Describing how that experience affected him, Zayd recounted, "Before I went to my country I didn't look into [being Palestinian] at all. I went back home and then I seen three people die in front of me and it was a big change." Before his time in Palestine, Zayd said he often told people he was "Spanish." However, his experiences with life under military occupation awakened his political awareness and, as a consequence, strengthened his sense of being Palestinian.

Zayd described the differences between his general lack of interest in Palestinian politics before he went to live there, and the jarring reality of the occupation:

> I went when I was, like, I was still new—like I heard [about Palestine] but, like I didn't care too much. Like I used to hear about the war, but I never really paid it no mind until I seen it. You know? And I seen gunshots, bloodshed, people dying, it's like, whoa.

Zayd reported being politicized by his experiences witnessing the shooting of youth who were protesting the occupation, and by being subject to numerous curfews.

Everyday life in the West Bank was significantly different from anything he had faced before. Zayd recalled:

> It was just crazy. Every night there would be helicopters and a curfew. You'd be in the street and after a certain time everyone [who was outside] would be in some sort of trouble. It's either in jail or shot. One time it was past curfew; it was past curfew. I didn't know. It was the first day of it [i.e., the curfew], and

they came into our village and they started screaming something. *Mamnū'*
al-tajawwul (curfew) or something, which is in Arabic meaning it's the shut-
down, lockdown, or whatever. But I didn't know that. So my friends said,
"Into your house fast and close the metal gates." And then we hear them, like
they're shooting outside. My mom was like scared 'til I got home. We closed
everything and when we came out next day, phew, there was like [a smell]—
something's burned.

Zayd was new to the experiences of occupation and local resistance. Unused
to the occupation's ubiquitous military presence, sudden imposition of curfew, and threats of violence or arrest, Zayd was quickly schooled by his more
savvy friends about how to respond.

Describing another similar incident, Zayd articulated the sharp contrast
between life in the United States and life under military occupation. Zayd
remembered:

> That night, the Israelis, they said that they had helicopters all over the place,
> and they just put curfews. Six o'clock, you had to be in the house. I didn't
> know this. I was—I went to the store, and my mom came out, saying, "We
> got to go in the house or they're gonna kill us." I was like, "Why are they
> gonna kill us for? For being outside? No, we have our rights." She was like,
> "This is not America." I was like, "So what?" and she was like, "Just get in
> the house."

Zayd's retort to his mother that "we have our rights" reflected the sense of citizenship born of his childhood in the United States—one that entailed rights
he presumed were universal. However, Zayd's experiences in Palestine challenged fundamental assumptions he had previously held about security, the
benevolence of the state, and access to basic civil and political rights. Zayd's
mother, who had grown up under the Israeli occupation, was well aware of
the serious danger involved in disobeying military orders; fearful for their
safety, she admonished him, "This is not America," meaning that the rights
he had in America did not travel with him.

As a consequence of his experiences with the occupation, Zayd returned
to the United States with a different sense of himself as a Palestinian Arab. In
contrast to the idealized portrait of Palestinian rustic life expressed by many
of his peers in the previous chapter, Zayd described his experiences in Palestine in a markedly different tone:

> I'm from the West Bank. Do you know what the West Bank is? You know? It's
> like in [this US city] there are thugs that steal from people. You know, I'm from
> the West Bank around people throwing a missile at you.

Zayd conveyed a sense of bravado as he spoke of the contrast between life in the big city in the United States where theft seemed the primary danger, and the warfare quality he ascribed to life under Israeli occupation.

Zayd's story illustrates a theme that reverberated throughout the stories of many of the Palestinian American youth. Encounters with the authoritarian, violent power of the state of Israel and its military occupation of Palestine solidified their sense of being Palestinian and belonging to its national community. At the same time, for many of these young people, it was their US citizenship, and the rights it guaranteed, that offered a reference point from which to assess experiences with occupation, war, and statelessness. Even though they often felt confused or conflicted about what "being American" meant for them personally, these young people identified politically with their US citizenship and its basic democratic guarantees of social, civil, and political rights. They were fully aware that even in the United States, and particularly for Arab and Muslim communities, basic guarantees of rights were not inviolate (Akram and Johnson 2004; Moore 1999; Murray 2004; Volpp 2002). Nevertheless, these young people believed that citizenship entailed rights—rights that should be guaranteed to all.[1] Moreover, as I show in part 2, their commitment to the ideals of democratic citizenship often led young Palestinian Americans to be critical of the failed promises of US democracy, and they called on this country to fulfill its stated ideals at home and abroad.

This chapter explores these young Palestinian Americans' lived experience of citizenship forged within transnational fields (see also Dyrness 2012; Maira 2009; Miller 2011; Sánchez 2007). If *being* Palestinian entailed a fundamental embodied sense of belonging to a land, people, and national community, these youth spoke of their identification with the United States in terms of citizenship and its attendant rights. Their understanding of citizenship was, importantly, developed in transnational fields and anchored by their knowledge of, and experiences with, the denial of rights that they and their families had experienced, most often, at the hands of other states, particularly the state of Israel. This intersection of the lived experience of democratic citizenship rights and encounters with states' power to deny these rights strengthened both their sense of belonging to the Palestinian national community and their political commitments to ideals promised by democratic citizenship—ideals they believed should be upheld in the United States and elsewhere. Palestinian American youth offer a twist on the "dual frame of reference" model

1. In many ways, these young people developed a grounded view of citizenship that echoes Somers's (2008) conceptualization of citizenship as "the right to have rights."

of immigrant incorporation, which shows that many newcomer communities are optimistic about the promises of US democracy because the educational and economic opportunities here compare favorably with the countries from which they migrated (see, for example, Gibson 1988; Ogbu 1987; M. M. Suárez-Orozco 1987). For the Palestinian American youth, this dual frame was dynamic, multidirectional, and *trans*national. US citizenship rights offered young people a comparative lens for critiquing the abrogation of rights and equality by other countries, and also by the United States.

Citizenship, broadly conceptualized, references not only a person's legal status but also his or her capacity to exercise a range of rights: civil, political, social, and cultural (Banks 2004, 2008; Castles and Davidson 2000; Kymlicka 1995; Marshall 1964; Rosaldo 1994; Somers 2008; Yuval-Davis 2011). Modern forms of democratic citizenship evolved initially to include civil rights, which guarantee individual rights, such as freedom of expression and equality before the law, and political rights, which grant people political power. In more recent times, democratic states have adopted social rights that offer citizens benefits, such as the right to work, equality of opportunity, and entitlements to certain standards of education, health care, and welfare necessary to guarantee their capacity to participate fully in their societies. Social rights can be difficult to define and guarantee. States continually debate how much and what social rights citizens should be guaranteed. Social rights have come under attack in the past few decades in many modern democratic states, as governments have curtailed individuals' rights to education, health, and welfare services. Most recently, *cultural rights*—the right to maintain linguistic, cultural, and group affiliation—have also emerged as key aspects of modern citizenship (Castles and Davidson 2000; Kymlicka 1995; Rosaldo 1994).

Citizenship, with its attendant rights, is a key site that regulates inclusion in and exclusion from the state. The question of who warrants consideration for citizenship has been, and continues to be, hotly contested across modern nation-states (see, for example, Bosniak 2006; Castles and Davidson 2000; Ngai 2004; Yuval-Davis 2011). This question shapes contemporary political debates and policies governing immigration. Citizenship mediates individuals' rights to live and work, but it also regulates who is and who is not entitled to the full protections[2] of due process. This distinction between citizen and noncitizen (and between belonging and not belonging) has had heightened salience since September 11, 2001. Although all citizens have been affected by the PATRIOT Act, Title I and Title II, the United States has curtailed the

---

2. In times of war, citizens' rights have also been routinely violated (see Delgado 2003).

rights of noncitizens (and focused on Arab and Muslim communities) to a greater extent than those of citizens[3] (Akram and Johnson 2004; Cainkar 2009; Cole 2003; Jamal 2008; Murray 2004; Volpp 2002).

For Palestinians, formal state citizenship holds particular salience. Many remain stateless more than six decades after the 1948 *Nakba*, and many more still face substantive barriers to full inclusion in the societies in which they reside. For example, Lebanon has refused to grant Palestinians citizenship, and until recently, Palestinians were restricted by law from working in more than seventy professions, from medicine and engineering to bus and truck driving.[4] Palestinians who are now citizens of Israel had to fight for that status, and still have not achieved equality (Kimmerling and Migdal 2003; Tocci 2010). The importance of legal and full citizenship for access to economic, civil, and political rights is not lost on the Palestinian community (Schulz 2003).

The status of having (or not having) legal citizenship profoundly shapes an individual's economic, social, and political opportunities. However, citizenship entails much more than one's juridical status. My work relies on anthropological approaches to citizenship that focus on "the everyday practices of belonging through which social membership is negotiated" (Lukose 2009, 6; see also B. A. U. Levinson 2005, 2011b; Maira 2009; Ong 1999). This definition focuses on citizenship as practice—practice that does not depend on either legal status or an alignment with dominant discourses of national belonging for its exercise. Even members of states who do not have legal residency or citizenship negotiate social belonging, and participate in the economic, cultural, and political spheres of the places where they live. Moreover, focusing on citizenship as practice acknowledges that legal citizenship is no guarantor of substantive inclusion in a nation-state. Normative definitions of belonging to the national imaginary constrain possibilities for substantive inclusion for communities whose members do not fit the profile of the imagined ideal citizen. The systematic discrimination experienced by racially/ethnically minoritized groups in the economic, cultural, educational, and political spheres of society reflects the relationship between the national imaginary and an

3. The abrogation of rights and targeting of Muslim communities did not begin with the PATRIOT Act (see Moore 1999).

4. In August 2010, the Lebanese government lifted some restrictions on Palestinians' right to work. Abolishing the fee for work permits, the law also permitted Palestinians to apply for some jobs previously denied them. However, Palestinians continue to be denied the right to public-sector jobs and high-status jobs such as medicine, engineering, and law. They continue to be denied the right to health care and education as well as the right to buy property. And they remain in Lebanon without citizenship.

individual's ability to exercise the full range of rights guaranteed by legal citizenship, a point I take up in part 2 of this book.

Examining the ways that the Palestinian American youth identify both as US citizens and as Palestinian nationals, this chapter explores citizenship as lived experience. On one hand, legal citizenship did not guarantee that these young people *felt* American. This sense of not quite being American had multiple sources that included their identification with the Palestinian national imaginary (fleshed out in chapter 1) as well as the exclusionary US nationalist discourses they experienced in their US schools and communities and the political disagreements they had with US foreign policy (which I take up in part 2). On the other hand, the diverse transnational experiences that these young people and their families had with both the exercise and the absence of rights—economic, civil, human, political, and economic—shaped their political perspectives about and commitment to democratic citizenship. Exploring the experiences that shaped these young Palestinian Americans' understanding of citizenship challenges normative models of citizenship that tightly interweave national belonging with the rights of citizenship. I argue that understanding the notions of citizenship these young people developed offers an alternate framework for thinking about citizenship and, as I discuss in the conclusion to this book, developing educational practices that align with the experiences of these, and many other, young people today.

Being American?

As illustrated in chapter 1, the Palestinian American youth expressed passionate commitments to their social, cultural, religious, and nationalist connections to Palestine. However, a majority spoke of their relationship to being "American" in more complex, and even at times tentative, terms. Kamal Sha'ban, whose words began part 1, spoke of his identity as continually "flipping between" Palestinian and American. Ali Khalidi, quoted in chapter 1, spoke about being "kind of in between." Some, such as Kamal and Ali, felt they were both/and. Others, such as Khalida Saba, acknowledged their status as Americans, but desired and felt more part of her Palestinian community. In the following exchange with my research assistant, Khalida responded to the question "Do you consider yourself to be American?"

KHALIDA: Most of, not most of the, most of the time I don't. Sometimes I do. Because the fact is that I do live in America, I'm considered American.
RESEARCH ASSISTANT: Who considers you American?

KHALIDA: A lot of people because, and I was born here, so that's why I'm considered American.

RESEARCH ASSISTANT: So what does American mean to you?

KHALIDA: Not much, really. It just means, it's just a place I was born.

Khalida often found herself questioning the meaning and significance of being American, at times distancing herself (as she did here) from her identity as an American. America signaled "just a place [she] was born" and lived. Khalida spoke of "American" as an identity that others put on her by virtue of her birthright citizenship. However, there were times that she was less tentative, asserting her rights to be treated fairly as an American, and lauding the civic, social, and political rights guaranteed by US citizenship. Khalida's sense of belonging to the United States, however, was less stable, more mutable and context-dependent than was her identification with being Palestinian.

Khalida's sister Leila was more certain about her identification with America. Leila appeared well schooled in the rights and responsibilities of citizenship as she explained:

> You have to feel some connection [to the United States], because you were born here and you carry their—you carry citizenship from here. So you're considered a citizen of the United States of America. So if you're considered a citizen, you have to commit to your duties toward the United States. . . . Every vote counts. Every voice can be heard like they say. And to me being a citizen, registering to vote is important, because like they have all the bulletins, "Register to vote because your voice could be heard." Every voice could be counted. One vote could make a difference. . . . So, once I turn eighteen, I'm going to register to vote.

Leila articulated a greater sense of connection to the United States than did her sister Khalida. This connection was based on her *citizenship* status, and the rights and duties that it entailed, rather than on a sense of national or cultural belonging. Leila expressed a commitment to fulfilling the traditional roles and obligations that citizenship involves. However, her words (here and elsewhere in her interviews) suggested hesitation and a tenuous relationship with Americans and the United States: "You carry their"—she broke off and then continued—"you carry citizenship from here." Thus, her words, similar to those of a majority of the Palestinian American youth, suggested that being "American" referenced their US citizenship, which they often described more as a set of rights they have rather than as an identity they inhabit.

Other Palestinian Americans expressed a firmer sense of being American. Hasan Hamadi, who, as noted in chapter 1, grew up in the United States but spent many summers in Palestine, described what it meant to him to be American:

> Being American is, it, it truly is *a blessing* to be, to be born here instead of in Palestine. Only for the reason that the education is better and you can, or, or more having whether it's better or not doesn't really matter, when you have a degree from [a local state university] it's better than having a degree from, from I don't know Al-Quds University. And like it's better, apparently better. And also, also you just have access to so many different things. It truly is a different place than, than other places. And I don't know, it's, it, in the beginning I used to say, I'm just American 'cause I was born here. Another thing is, remember I said [earlier] I'm not American. I don't agree with America's stance on the war on Palestinians. But now I say I'm American because, like again aside from the fact that I was born here is just because of my experiences here. Just not all of them bad, I guess just a childhood that wasn't, it wasn't terrible, or it was terrible but essentially it made me who I am.

Although Hasan laid stronger claim to his identity as an American than did many of his peers, his words suggest that this identification reflected a developmental process, and was not unmitigated. With a comparative frame of reference, Hasan described being American as a "blessing" because of the opportunities and rights it affords, rights and opportunities that are unavailable to their family members in Palestine. At the same time, Hasan described an earlier time when, similar to many of his peers, he had felt conflicted about claiming an "American" identity—it was "just" a place he was born. He had felt distant from being American because of US foreign policy in Palestine. However, in the end he came to adopt "American" as part of who he is, because childhood experiences in the United States "made me who I am."

The complex, often ambivalent, feelings these young people expressed about being American had multiple roots. As described in chapter 1, their experiences growing up as part of a transnational community contributed to the development of their consciousness as Palestinian nationals seeking to gain an independent homeland. However, to focus solely on the effects of the Palestinian transnational experience would be to miss two critical factors that made it difficult for Palestinian American youth to *feel* American. First, they were strongly opposed to the United States' foreign policy, in relation not only to the Palestinian-Israeli conflict but also to the wars in Afghanistan and Iraq (see Stockton 2009 for similar observations about Arab American opinions on foreign policy). Second, and more important, they were deeply conscious of the exclusionary, nationalist, and racialized discourses and practices that affected their everyday experiences in schools and communities. When Leila hesitates in her use of pronouns—when she talks about carrying "their" citizenship—

she is, in some large part, also signaling the ways that Palestinians have been excluded from full membership in the American national imaginary. In part 2, I take up the ways that the Palestinian Americans encountered (and resisted) racialized discourses that positioned them as dangerous outsiders to the American national imaginary. In the remainder of this chapter, I show that although, for these youth, a sense of *being* American seemed hard to achieve, a democratic sensibility of what citizenship entails was not (for similar observations about Palestinian Swedes, see Schulz 2003). I argue that this sensibility of rights was forged largely in the gap between their experiences with US citizenship rights and the lack of those same rights in Palestine.

Citizenship as Rights

Not feeling American did not translate into a sense of alienation from or discord with everyday life in the United States. These young people were appreciative of the basic rights that they and their families were able to exercise and enjoy because of their status as US citizens. Their understanding of the importance of these basic rights was fundamentally shaped in contrast to the living conditions of the occupation. Many of the Palestinian American youth recognized and appreciated US citizenship as a privileged status, highly valued for the political, civil, and social rights it offered these young people and their families.

Perhaps the most important function of US citizenship (and legal residency) for the youth was to facilitate social rights—economic and educational opportunities—that were unavailable "back home" to Palestinian families due to the harsh conditions of the occupation. Adam dreamed of a future in which he could "go back home," but he argued that the current conditions in Palestine made this impossible in the near future:

> Back home in this time, it's hard to find a job. And it's hard to go to school. Over here you're free. You can do whatever you want. And we own two stores, and we're working. We're getting money, and we're sending money back home.

Adam's reference to the idea that "over here you're free" invokes the notion of rights that his community sought in the United States—rights they were leveraging to support people back home.

Samira also viewed her privileged citizenship status in terms of the responsibility it entailed to family members in Palestine:

> For me and other Palestinians living in the United States of America, I think that there is a reason why they are living here. I think there is a big reason why

my family and me are living here. And while we are living here, we are supporting those in Palestine. I have relatives who live there, and my dad is working here in America, and he's taking the money and sending it to Palestine in
order for them to pay their bills or get food or clothes and everything else. So
over here I feel it is our duty to work and, you know, help out the people over
there because over there right now there are no jobs.

US citizenship afforded Adam, Samira, and other Palestinian families the opportunity to work and earn money to support their families in the West Bank,
families that faced extreme financial hardship living under military occupation. The contrast between the availability of work in the United States and the
lack of jobs in Palestine highlights the ways that opportunities (to work and
to go to school) are rights necessary for full participation in society. Samira's
observation that "it is our duty to work" invokes (albeit unconsciously) the relationship between rights and responsibilities, typically embedded in notions
of citizenship. Thus, like many transnational im/migrants who are driven to
migrate from their homelands because of political and economic conditions,
these Palestinian families look to US citizenship to realize social rights—such
as the right to work and opportunities for education—while working on behalf of and maintaining a relationship with those "back home."

Palestinian youth often emphasized social rights, especially the right to an
education, as important features of US citizenship. As discussed above, social
rights include a broad range of rights that guarantee citizens minimum standards for economic security, well-being, and social inclusion, such as the right
to work, equal educational opportunity, and entitlements to health and other
welfare services (Abowitz and Harnish 2006; Castles and Davidson 2000;
Marshall 1964; Yuval-Davis 2011). Many students experienced how difficult it
was to get an education in Palestine because of the military occupation and
the frequent closure of schools imposed by the military authorities. Others
spoke positively about some aspects of US education, contrasting the stricter,
more traditional schooling system in Palestine with the more relaxed atmo-
sphere in US schools. Some of the girls noted that there were more opportunities in the United States for them to finish high school and attend college. A
majority of the students spoke about their parents' desire for them to obtain
professional training.

Khalida pointed to important social rights in the United States that did
not exist to the same extent in Palestine:

In a way, I feel comfortable here because we have a lot of rights here, for example, child abuse. A lot of people abuse their children there and no one can
do anything about it. And where I live [in Palestine] there is no source of

medical attention, no hospitals, no clinics. We have to like transfer and take
transportation like about fifteen to twenty miles away from where we live just
to get medical attention and medical help. And now with the checkpoints it
takes even longer. So a person can die just on the way there. And here every
other county, not a county, just a neighborhood, there's a clinic or a hospital or
somewhere you can go. That's the only difference.

Khalida contrasted positively the social services—social rights that guarantee
individual health and welfare—available in the United States to the lack of
comparable services in the occupied West Bank. However, it is important to
note her reference to checkpoints, a routine part of everyday life in Palestine,
that deny people basic civil and human rights. Khalida's observation that, for
some Palestinians, the checkpoints have resulted in a denial of health care is
a well-documented reality of everyday life in Palestine (Makdisi 2008). The
raw power of the Israeli state to deny Palestinians basic civil and human rights
simultaneously impedes them from accessing social rights. Even with the ongoing erosion of the welfare state in the United States, the guarantees of social
rights far exceed those that exist in the occupied West Bank.

These young people also described the importance of US citizenship in
terms of other freedoms that involved their political and civil rights. Some
students referenced access to a legal system (through which, for example, they
could attempt to contest unfair school expulsions) and the right to vote as
valued freedoms that they and their relatives in Palestine struggled to exercise under the conditions of the military occupation. At our first after-school
club meeting following the 2004 US presidential election, Adam bounded
in, excited to announce that he had voted for the first time, even though he
expressed disappointment that his candidate had not won.

Most fundamentally, US citizenship provides a basic human right denied to many Palestinians (and other refugee populations): the right to move
across borders. For many, US citizenship facilitated travel to and from their
village in the West Bank. Zena Khalili, who grew up in the United States and
traveled during the summer to Palestine, put it this way: "As an American
citizen, you have the right to go and come back and do whatever you please. It
gives you more respect, I think." Zena's words suggest that holding US citizenship is both a legal permit that allows border crossing as well as a source of
some degree of "respect" and protection from the routine harassment that
many Palestinians have experienced at borders across the globe. Importantly,
the power of US citizenship is tethered to this nation's global dominance: US
citizenship (as well as that of Western European nations) afforded members
greater economic, political, and civil rights than those of many other nations.

Border crossings hold a particular place in Palestinian consciousness. Rashid Khalidi (1997) writes:

> Borders are a problem for Palestinians since their identity—which is constantly reinforced in myriad positive and negative ways—not only is subject to question by the powers that be; but is also in many contexts suspect almost by definition. As a result, at each of these barriers which most others take for granted, every Palestinian is exposed to the possibility of harassment, exclusion, and sometimes worse, simply because of his or her identity. (2)

The borders of nation-states have separated Palestinian people from their places of birth and from their family members. Many Palestinians carry no citizenship but instead are issued travel documents by Israel, Egypt, Iraq, or Lebanon, listing them as stateless Palestinians and allowing them limited mobility across national borders (R. Khalidi 1997). Even Palestinians who do carry the citizenship of a powerful nation, including that of the United States, are often treated differently at borders. They may be granted "more respect," as Zena suggests, but they are not guaranteed freedom from harassment or exclusion, since exercising their right to move across borders is often accompanied by increased surveillance, harassment, or questioning such that their freedom of movement is constrained. Nevertheless, Palestinian youth were well aware that US citizenship offers them relative freedom to traverse borders that many Palestinians typically lack. These border crossings highlight the contradictory nature of the modern era: amid global flows of people, information, technologies, and products, nation-states maintain a strong, central role in regulating and enforcing their own borders (Castles and Davidson 2000; Soysal 1994; Yuval-Davis, Anthias, and Kofman 2005; Yuval-Davis 2011).

Whereas for some, such as Zena, US citizenship offered more "respect" than citizenship from other nations, for others, such as Kamal and Zayna Sha'ban, US citizenship was a lifeline out of statelessness. Like many Palestinians, Kamal and Zayna's great-grandparents and grandparents (who were children at the time) were exiled from Palestine in 1948. Their families became refugees scattered across Jordan, Syria, and Iraq. Although some members of their family who had made it to Jordan were granted Jordanian citizenship, others who ended up in Syria and Iraq remained without citizenship, their statelessness leaving them with no right to travel. Some members of their mother's family eventually came to the United States and became citizens. In time, Kamal and Zayna's maternal aunt, a US citizen, applied for a green card for their mother, Amira. As discussed in chapter 1, when Amira was pregnant with Zayna, she came to the United States to deliver her so that

Zayna would be a citizen, and she did the same when, five years later, she had Kamal. After each delivery, she returned to Syria and later Iraq to be with her husband, who remained a refugee-status Palestinian without citizenship or even the right to travel. As Zayna explained:

> My mom is a Jordanian citizen, but she can't give us her citizenship, 'cause it's passed down through the father, not the mother. We would have, had we not been born in the United States, we would have been refugee-status Palestinians, like my dad. And that means we can only, we can be in Iraq and maybe get a visa into Syria. So she had us here. And then my dad went [from Syria where he was working] to visit his family in Iraq, and the [first] Gulf War broke out. And he got stuck there, 'cause nobody knew that the United States was going to invade and put sanctions on and—or at least he didn't. So when Iraq was sanctioned he couldn't go in and out anymore, 'cause the only place he could go to was Syria and the border was closed.

For Zayna and Kamal, US citizenship spared them the fate of becoming members of a fourth generation of statelessness. Her parents' experiences with statelessness led Zayna to develop a nuanced understanding of how citizenship constrains or enables possibilities for work and travel across borders—possibilities and constraints that have an impact on access to a range of rights that guarantee security and well-being.

The story of Zayna and Kamal's childhood offers a window into the complex ways that their parents navigated between statelessness and citizenship. After each child's birth, Amira returned to Syria, and later Iraq, to be with her husband, whose lack of any legal citizenship prevented him from traveling. However, after the war directly threatened their family, Amira and her husband decided she should leave him and bring their children back to the United States permanently. They moved close to their relatives in the United States, and Amira worked full-time in local small businesses to support her children while she obtained her citizenship and applied for her husband to join them. As young adults, Zayna and Kamal felt close to their parents, ever aware of the dangers and separations they had endured to obtain citizenship. They also admired their parents' early histories of community activism in the refugee camps in Syria. Speaking of what she had learned from her mother about citizenship, Zayna said, "And she still taught us that we were stateless, but that like we had rights." Zayna's, as well as her brother Kamal's, sense of being Palestinian, and their explicit political commitment to Palestinian statehood, grew from knowledge of their family's experiences with statelessness and their struggles to obtain rights afforded by democratic citizenship.

These experiences shaped a view of rights that transcends the boundaries of national citizenship.

This complex picture of how citizenship works for people who are trying to navigate between a broad human need for basic and inclusive rights and the realities of nation-state-based citizenship is often lost in contemporary, conservative political debates that decry the actions of women such as Amira. The Sha'bans' story shows the disjuncture between two conceptions of citizenship and rights: one notion ties these rights to nation-states (and the different range of rights each nation guarantees), and a second ideal treats all humans as equally deserving of these guarantees (as enshrined in the United Nations Charter). The Sha'bans' struggles for citizenship illustrate the human cost of the first view of citizenship—a view that frames a wide range of policies, from those that drive immigration laws to those that shape citizenship education in our schools (Abowitz and Harnish 2006). Implicit in Zayna's observation that statelessness should not equate with a lack of rights is a normative claim that rights are due to us as human beings, not just as citizens of particular nation-states.

Encountering the State of Israel

For Zayna and Kamal, it was their parents' struggle to obtain citizenship that brought into relief the power of nation-states to dictate the parameters of people's lives. For many of the young people, it was through direct encounters with the state of Israel that they developed their political sensibilities, as illustrated earlier by Zayd's experiences with the occupation. It is important to remember that Zayd returned to the United States the summer before the outbreak of the second intifada, and his experiences reflected the fact that the occupation made life in the West Bank and Gaza anything but normal well before September 2000. However, the start of the second intifada marked a significant break that many youth reported as a reason for their return to the United States. Ali Khalidi, for example, explained:

> The town where we used to live in didn't have too much problems. It's just the way, like if we wanted to go to the city. My school used to be in Jerusalem. So when we used to go there we have to cross a checkpoint. And until the intifada—the one in 2000 happened—and they wanted to build the wall, that's when we left because they closed the school down. So we got, we had to leave and then, after that we just go there for a visit, so [we came back] 'cause of the intifada. If it wasn't for that I was supposed to finish high school there, graduate from there, *tawjihi* (end of high school exam). So we came here. Right now

we go to *Falasṭīn* (Palestine) in the summer; but when we were there we used
to come here in the summer.

Ali, similar to many of the youth who came from his village, reported few
problems before the intifada. Of course, the reality that children needed to
travel through a checkpoint to get to their school—a circumstance he reported here so matter-of-factly—illustrates the everyday impediments of the
occupation that predated the outbreak of the second intifada. Checkpoints
have been a routine part of Palestinian life under Israel's military occupation
(see Makdisi 2008), a key site at which the exercise of state power becomes
highly visible.

Everyday life changed significantly in the aftermath of the intifada, and
securing a culturally appropriate education—the primary reason that parents
had sent their children back to Palestine—became an erratic enterprise. Ali
described his school experience when the intifada started:

> But I mean then when we're in school like I remember when it [the intifada]
> first started because we're like ten, fifteen minutes from the *al-ḥarām al-sharīf*
> (Noble Sanctuary), the *qubbat al-sakhra* (Dome of the Rock). So it's like where
> the incident happened, when like [former Israeli prime minister] Sharon went
> in. And like I remember like right across from us is a checkpoint. So when
> people used to throw rocks at them [the Israeli soldiers], the soldiers used to
> throw gases, and all the gases used to come into the school. So I remember
> like we're sitting in class and then oh you hear something inside the classroom
> going or like bullets or whatever they used to throw. So it became crazy like
> now your life is threatened. You know what I mean? So that's when my dad
> found like it's not even worth it like.

Here Ali was referencing the incident that precipitated the second intifada in
September 2000. Ariel Sharon, then the prime minister of Israel, visited the
al-ḥarām al-sharīf with a contingent of Israeli soldiers; the visit was highly
provocative and sparked mass demonstrations precipitating the second intifada against the occupation. This incident and the ensuing demonstrations
had an immediate disruptive effect on Ali's education, and his father made the
decision to return his family to the United States, where his children's safety[5]
and education could be guaranteed.

Hania Nabulsi, whose idyllic recollections of her two-year sojourn in Palestine quoted in chapter 1 had a hyperbolic quality to them, also spoke of the

---

5. Ali and his family lived in a major US city with a significantly high murder rate, and their
working-class neighborhood was not completely immune to this violence. However, on balance
their lives were relatively secure, and Regional High had a very low incidence of violence.

changes wrought by the second intifada. She contrasted her memories before 2000 to those that followed the outbreak of the uprising:

> When I was there in 2000, then they [i.e., the Israelis] attacked. After I came back, they attacked again. Ramallah was closed and all these other *yahūd*[6] like [before] we went to a lot of places where the *yahūd* was there; but Arab also were there too. Like now they [the Israelis] ask them for their passports and you might, in Quds [Jerusalem] you can't even go in with, without—like if you have a *hawiyya* (Israeli identity card)[7] you can't go and like only if you're an American citizen, or even if you're old, senior citizen you can't go there, and it's not fair that they get to make all these rules. My aunt, *rawwaḥat* (returned home) last year to the *bilād* (homeland) and she was right there *fi* (in) Tel Aviv *yaʿnī* (I mean), and she's like what an hour away from [her village]. And they said no and they sent her all the way back to America. *Yaʿnī*, you're right there you see it with your own eyes yet you can't go and touch it because of what, *yahūd* they're setting the rules? You can go, you can, you can't go, you have to get this, you can't get that.

Life changed palpably after the start of the second intifada. Here Hania noted almost in passing the violence that ensued. But her focus was trained on the fundamental ways that normal everyday routines were shattered. She mentioned the fact that before the intifada, Palestinians and Israelis sometimes shared the same spaces (these occurrences, while not commonplace in the occupied West Bank and Gaza, were most likely to take place in family resorts, for example, on the Dead Sea). Hania also attended to the restrictions of movement now faced by Palestinians. For example, it became exceedingly difficult for Palestinians who resided in the West Bank and Gaza to get permits to go to Jerusalem. Moreover, even Palestinians with US citizenship—a status that normally guaranteed the right of travel—were sometimes turned back at the borders, refused entry to visit their homes. (Lena Deeb's poem, cited in chapter 1, told a similar story of the Israelis refusing her grandfather entry, and she was upset that "the world have let it gone this far.") In commenting on the unfairness that the Israelis get to "make all these rules," Hania

---

6. *Yahūd* is the Arabic word for Jews. Palestinians living in the Occupied Palestinian Territories often use *yahūd* to mean Israeli Jews, both the soldiers and the settlers, who are typically the only Jews they ever meet.

7. The *hawiyya* is the identity card that Israel issues to Palestinians living under occupation. It regulates where they can live and work. Israel has cut off access to occupied East Jerusalem for most Palestinians. Through a series of administrative measures, Israel has also been systematically depopulating East Jerusalem by rescinding the residency rights of Palestinians from East Jerusalem (see Makdisi 2008).

implicitly invoked the presumption of democratic rights to shared decision making. Hania's (and Lena's) outrage that Israelis have been allowed to violate fundamental civil, human, and political rights indicates a sensibility of democratic rights developed, at least in some part, through their experiences with citizenship in the United States.

Although US citizenship did not completely protect Palestinians from the harsh rules of the military occupation, the Palestinian American youth were well aware of the ways in which it often offered them powerful rights not afforded to other Palestinians. At the most basic level, families with US citizenship could leave Palestine in order to ensure that their children could continue their education. In discussing his family's decision to return to the United States after the inception of the intifada, Ali said:

> I mean it was the talk of that time about the intifada, 'cause we weren't the only one who left. It was many, many Americans who had the American like passports and stuff that they can leave. They left too because of the schools. And, over there, you have to know when they stop, everything stops—like schools, going shopping, going anywhere like leaving the town. So missing school's like missing a whole year, and you can't just do that. So most of the people whoever can get out, leave, they left.

US citizenship is a strategic resource that allowed Ali and other Palestinian families access to basic civil and social rights denied by the Israeli military occupation: the right to move about and conduct routine daily business, and the right to pursue an education for their children.

Thus, many of the youth, particularly those who had spent most of their lives in the United States, interpreted their experiences with Israeli state power through a lens of US democratic citizenship that, at least in the ideal, guarantees basic civil, social, human, and political rights. For example, as expressed in the story that began this chapter, Zayd's incredulity at his mother's fear that they would be in physical danger if they violated the curfew imposed by the Israeli army grew from his conviction that "we have rights." The enabling power of their rights-bearing citizenship offered these young people a critical perspective on the extreme ways that the state of Israel curtailed the lives of Palestinians through the military occupation.

After graduating from high school, Samira Khateeb went to spend the summer with her relatives in Palestine—her first visit since she was a toddler. I analyze in detail her lengthy narrative about the visit because it shows the kinds of everyday confrontations that Palestinians have with the state of Israel, and highlights the major argument of this chapter. Samira's description of her awakening to the nature of Israeli state power shows that, because of her life in the United States, she had come to expect and embody the safety and security of rights conferred by citizenship. Moreover, through her narrative, Samira conveyed the range of emotions—shock, fear, confusion, and humiliation—she experienced as her understanding of citizenship rights was upended, and she confronted the punitive nature of the Israeli occupation that many of her relatives in Palestine experienced as normal.

Samira's stories illustrate a range of constraints that Palestinians routinely face because of this occupation. Samira's narrative began with her nine-hour detention at the Tel Aviv airport:

> Once I reached Tel Aviv airport, I was there for nine hours and supposedly it was security testing or whatever, that I was—I mean when I—I asked a lot of people and not just people who work at airports but anybody that's around there, I asked them why they think they kept me there and they just tell you it's just for security reasons. But I don't see why an eighteen-year-old girl had to stay nine hours at an airport for security reasons when they—I mean I can understand if I had anything in my background or history but it was my first time there. And basically what I asked my family and a lot of my cousins why do you think they did that? It's for one reason: they don't want you to go back, so they try to scare the hell out of you so you don't never want to go back. And it worked.

The lengthy detention of Palestinians at the Tel Aviv airport has been routine for decades. Samira, however, was unprepared for and confused by this treatment. The explanation that this was for "security" reasons made no sense to her, and she could not imagine any threat posed by an eighteen-year-old girl who had grown up in the United States. Her observation that she could "understand if I had anything in my background" suggests her implicit assumption of presumed innocence enshrined in an American sense of rights. From the perspective of her Palestinian relatives, the purpose of the detention was to intimidate Palestinians and curtail their desire to return to their homeland.

Samira continued her description:

> At first I was waiting for at least three hours by myself in the airport and I had no contact with anybody. They told me to sit in the back of the airport near their office. But when you go inside the office there's like a lot of rooms that they, I don't know what they do in there but I was sitting there for about three hours alone. So I started to get scared and I was like you know the driver who's here to pick me up probably left and the airport was like basically empty, because flights they're not always landing there. And then after like three hours more people started coming in from different flights and then I met Arabic families and they saw me crying and they would come and ask me, "Are you

OK?" and "Give us your phone number when we . . . once we get out of the airport we'll call them and don't worry, you know, this is you know normal." And *it wasn't normal for me.* So after the three hours one of the guys came out and he looked at me and he was like, "Why are you crying? We're not gonna bite you," and, "It's OK," and da-da-da-da-da. And I was like you know, "Can I use the phone? I need to call my aunt." And he told me, "Let me, I'll ask the people inside." So then a girl came out asking the same question. I told her that I need, really need to use the phone and then they finally did let me use the phone. Once I used the phone I called my aunt who lives back home and I told her you know they're keeping me here and she heard me crying over the phone she told me, "It's OK, it's, you know, don't show them that you're scared. Tough it out." But I, I just couldn't do it. I was like a little . . . I, I, not even a mouse. A mouse probably, a mouse's heart is probably braver than mine. But I was just, I was in tears for basically six hours nonstop. (emphasis added)

Samira's abject fear—palpably expressed by her sense that a mouse's heart would be braver than hers—stood out in this context in which other Palestinians tried to comfort her and reassure her that this was routine. Their expressions of care, and confirmation that this was normal, did little to assuage her feelings of dislocation and powerlessness in the face of a situation that was anything but normal for her. As a young woman who had grown up entirely in the United States, her definition of "normal" was grounded to a different assumption of guarantees of basic civil and human rights. Samira retained this sense of normal guarantees of democratic rights even though many of those rights had been compromised for members of Arab and Muslim communities in the United States both before, and even more so after, September 11, 2001 (Akram and Johnson 2004; Jamal 2008; Moore 1999; Murray 2004; Volpp 2002).

Samira continued:

And then finally after a couple more hours, two guys came out. One sat on the right of me, one on the left asking me questions. And they gave me a paper and pen told me to write down everybody that I know that's in Palestine. They asked me how much money do you have and, you know a couple of other questions and then, after maybe another hour the same two guys came, pulled me into a room and there was a third guy there. One was behind the computer in front of me, one on the right one on the left, and the room was [tiny]. And, I even asked them for a cup of water because I was really feeling bad. And they got me hot, hot water to drink. Yeah so I, I didn't drink it and, and I left it there and I asked them how long this is gonna take. They said just, you know, don't, like when we're done we're done, don't even ask. So I told them

OK. They asked me who's my grandfather. They put his name in the computer they got, put a picture of my grandfather on the computer and they asked me if it's him. I said yes, and my grandfather is dead. And then they asked me all these other questions that I, you know, I didn't even know the answers to. And they were talking to me in Arabic and I asked them not to talk to me in Arabic. For one their Arabic I didn't understand it and for two I really didn't want them talking to me in Arabic. I asked them talk to me in English. I really couldn't understand them talk. You know, anybody that's learning another language talks it slightly different than our country exactly. Then I even have trouble sometimes understanding, you know, other Palestinians. But I mean with them I asked them not to talk to me in, in Arabic. And they just kept on asking me questions and then they told me go sit outside again. I sat outside and I kept waiting, waiting. And then finally one lady came out and she gave me my passport and she said you're good to go. So I told her OK and I just grabbed it and I just ran out—couldn't wait to get out.

Unfamiliar with the powers of a security state, Samira seemed particularly surprised by the capacity of the Israeli officers to pull up information and a picture of her deceased grandfather. Samira appeared disoriented and frightened by an interrogation she could not completely follow because of the differences between the Arabic she and the officers spoke. At the same time, her insistence that they speak with her in English subtly invoked her American identity in a context in which her citizenship appeared to have little to offer her in terms of protection.

Samira's airport ordeal did not end with her release. She continued:

And, once I got out I went to go get my luggages. And when I got there my luggages been laying there for hours. And I got there my luggages were open and half my stuff was on the floor. When I looked my luggages were black. When I looked there was footprints on them, people were stomping on my suitcases. So I sat there and I, I started picking up my stuff and my luggage was really heavy, and the people that work with the airline and they're responsible for your luggages. . . . So I was picking it up and they saw me having trouble with it nobody asked, "Do you need any help?" There was two guys and they literally just sitting there laughing. So I ignored it and you know I just picked it up and I was so, so mad that I you know I had all the strength and everything to just pick it up and throw it on the cart. So then I, I did ask them, "Aren't you supposed to pick it up and put it behind the counter?" And he was like just take your stuff and go, and I was like let me just shut up 'cause I don't want them to keep me here again. So I just picked them up and I ran out and my driver was there and he took me home. I arrived at my village at 1:00 a.m. when I was supposed to be there at 5:00. It was a horrible experience.

Samira's words conveyed a sense of degradation and humiliation as her belongings had been carelessly dumped on the airport floor, and her suitcases stepped on and blackened. Even the airline service personnel whose job should have been to help her refused to come to her aid. Although it is impossible to know for certain what motivated the airline personnel to treat Samira (and her belongings) with such indifference, her story is consistent with the racialization of Palestinians in Israeli society (Tocci 2010). From the first moment of entry, Samira was learning a new landscape of citizenship.

Samira's experience in the airport was only the first in her education about security states and dealing with everyday life under military occupation. In her description of a trip she and her mother took to travel from their West Bank village for a visit to Jerusalem, Samira revealed the disjuncture between the rights she assumed she had as a US citizen and the reality on the ground:

> And then while I was there, me and my mom at one point decided to go and visit Jerusalem. And from what I knew if you're an American citizen, you're allowed to go wherever you want anytime you want. They won't ask you anything, but that's—it was bullshit. We, me and my mom, you know we got dressed we woke up early in the morning ready to go to Jerusalem. We got in the car and there was a couple of other people with us in the car but they weren't Americans. Me and my mom were the only Americans in the car. There was about seven people. And as we were leaving the village there was a checkpoint. So they stopped us and they asked for everybody's ID. So me and my mom pulled out our passports and we gave it to them. The guy came back and he said, "Everybody's allowed to go. Two American passports, go back." So I looked at my mom I was like, "Ah, you know are they serious?" And my mom was like, "Yeah." So everybody in the car was used to seeing this 'cause they were people who lived there. But—and my mom you know she was OK with it. But me, I you know I wasn't. I was like you know why can they tell us when to leave the village and when to enter the village? OK the village people I can understand if they tell them to go back, but why us?

With the rights of US citizenship as her point of reference, Samira was ill prepared to confront the harsh and capricious rules of the military occupation of Palestine. She assumed that her US passport would guarantee her basic civil and human rights and separate her from the everyday violations that the Palestinians in the village routinely experienced. Her mother's apparent resignation to the situation contrasted sharply with her own anger at the power of the Israelis to regulate their rights of movement.

But then, in what seemed a surprising and risky move, her mother and the other passengers in the car told Samira to use her status as a US citizen to negotiate with the military personnel. Samira continued:

So my mom and everybody in the car told me to go down and talk to them in English. So I looked at my mom and I'm like, "I'm not going down. You know they have guns." And I'm like I thought it was like here you know over here you're not allowed to open your door if a police pulls you over. You know you honk your horn until he comes to you. You're not allowed to go up to him. So I was like to my, I mean if you open the door and get out they have the right to shoot you. So I was like to my mom, "If I step foot out you know, how do you know they're not you know gonna pull the trigger?" And my mom's like, "Just do it." So I got out, and I was like you know I'm gonna do it. So I got out and I walked to the guy and they as soon as they saw me get out the car all of them just ran to me. They, they, they don't know what to expect you know I could have, to them I could have bombs under my, what I was wearing. And so they came to me and I started talking to them in English. Well first they, they didn't dare to come near me until after like two minutes I was just yelling so they can hear me, and I said I want, I need to talk to you, and they couldn't understand English that good. So when he came to me he asked me what do you want and I told them why you're not letting me and my mom go through? We're here on vacation and you know I want to go sightseeing, you know. And he was like, where you're from? And I told him the US and he was like where? And I was like the US and then I was like America? And, and he doesn't know when I said the US he didn't know where I was from and he looked at my passport he didn't know what kind of passport it was what, from what country, nothing. So then he just told me show me your visa, and I opened my passport and I showed him and he was like all right go ahead. So I went back in the car and I was like he said go ahead and he let us through.

It is difficult to know what spurred Samira to overcome her fear that she might be exposing herself to being shot; but she did, and, remarkably, she was able to use her status as a US citizen to assert her and her mother's right to visit Jerusalem and simply be tourists. She used English and waved her passport, symbolically invoking her difference from ordinary Palestinians. Samira's encounter with the soldiers at the checkpoint illustrates the shifting, unpredictable power of citizenship as she attempted to leverage the status of her US citizenship to assert her right to travel to Jerusalem. At first, their status as outsiders—persons with US citizenship but without the appropriate Palestinian identity cards—marked Samira and her mother as different for the purposes of exclusion: as Palestinian Americans with fewer rights than their fellow passengers. In her initial confrontation with the soldiers, Samira's US citizenship was visibly meaningless; the soldiers did not seem to know what her passport signified, and her citizenship status conveyed no rights within this system of military occupation. However, eventually, Samira and her mother were marked as different from the other Palestinians—tourists with visas on a sightseeing vacation. Samira's story shows how citizenship unfolds as a negotiated practice, as she, in collaboration with her fellow travelers, pushed back at the soldier's exercise of authoritarian power to assert basic rights that she (and her fellow passengers) assumed she should have.

Samira's experiences with the occupation rattled her sense of security in more profound ways than similar encounters that her peers reported. Perhaps the intensity with which she felt violated by the power of the occupation was due to the fact that she had lived her entire life in the United States; her internalized sense of the guarantee of basic rights was deep. Her experiences with the Israeli occupation—from her extended detention in the airport to travel restrictions within the West Bank and encounters with the military in the villages—were fundamentally jarring, and she returned to the United States plagued by anxiety and nightmares.

The direct experiences that Samira and many of her peers had in the West Bank taught them much about everyday life Palestinians share under the Israeli military occupation, and in doing so, it strengthened their sense of being part of the Palestinian national community and their commitment to the cause of Palestinian independence. At the same time, their grounded experiences of US citizenship offered a framework of democratic rights from which they narrated, made sense of, and, occasionally, tactically avoided Israeli state coercion and discipline.

Landscapes of Belonging, and Citizenship in Transnational Fields

Samira first went to Palestine when she was eighteen in order to meet her fiancé. She knew that she would likely spend summer vacations in Palestine, but she planned to make an adult life in the United States, teaching, raising children, and being politically active on behalf of Palestinian independence. Adam dreamed of returning "back home." Kamal anticipated a medical career dedicated to working with Palestinians in refugee camps. At times Khalida wished she could return to the quiet life of her family's village in Palestine; at other moments she looked forward to becoming a teacher and living close to her family in the United States. The lives of all of these young Palestinian Americans were interwoven with the imagined and material landscapes of Palestine and the United States, and as a result, they developed rich and complex affiliations across these two communities. Their everyday lives in the United States were intimately bound up with the cultural, economic, religious, and political ties they maintained with a Palestinian "homeland" and the political quest for an independent state. The multifaceted and at times conflicted ways they talked about their identifications as Palestinians and as

Americans evolved from their experiences growing up in transnational fields and (as I explore in part 2) from the position their community held in the post-9/11 US political context. These experiences must be understood to be fundamentally *educative* in nature: they constitute a transnational citizenship education woven through the fabric of everyday life in families, communities, and society.

In describing their connections to the United States, a majority of the Palestinian American youth drew a distinction between citizenship and a sense of national belonging—between "having" US citizenship and "being" Palestinian. They continually discussed and negotiated the shifting boundaries between "ours" and "theirs." At times, they spoke of the United States in terms that highlighted their position as outsiders: they described "living in *their* country" and "carrying *their* citizenship." However, they also wore the protective coat of their US citizenship proudly, and they were knowledgeable about, and appreciative of, the range of important rights it afforded them. Their Palestinian community, similar to many other transnational communities, was compelled to migrate by the unequal global distribution of social, economic, political, and civil rights. This community mobilized social, political, and economic resources across national borders to respond to shifting political and economic conditions. Although these strategies are similar to Ong's (1999) description of those used by elite transnationals exercising what she calls "flexible citizenship," there is a critical difference for Palestinian (and many other) transnational communities. These flexible citizenship practices are a response to conditions of oppression—conditions under which they are unable to realize economic, civil, social, and perhaps most important, *political* rights (see also Maira 2009). The creative deployment of citizenship serves as a reminder of the tenacious power that nation-states hold to regulate individuals' access to rights, even in this time of globalization and widespread transnational migration (see also Castles and Davidson 2000; Yuval-Davis 2011).

To a large extent, the experiences that Palestinian American youth have with belonging and citizenship reflect the particular political context of their stateless community and its aspirations for national independence. As Musa eloquently put it in the previous chapter, they are "trying to have an identity without a place in the world." The capacity to realize a place in the world depends on sustaining a national imaginary, and this work occurs in the everyday practices through which linguistic, cultural, and religious practices and national histories are produced. However, it also entails a view of rights to which all people should have access (rights instantiated in the United Nations Declaration of Universal Human Rights). For the young Palestinian Americans with whom I worked, this understanding of rights was forged out of the contrastive experiences of rights-bearing citizenship and the abject conditions brought about by exile, statelessness, or military occupation. Citizenship entailed much more than their legal status in the United States. It offered a vantage point for understanding and engaging in transnational citizenship practices—practices through which they navigated social, cultural, and political belonging in relation to more than one place. Although related to the observation that youth from many im/migrant communities have a "dual frame of reference" (M. M. Suárez-Orozco 1987; see also Gibson 1988; Ogbu 1987)—one that that makes them more willing to accept and integrate into US society—my research highlights the ways that these contrastive experiences strengthen *transnational* sensibilities and lead Palestinian Americans to take up critical citizenship practices that highlight, and work against, oppressive conditions and violations of promised equality, both outside of and within the United States (as I show in more detail in part 2).

Despite the particularities of the Palestinian case, the questions about belonging and citizenship raised by this transnational community are not unique. They resonate with the experiences of many young people in this era of global migration—people whose sense of belonging and citizenship is no longer hitched primarily to one nation-state (Abu El-Haj 2007; DeJaeghere, and McCleary 2010; Ewing and Hoyler 2008; Fouron and Glick-Schiller 2002; Grewal 2014; Maira 2009; Sánchez 2007). As more and more people migrate to realize economic, cultural, or political rights denied in their home countries, they are reimagining belonging and citizenship in ways that do not line up with dominant conceptions that structure both political debates and—of more relevance to the argument I make in this book—educational practices.

Although dominant conceptions of citizenship take divergent forms, the nation-state is presumed to be the locus for identification and citizenship. This conception is evident in discourses and practices that represent a variety of political positions. From the perspective of American conservative political discourse about immigration, the kinds of creative citizenship practices enacted by this Palestinian American community are often read as problematic and threatening to the integrity of this nation. For example, Amira's decision to deliver Zayna and Kamal in the United States would fuel conservative vitriol over "anchor babies" that leads some to call for repealing birthright citizenship enshrined in the Fourteenth Amendment. Practices of sending economic remittances to family members and taking political action on behalf of Palestinians would be viewed as signs of a problematic, utilitarian approach to the benefits of US citizenship, and insufficient assimilation to this country. Similarly, educational language policies that require English-only instruction within two years of arrival in the United States imply a version of citizenship that requires abandoning ties to other places. However, even educational policies that can be viewed as more politically liberal (for example, multiculturalism and most approaches to civic education) share a presumption that the nation-state should be the locus of young people's primary sense of belonging and citizenship.

In contrast to this dominant framework instantiated in much public political discourse and educational policy, the transnational citizenship practices enacted by the Palestinian American youth offer a picture of the changing face of citizenship. Because these young people's citizenship practices developed in transnational fields—forged across the various spaces they inhabited, physically and imaginatively—their lives were inextricably bound to more than one nation-state. Their experiences, perspectives, and practices illustrate the ways in which many young people are educated into citizenship identities "glocally." This reality led them to a view of rights that transcended the nation, and Palestinian American youth expressed a commitment to the values and ideals of democratic rights-bearing citizenship for all. This sensibility for democratic citizenship among the Palestinian American youth implicates an aspirational component of their transnational citizenship—an implicit demand that certain rights should be inalienable for all people, not just conationals. Thus, as these young people became active participants in their society, they engaged in cultural, economic, and political activities that spanned the borders of nation-states. Neither belonging nor citizenship was nation-state bound.

Unfortunately, as I show in part 2, these multilayered affiliations that the youth developed through transnational fields were at odds with the normative definitions of citizenship they encountered in their US schools. Teachers, for the most part, expected that Palestinian youth would abandon their affiliations with Palestine and become "Americans" even as the conditions for being or becoming American precluded the cultural, religious, and political commitments of these young people and positioned their community as fundamentally Other. Although, in part 1, I have focused on the ways that these young people's lives are interwoven with their community's aspirations for an independent nation-state, their sense of belonging and citizenship has also been fundamentally forged in a post-9/11 US political landscape, and this country's "war on terror." Importantly, within this context, the Palestinian-Israeli conflict has played a particular discursive role that has in many ways marked this community as the quintessential representatives of terror. In part 2, I take up the question of the role that US nationalism and this country's colonial ambitions played in shaping Palestinian American youths' experiences with citizenship and belonging, and I examine the disjuncture between Palestinian American youths' lived experiences of transnational belonging and citizenship and the normative expectations for citizenship they encountered in school and society.

PART TWO

"I Know How the Men in Your Country Treat You": Everyday Nationalism and the Politics of Exclusion

On a brisk March day in 2005, I waited for Samira Khateeb at the school's entrance, watching as the long line of students going through security slowly dwindled well past the morning bells signaling the start of the school day. Samira showed up fifteen minutes late, wearing her usual black scarf, neatly and expertly tied, with a bright red sweatshirt and jeans. She apologized for being late. She had the car today, and her brother had asked her to drop him off at school. This proved to be another typical school day for Samira—one in which she dutifully went through the necessary motions to do what was required of her. After a brief assembly in which students sat listlessly through announcements about sporting events and the guidance counseling process, Samira proceeded through a day of classes characterized mostly by rote exercises and copying activities. She spent fifty minutes in her cooking class washing mint leaves, peeling them off of their stems, and handing them to a boy whose task it was to chop them. In social studies class, students spent a third day copying from the board the same, barely legible, outline of a chapter about corporations. They were referred to their textbooks—books they could not take home—to fill in missing definitions. The only significant verbal interaction the teacher had with the class (other than to grant permission to use the bathroom) consisted of a monologue on senioritis and his academic goals for the students. He stated, "I want you to remember that I care. So if I see you shutting down, I'm going to call your parents," and "My main goal for you is for you to learn how to outline a text because that's what you'll do in college." For one hour in her child psychology class, Samira copied fifteen vocabulary words and definitions that another student was asked to write on the chalkboard while the teacher sat on his desk and looked at his textbook. In chemistry class, the students followed step-by-step directions for an experiment that involved popping popcorn and subtracting the weight of the popped kernels from that of the dry ones to figure out the water content of the kernels. Samira sat at a laboratory table with two male students. She counted out corn kernels and copied the answers that one of the boys figured out. Although most of the problems entailed simple subtraction, when the students got to a question that asked them to figure out a proportion, none could set up the equation and their work simply came to a halt. I had to wonder how Samira would handle the college-level math and science courses required to become a registered nurse—her career goal at that time.

The one striking interaction of the entire day occurred in Samira's chemistry class. Two boys seated at another table suddenly called out to Samira to settle a dispute they were having. It took them a few minutes to get her attention, as they didn't know her name, even though it was March and these students had been together all year. When the boys were able to catch her attention, one said, "You're married, right?" Samira (with incredulity) retorted, "No." The second boy was surprised, reflecting, "Oh. I thought you were because of that thing you wear," referring to her headscarf. On its own, this interaction may simply have demonstrated these two students' ignorance about the significance of the headscarf. However, myriad similar interactions indicate another interpretation. Although Samira typically went through her school days almost completely silent, seemingly invisible to her peers and teachers, on occasions such as this one she became highly visible as a Muslim because she wore a headscarf—or *mandīl*, in her dialect—which marked her as an outsider.

When I first met her as a sophomore, Samira did not cover her hair; she had chosen to adopt a *mandīl* the summer before she began her junior year. Telling me about the first day she came to school wearing her headscarf, she recalled her grade adviser's response:

> Only when I first came in with the *mandīl*, my adviser told me to take it off. My adviser. I still remember that. He told me to take it off because it's not allowed in the school. I looked at him and I was like, "This thing ain't coming off my head, whether you like it or not, and it's for religious purposes." So then he just shut up, and then at the end of the period, he called me outside and he talked to me. And he was like, "Well, I didn't know that you're going to keep it on, but since you have it on now you're not allowed to take it off," and this and that. And I was like, "It's not up to you, it's up to me." And I was like, "It's not coming off, but if I wanted to, I will take it off."

The reasons this particular teacher would tell a Muslim student to remove her headscarf were not completely clear; however, it is difficult to separate this confrontation, in 2004 in the United States, from the existing politically

charged climate in which Muslim women who wear the hijab become visible
to non-Muslims. All of the girls who wore headscarves had stories to tell of
encounters they experienced in school or in other public spaces. Curiously,
Samira was one of the few students who remarked that she had not faced
obvious discrimination after September 11, 2001, and yet she, like a majority
of her female peers, told several stories of times when her *mandīl* became a
source of public commentary or blatant conflict.

The significance of her headscarf was not lost on Samira in the most explicit confrontation that she and several of her peers who also wore headscarves had with a substitute teacher one day. As she described it:

> [My friends and I were] all sitting down on the computer, and we're munch-
> ing on a couple of snacks. The teacher never ever told us put away the snacks.
> And we're sitting down on the computer and we were talking, I think. And the
> guy [i.e., the teacher] was giving us rude looks ever since we went in there. So
> he comes to us and he tells us, he tells my friend, "Put the food away. You're
> eating like a pig over the computer." So when he said that, you know, we like
> freaked out. What do you mean? He just called you a pig? So my friend tried
> to get back at him, and she's sitting there yelling at him and he's yelling at her.
> And then he starts telling her, "I know how the men in your country treat you.
> I've been to your country twice already. If you talked to your family member
> like that he would smack you across the face." I said, "This is our country.
> What country did you visit?" And so he's like, "Trust me, I know, I know."

In the face of a challenge to both the rules of the classroom and his authority, this teacher's reaction was to frame the girls as outsiders who belonged
to another country—placing these Palestinian American citizens outside of
the national borders. Hostile encounters such as this one suggest how rap-
idly a sense of "American" national identity could be mobilized to stake out
the borders of belonging to the United States. However, equally important,
the boundary he constructed between the United States and "your country"
turned on certain assumptions about the oppression of Muslim women. In
signaling the way "men in your country treat you"—violently, by "smack[ing]
you across the face"—this teacher implicitly contrasted the putative oppressive
treatment of Muslim women with an assumption that equality and freedom
define life in the United States for American women. On its own, this might
seem a large leap of interpretation from this one teacher's comments about
"men in your country." But, as I show in the following chapters, his words
reverberated with assumptions I heard expressed repeatedly by teachers and
administrators at Regional High—assumptions reflective of broader political
discourses. Educators often asserted that fundamental to being "American" is
having individual liberty and being free, conditions that a majority believed

were denied to Muslims in general, and to Muslim women in particular, by virtue of their religion and culture (Abu-Lughod 2002, 2013; Haddad, Smith, and Moore 2006; Zine 2006).

In part 1, I explored the ways that the experience of growing up in transnational social fields led Palestinian Americans to develop a sense of belonging to the Palestinian national imaginary while also drawing on their rights-bearing American citizenship to exercise economic, social, civil, and political rights denied to many Palestinians. Although these young people spoke of a primary sense of being Palestinian, they also described complex, fluid, and dynamic processes through which they forged connections and a sense of belonging to multiple places.

In part 2, I turn my attention to the normative discourses of American nationalism that positioned the Palestinian American youth as "impossible subjects" (Ngai 2004)[1] of this national imaginary. These normative discourses circulate in the public domain through political speech, media, and popular culture, but they are also expressed in everyday life in schools and communities. These discourses structured how educators spoke about and interacted with the Palestinian American youth at Regional High. In part 1, I focused on the ways that imaginative and actual movement across borders shaped young people's lives. In part 2, I examine how these young people encountered rigid barriers to belonging created by dominant discourses of American nationalism in the wake of September 11, 2001.

Nationalism is usually discussed in relation to new nation-states, independence movements, or extreme right-wing movements, with cautionary warnings about the powerful, and potentially dangerous, emotions associated with it (Benei 2008; Billig 1995). In more established nations, it tends to be discussed as patriotism, and while there are debates about the usefulness and parameters of the love of one's country (see Nussbaum and Cohen 1996), patriotism is often cast as less problematic than its close relation nationalism. However, nations are not natural givens. They are made and remade, in part through the practices of everyday nationalism that continually organize people's sense of belonging to particular nation-states (Anderson [1983] 1991; Appadurai 1996; Benei 2008; Billig 1995; Calhoun 2007). Even long-existing nation-states must continually reestablish the nation, constructing a national imaginary that articulates its normative values and beliefs, along with the parameters of belonging (and exclusion). Moreover, the boundaries of national belonging are fluid, negotiated over time in relation to different groups of people (Anderson [1983] 1991; Hall 2002; Ngai 2004; Yuval-Davis, Anthias,

---

1. See n. 4 in the introduction.

and Kofman 2005; Yuval-Davis 2011). Wartime is a period during which these discursive constructions of the nation are rearticulated—the edges of belonging and not belonging sharpened (O'Leary 1999). However, although these edges are hardened in the face of war, they rely on boundaries that already exist.

In part 2, as I unpack normative discourses about what it means to be "American" and what "America" stands for, I focus primarily on dominant discourses of American liberal nationalism. Liberal nationalism, also referred to as civic nationalism, is defined as nationalism that draws on liberal values such as freedom, individual rights, and equality—values that are presumptively universal—as its defining tenets (see Calhoun 2007; Gerstle 2001). This brand of nationalism is distinguished from ethnic (or racial) nationalism, which relies on ethnicity to define the parameters of the nation.[2] Moreover, as I discuss further in chapter 3, since the end of World War II, discourses of multiculturalism have been sutured to the dominant discourses of American liberal nationalism, highlighting the centrality of the value of multicultural diversity to this national imaginary (Melamed 2006; Moallem and Boal 1999). My aim in the following chapters is not to engage in debates about liberal (multicultural) nationalism as a political philosophy.[3] Rather, I analyze this nationalism as a discursive construction that does work on the ground, and illustrate the effects of its everyday expression on the lives of the Palestinian American youth.

Liberal multicultural nationalism is not the only expression of nationalism in contemporary US society. There are other expressions of nationalism that articulate explicitly racist and xenophobic beliefs about im/migrants, members of racially/ethnically minoritized communities, Muslims, and so forth (Gerstle 2001). These expressions can be found, for example, in the ongoing violent attacks on individuals believed to be Muslim in the wake of national or international events. The strident opposition to the building of mosques in communities across the country also signals a more explicitly xenophobic form of nationalism.[4] Moreover, these more virulent forms of nationalism do not attach only to Arabs and Muslims. Recent state legislation targeting Latino communities—for example, in Arizona and Georgia—reflects similar nationalist sentiment. I focus on liberal multicultural nationalism for several

2. This distinction itself has been called into question (Calhoun 2007).

3. Liberal nationalism as a normative project and the distinction between civic and liberal nationalism have been much debated by political theorists; however, these debates are well beyond the scope of my work. See, for example, Calhoun 2007; Kymlicka 1995; Tamir 1993.

4. See "Map—Nationwide Anti-mosque Activity," the ACLU's documentation of this, at https://www.aclu.org/maps/map-nationwide-anti-mosque-activity.

reasons. First, it was the primary expression of nationalism reflected at Regional High. Second, rather than being completely distinct, it is, and has always been, hitched to other, more explicitly virulent, forms of nationalism (Calhoun 2007; Gerstle 2001). Finally, and most important for the argument I am making, liberal multicultural nationalism is hinged to the United States' imperial project, justifying its role on the global stage and discursively framing an oppositional relationship between Americans and Muslims (Brown 2006; Melamed 2006).

Liberal multicultural nationalism articulates a set of tenets that fundamentally defines what America stands for and what it means to be American, constructing a dominant national imaginary that posits the United States as the beacon of freedom, diversity, and tolerance worldwide. These norms of liberal multicultural nationalism are not created in a vacuum. Rather, they simultaneously define self and other, insider and outsider. Though they function under the conceit of neutrality and universality, they are, in fact, a result of particular historical and sociopolitical processes (Brown 2006; Melamed 2006). They create—even as they hide—a set of norms that function to exclude those people who are presumed to be incapable of participating in the ways set out by liberal multicultural nationalism. Set in motion long before September 11, 2001, the hegemonic American national imaginary is, at this historic moment, being constructed largely in the shadow of Islam. When Samira's teacher claimed to know "how the men in your country treat you," he was implicitly drawing on presumed norms that simultaneously position "American" women as free and Muslim women as oppressed. For this teacher, Samira and her friends were easily identifiable as outsiders because they were Muslims. Recognizing the oppositional relationship that has developed between the contemporary American national imaginary and Muslim Otherness makes visible the ways in which US nationalism continues to be intimately interwoven with the United States' role as an imperial power on the global stage.

In the following three chapters, I argue that in order to understand how the young Palestinian Americans were positioned as "impossible subjects" of the United States, we must focus on the everyday effects of American nationalism. Paying attention to the imbrication of US nationalism, with its imperial ambitions, deepens our understanding of the processes of racialization. These processes have been and continue to be not only about racial domination and subordination inside the boundaries of the nation-state, but, just as important, inextricably linked with the United States' ongoing role as an imperial power (Cainkar 2008; Naber 2008; Puar and Rai 2002; Rana 2011). This relationship is one that is underexamined in the literature on contemporary US education, which tends to ask how im/migrant youth get dragged into the existing racialized hierarchy of the United States without careful attention to the ways in which the norms defining what it means to be American (and thereby where one goes in the hierarchy) are tied to norms of liberal nationalism that also serve to justify imperial ambitions (Brown 2006; Melamed 2006).

In part 2, I scrutinize how these normative discourses of liberal multicultural nationalism—discourses that are interwoven with imperial projects—manifested in everyday practice at Regional High, affecting how educators saw and understood their young Palestinian American students. These discourses shaped educators' desire to "Americanize" the youth while also making it impossible for these young people to be fully included in this nation. I show as well how the seemingly benign norms of liberal nationalism—those that focus on freedom, diversity, and tolerance—could turn quickly into ugly expressions of silencing and exclusion.

In order to contextualize the analysis of everyday nationalism at Regional High, in chapter 3, I focus on widely circulating public discourses of liberal multicultural nationalism and show how these get expressed at the level of school curriculum. I draw on cogent analyses of the cultural politics that developed around the "war on terror" (Abu-Lughod 2002, 2013; Asad 2007; Brown 2006; Das 2001; Gregory 2004; Kinsella 2007; Mamdani 2004; Melamed 2006; Pease 2009; Puar and Rai 2002) to illustrate broad public expression of this form of nationalism. Chapter 3 sets the ground for the two chapters that follow. In chapter 4, I track the discourse of liberal multicultural nationalism to Regional High, illustrating how it set educators up to view Palestinian American youth as impossible subjects of the United States. The final chapter in part 2 examines the political conflicts that emerged between educators, who drew on presumptions of liberal multicultural nationalism, and the Palestinian Americans, who had developed critical perspectives on the United States and its ally Israel through their transnational lives. Chapter 5 then offers a picture of how these young people forged alternate discourses that challenged the dominant exclusionary discourses of nationalism, making "bids for citizenship"—claims for belonging and rights for their community.

3

"The Best Country in the World":
Imagining America in an Age of Empire

Freedom itself was attacked this morning by a faceless coward. And freedom will be
defended.

— PRESIDENT GEORGE W. BUSH, September 11, 2001

In the immediate aftermath of the terrifying tragedy of September 11, 2001,
President Bush opened his remarks to the nation with the idea that it was
"freedom itself" that was under attack, and, thus, freedom that would be "defended." In invoking the notion that freedom—rather than the United States
or its financial and military core—was under attack, President Bush signaled
that this country is (and has been) symbolically imagined in relation to a set of
ideals such as freedom that are taken to be simultaneously deeply "American"
and universal. This chapter analyzes the dominant discourses of American
liberal multicultural nationalism as they were rearticulated in the post-9/11
era—discourses that link America and Americans to a set of liberal values for
which the nation stands. Critically, I examine how this dominant discourse
of liberal multicultural nationalism implicitly and explicitly co-constructs self
and Other, belonging and not belonging, civilization and barbarism.

I explore the ways in which this dominant national imaginary is deeply
interwoven with the United States' imperial ambitions, mitigating its economic, political, and military interests in the Middle East and South Asia.
At this historic moment, the normative articulations of what it means
to be American—and the values and beliefs that this nation is imagined to
embody—have been drawn in relation to a particular discursive construction
of Islam and the "Muslim world."[1] The discursive construction of opposition
is critical to the production of "us" and "them," belonging and not belonging.
America's love of freedom is placed in stark relief against the hatred of liberty
ascribed to radical Islam. America's commitment to diversity is positioned

1. See n. 9 in the introduction.

against Muslims' intransigent monoculture. "Our" tolerance is pitted against the intolerance of Islamic fundamentalism and the undemocratic regimes in many parts of MENA and South Asia.[2] Here, I analyze the broader, public, dominant discursive construction of the American national imaginary and its articulation of difference from the "Muslim world," because, as I show in chapters 4 and 5, these broader public discourses tracked into everyday practice at Regional High, generally positioning Palestinian Americans on the "wrong" side of this oppositional relationship.

Although my focus is the post-9/11 US context, current beliefs about the "Muslim world" do not arise from nowhere. As Edward Said traced in his seminal work, *Orientalism* (1978), there is a long history of knowledge production about the "East" that simultaneously created the "Orient" and "Orientals." Said argued:

> For Orientalism was ultimately a political vision of reality whose structure promoted the difference between the familiar (Europe, the West, "us") and the strange (the Orient, the East, "them"). This vision in a sense created and then served the two worlds thus conceived. (1978, 43)

For Said, the critical insight is that knowledge produced about the Other is political, and produces power in its wake. Although the particular actors shift over time, and the forms of knowledge production change with the decades, Orientalism remains steadfast in not only justifying but, as Said points out, *producing* the Western colonial relationship with the East—a relationship that in the post–Cold War era has increasingly trained the United States' focus on the "Muslim world."

At this moment, liberal multicultural nationalism constructs *America* in relation to the shadow of (radical) Islam. I put "radical" in parentheses because although some political discourse makes a distinction between what is taken to be "true" Islam and its radical variants, there is constant slippage— slippage that reflects the widely circulating theory of a fundamental "clash of civilizations" between Islam and the West (B. Lewis 2002; Huntington 1996). This theory, which was developed well before September 11, 2001, posits an opposition through which the West in general and the United States in particular come to stand for modernity, progress, and their attendant values— individualism, equality, democracy, diversity, secularism, tolerance, and freedom—and Islam is characterized in monolithic terms as a backward "cul-

2. It is not only in relation to Islam that the contemporary American national imaginary is articulated. In political discourse, China, for example, is also positioned in contrast to American norms and values.

ture" that is, at its core, undemocratic, oppressive, and violent (Abu-Lughod 2002, 2013; Brown 2006; Mamdani 2004; Said 2001).

Using former president George W. Bush's speeches as exemplars[3] of normative discourses of liberal multicultural nationalism,[4] I explore three related issues in this chapter. First, key elements of this discourse construct the United States as a beacon for liberal values of freedom, diversity, and tolerance worldwide. Second, this discourse is mobilized such that it co-constructs Muslims and the "Muslim world" as Other, and as potential threats to democracy. Finally, this discourse of liberal multicultural nationalism hides the United States' role as an imperial power behind a mantle of "radical innocence" (Pease 2009), rendering invisible the ways this country has supported policies that belie its claim to be the beacon for democratic values worldwide. I draw on a decade of scholarship on the cultural politics of the "war on terror" (Abu-Lughod 2002, 2013; Brown 2006; Das 2001; Gregory 2004; Kinsella 2007; Mamdani 2004; Pease 2009; Puar and Rai 2002; Joseph and D'Harlingue 2008) in order to illustrate the connection between these broad political discourses of nationalism, and the everyday nationalism that, as I show in the following two chapters, Palestinian American youth encountered in their schools and communities. In this chapter, after tracking the dominant terms of liberal nationalism, and showing the relationship between American liberal nationalism and the United States' imperial ambitions, I turn my attention to three examples of how these discourses enter the sphere of public education.

The Tenets of Liberal Multicultural Nationalism

FREEDOM AND DEMOCRACY

It may be understandable and predictable that in the face of the traumatic loss, pain, and shock of the 9/11 attacks, President Bush and other political leaders would draw on the language of freedom and democracy to craft a

3. I use former president Bush's speeches because it is possible to see how immediately these articulations of liberal nationalism were mobilized after September 11, 2001. These articulations, however, are apparent not only in conservative political discourse. They can be heard in President Obama's rhetoric too. They echo (with some difference in emphasis or tone) throughout American political discourse of both major political parties.

4. As noted in the introduction to part 2, I focus on the discourse of liberal nationalism, and the liberal, multicultural imaginary it constructs, because it is the dominant discourse, not the only discourse, circulating in public venues, and at Regional High. As I show, at particular moments, it articulates with more explicitly racist and xenophobic nationalist discourses.

common response and purpose for the nation. However, this language must be analyzed for the work it did in simultaneously articulating national ideals while justifying the United States' reinvigorated role as a global military power. This political rhetoric cast the United States not simply as one of many democratic states in the world, but as the standard-bearer for freedom worldwide (Gregory 2004; Pease 2009). As President Bush intoned, "Human freedom . . . now depends on us" (September 20, 2001). Thus, the impulse to pull a nation together in its grief by asserting a set of binding national values was inextricably linked to a mission to champion its ideals as a set of universal values, and a universal way of life to which all people do (or should) aspire (Das 2001).

This expression of liberal nationalism simultaneously produced a diffuse enemy that was this nation's inverse self. As President Bush asserted in his September 20, 2001, address to a joint session of Congress:

> Americans are asking, why do they hate us? They hate what they see right here in this chamber—a democratically elected government. Their leaders are self-appointed. They hate our freedoms—our freedom of religion, our freedom of speech, our freedom to vote and assemble and disagree with each other. . . . These terrorists kill not merely to end lives, but to disrupt and end a way of life.

Against the lovers of freedom President Bush positions the enemies of freedom. Against a pluralist society that values diversity (of religion and opinion), "they" stand in rejection of such openness. Against democracy stand the terrorists who threaten democracy itself.

This rhetorical construction of an enemy at war with democracy framed the fight for freedom as a "civilizational" conflict against a diffuse enemy that knew no national boundaries. Consider President Bush's words a year after the 2001 attacks in his address to the United Nations:

> Above all, our principles and our security are challenged today by outlaw groups and regimes that accept no law of morality and have no limit to their violent ambitions. In the attacks on America a year ago, we saw the destructive intentions of our enemies. This threat hides within many nations, *including my own*. In cells and camps, terrorists are plotting further destruction and building new bases for *their war against civilization*. (President G. W. Bush, September 12, 2002; emphasis added)

The United States' response to the crimes committed on September 11, 2001, framed the conflict as one between *civilization* and outlaw people and states. The enemies of freedom were everywhere—represented in both outlaw groups and regimes, present both within and outside of the nation. This sense that enemies lurked not only in foreign lands but also within the borders of the United States effectively cast suspicion on *all* Muslim Americans, who might be members of sleeper cells readying for their "war against civilization." Evidence that distrust of Arabs and Muslims living in the United States goes deeper than political rhetoric can be found in the consistency with which polls continue up to the present to show unfavorable, negative attitudes toward Arabs and Muslims on the part of the general American public (Arab American Institute 2012;[5] Gallup 2014). Moreover, President Bush's dichotomous view of the world—with the light of civilization posited against the shadowy omnipresent barbarisms of radical Islam—left little room for dissent and complexity. As President Bush reminded the nation in the immediate aftermath of 9/11, "Either you are with us, or you are with the terrorists" (joint session of Congress, September 20, 2001).

This political discourse of liberal nationalism creates an "imaginative geography" (Said 1978, 49) that simultaneously constructs the US national community as one that loves freedom and democracy, and Other spaces—spaces that exist *both* inside and outside this nation—inhabited by suspect Muslims who "hate our way of life" (see also Gregory 2004). These ideas—that Americans love freedom and democracy, and Muslims do not—would, as I show in the next chapter, track into the school, and shape particular relationships for the Palestinian American youth, who were often imagined to belong to those antidemocratic geographies of violence.

MULTICULTURALISM

If the dominant American national imaginary rests on the idea that freedom and democracy are core American values, it also turns on the image of the centrality of multicultural diversity to this nation. After September 11, 2001, Muslims and other people who were taken to be Muslims faced violent attacks across the nation (Ahmad 2002; Bakalian and Bozorgmehr 2009; Cainkar 2008; Ibish 2008).[6] In a speech to the Islamic Center of Washington delivered on September 17, 2001, President Bush sought to reach out to the American

5. This poll showed there were significant differences between Democrats and Republicans in their attitudes toward Muslims and Arabs. At the same time, Arabs and Muslims had the highest unfavorable ratings of any ethnicity or religion.

6. It is critical to note that attacks on people presumed to be Muslim occurring in response to international or national events did not begin on or end with September 11, 2001. As with other racial/ethnic groups perceived to be foreigners, events that are viewed as international in scope are often accompanied by local violence against communities seen to be related to those events. Moreover, these hate crimes continue to the present day.

Muslim community to reassure them of their place in this multicultural democracy. In his talk, President Bush directly addressed the prejudice and hostile climate that Muslims were facing across the United States. He stated:

> The face of terror is not the true faith of Islam. That's not what Islam is all about. Islam is peace. These terrorists don't represent peace. They represent evil and war. When we think of Islam we think of a faith that brings comfort to a billion people around the world. Billions of people find comfort and solace and peace. And that's made brothers and sisters out of every race—out of every race. America counts millions of Muslims amongst our citizens, and Muslims make an incredibly valuable contribution to our country. Muslims are doctors, lawyers, law professors, members of the military, entrepreneurs, shopkeepers, moms and dads. And they need to be treated with respect. In our anger and emotion, our fellow Americans must treat each other with respect. Women who cover their heads in this country must feel comfortable going outside their homes. Moms who wear cover must not be intimidated in America. That's not the America I know. That's not the America I value.

Distinguishing the "true faith of Islam" from that of the terrorists (Mamdani 2004), and framing it as one that makes "brothers and sisters out of every race," the president implicitly invoked the multicultural discourse that grounds both "true Islam" and this national imaginary. Our right to express our differences in public—symbolized here by the need for Muslim women to feel safe in public—is critical to a functioning democracy. This multicultural respect, rather than the hateful attacks on Muslims after 9/11, symbolizes the America the president knows and values.

The president's words reflected a trope of multiculturalism that has, over the past half century, become a central feature of the contemporary American national imaginary (Brown 2006; Melamed 2006; Moallem and Boal 1999). I want to focus here on two aspects of the multicultural national imaginary symbolically invoked in President Bush's speech: its development over the past half century in relationship to the United States' emerging role as an imperial superpower, and the version of culture that it entails.

It is only very recently that the American national community could even be imagined as a multicultural one. For most of its history, the United States was configured as a separatist racial state. This began to change as the structure of racialization shifted from one instantiated by law to the more diffuse, but still pervasive, system existing today (Omi and Winant 1986; Winant 2004). Multicultural discourse has played a critical role in hiding, and thus sustaining, the racialized post–civil rights era structure of US society (Melamed 2006; Moallem and Boal 1999). Indeed, at the very same moment that President Bush was reassuring Muslims that America valued diversity, across the country government agents were detaining Muslims, deporting them without due process, and targeting them for increased surveillance.

The development of this liberal multicultural imaginary is intertwined with the United States' post–World War II ambitions as a global superpower. In the postwar period, the United States was called to task for the contradiction between its internal racial inequality and its desire to spread US political, economic, and military power worldwide. Jodi Melamed (2006) argues that as the civil rights movement dismantled the United States' de jure racial segregation, a new racial formation emerged that "suture[d] an 'official antiracism' to U.S. nationalism" (2). Melamed argues that the United States' role as a multiethnic democracy "obligates [it] to secure 'political and economic liberty' for 'every person and society'" (2006, 17). Thus, over the course of the last half of the twentieth century, multiculturalism was transformed into an American value—a symbol of this nation that has not been achieved (at least not to the same extent) in other nations. This interweaving of multicultural liberalism[7] and nationalism reverberated under the surface of President Bush's declaration that the America he "knows" and "values" is one that respects diversity.

If the ideal of multicultural diversity was inextricably woven into the American national imaginary, "culture"[8] became a shibboleth in the "clash" between the United States and Islam. Dominant political discourses constructed a conflict between the United States' flourishing cultural diversity and the putative rigidity and backwardness of Islamic "culture." In the United States, diversity of religion, language, ethnicity, and so forth are all treated as equivalent matters of individual choice and conscience. Cultural diversity as an individual affair is to be protected in this multicultural democracy. Individuals should feel free to pray to the god of their choosing. Women should feel comfortable covering (or not covering) their hair. These expressions of diversity are treated as fundamentally individual and private—flavoring but making no political demands on the public sphere (see Kymlicka 1995 and Taylor 1992 for critiques of this model of democracy).

This version of culture comes into particular relief when it is set against

---

7. This multicultural liberal national imaginary is one that—while representing itself as a universal ideal—reflects the particular culture of liberalism. There is a rich literature critiquing liberalism's claim to universality that I cannot address here. (See, for example, Asad 2003; Brown 2006; Mahmood 2005.)

8. Melamed (2006) argues that with time and the emergence of neoliberalism, the earlier racial formation she calls "racial liberalism" gave way to a new racial formation that broke with older racism's dependence on phenotypes, and "deploys economic, ideological, cultural and religious distinctions to produce lesser personhoods laying new categories of privilege and stigma across conventional racial categories" (14).

culture as it is putatively lived in the "Muslim world" (Abu-Lughod 2013; Brown 2006; Mamdani 2004; Melamed 2006; Said 2001). If, in the United States, culture is viewed as a matter of individual choice and conscience, in the "Muslim world" it is purported to dictate people's beliefs and actions according to ancient, ossified traditions and practices. In contrast to Americans who are freely choosing subjects, Muslims are viewed as cultural captives driven by blind commitments to an essentialized and fossilized culture. Critically, within this putative Muslim culture, women are viewed as particularly trapped, subject to oppressive religious beliefs and practices (Abu-Lughod 2002, 2013; Haddad, Smith, and Moore 2006; Zine 2006). This view of Islam as uniformly harsh toward women held sway well before September 11, 2001, but in its aftermath, rescuing "women of cover" even became part of the rationale for the US war in Afghanistan (Abu-Lughod 2002, 2013).

Mamdani (2004) has argued cogently that "culture talk" reduces political conflicts and complex and particular historic engagements between the United States and the "Muslim world" to an essential clash of cultures. Political, military, and economic conflicts (and vested interests) disappear under the veneer of the benevolent project of American liberal multicultural nationalism. Thus, these two versions of culture—the American one in which culture is a matter of individual choice, and the Muslim one in which culture mechanistically drives individuals' beliefs and behaviors—play a key role in ideologically supporting the United States' mission as an imperial power.[9]

If "culture talk" simultaneously defines Americans as freely choosing subjects, and Muslims as cultural captives of their religion, then what of Muslim Americans? Mamdani (2004) points out that after 9/11, dominant US political discourse tried to distinguish between "good Muslims" and "bad Muslims," urging the former to fight against the latter. President Bush signaled this distinction in a news conference he held on September 19, 2001, addressing possible retaliation by the United States. Asked by a reporter whether he was worried that the attacks signaled a religious war, the president responded:

> The Muslim faith is a peaceful faith. And there are millions of good Americans who practice the Muslim faith, who love their country as much as I love the country, who salute the flag as strongly as I salute the flag. And for those who pit religion against religion, our great nation will stand up and reject that kind of thought. We won't allow that to creep into the consciousness of the world.

---

9. Public opinion research undertaken by the Detroit Arab American Study Team found that the general public was much more likely than Arab Americans to believe that a clash of civilizations (45 percent to 22 percent) or conflict of values (37 percent to 22 percent) was responsible for the September 11, 2001, attacks (Stockton 2009).

We're going to lead the world to fight for freedom and we'll have Muslim and Jew and Christian side by side with us.[10]

President Bush's words leverage the national imaginary of a peaceable multicultural democracy in which Muslims, Jews, and Christians work side by side to support the United States' global ambitions. Being a "good" American Muslim becomes one and the same as being a patriotic, national citizen aligned with the ambitions of the state.

Tolerance and Its Role in the National Imaginary

Ours is a country based upon tolerance and we welcome people of all faiths in America. (remarks by President George W. Bush in a statement to reporters during a meeting with UN secretary-general Kofi Annan, White House Oval Office, Washington, DC, November 13, 2002)

The implicit glue in this multicultural democracy is the value of tolerance. The belief that the United States is, at its core, a tolerant nation, and that intolerant behaviors are exceptions to a national ethic, is pervasive—reflected throughout our political discourses, schools' mission statements (including Regional High's), religious institutions, and more (Brown 2006; Wemyss 2009). In a brilliant analysis of the shifting and various logics of tolerance as a political discourse (rather than an individual virtue), Wendy Brown (2006) argues that tolerance has become a "telos of multicultural citizenship" (5) and, after September 11, 2001, a powerful tool as a "civilizational discourse distinguishing Occident from Orient, liberal from nonliberal regimes, 'free' from 'unfree' peoples" (6).

Brown (2006) shifts from a view of tolerance as a moral value to tracking its development as a political practice that renders identity its object. Rather than being a practice that protects differing political or religious opinions and practices, modern tolerance discourse is addressed to people's group identities. Brown argues that, as a political practice, tolerance produces identities as cultural and essential, often "conflating culture with ethnicity or race, belief or consciousness with phenotype" (14). In doing so, she argues, tolerance discourse depoliticizes conflicts in two important ways. First, in its contemporary iterations, it "reduces conflicts to an inherent friction among identities, making religious, ethnic, and cultural difference itself an inherent site of con-

10. "Text: President Bush on Possible Retaliation," *Washington Post*, September 19, 2001, http://www.washingtonpost.com/wp-srv/nation/specials/attacked/transcripts/bushtext2_091901.html.

flict, one that calls for and is attenuated by the practice of tolerance" (15). However, in focusing on identities—on tensions between individuals—the practice of tolerance becomes about tolerating difference itself rather than exploring the historical circumstances and power interests that underlie the conflicts at hand.

This leads to the second way that modern tolerance discourse depoliticizes conflict. It "substitutes emotional and personal vocabularies for political ones in formulating solutions to political problems" (Brown 2006, 16). We can see this move at work in President Bush's speeches to the nation after 9/11. On the one hand, he argues that Muslims, as Muslims, must not be targeted by intolerant behaviors. However, even as individual, mainstream Americans were being asked to "tolerate" Muslims, there was no acknowledgment of the racialized power structure that rendered Muslims a special category of persons subject to particular treatment by government policies.

Finally, Brown (2006) analyzes the important turn that tolerance discourse took after 9/11, functioning as a civilizational project justifying the state's newest imperial ambitions. Positioned as a virtue that liberal societies and their liberal subjects are capable of, tolerance does important work in creating the self and the Other—the tolerant and the intolerant. Tolerance as a civilizational discourse makes it possible for "us" to refuse to tolerate the intolerable (see also Mamdani 2004). It justifies a range of actions against those "civilizations" deemed intolerant, everything from violent military interventions to bring Others liberal democracy to the abrogation of basic rights and democratic principles at home. Tolerance discourse, as I show in chapters 4 and 5, also operates at a much more local level as an everyday practice inside schools.

Radical Innocence and Colonial Amnesia

As I have already noted, liberal multicultural nationalism promotes the United States as a nation standing outside of history, championing human freedom and dignity everywhere. As such, this discursive framework produces a kind of "colonial amnesia" (Gregory 2004) that obscures the United States' role as a historic and contemporary imperial power. The narrative that imagines this nation as a beacon for freedom and democracy worldwide works only by rendering invisible both the ongoing structural inequalities woven into US institutions and society and the nation's contemporary role as an imperial power that leverages a range of strategies of global dominance. In the aftermath of the 9/11 attacks, the rearticulation of this liberal multicultural nationalism obscured the United States' deep and complex engagement in

MENA and South Asia over the course of the twentieth century, making this history either invisible, or irrelevant, to the rationale for the military invasions of Afghanistan and Iraq, and, over time, the drone wars that expanded to include other countries.

Without an understanding of the historic involvements that this nation had with particular states in MENA and South Asia, many Americans remained largely ignorant of the roots of the conflicts that subsequently landed on US soil (see Gregory 2004; R. Khalidi 2004; Mamdani 2004), and a majority were quick to support the military campaigns in Afghanistan and later in Iraq.[11] Many Americans seemed perplexed by the roots of radical Islam, which appeared to emerge not from particular historical circumstances in which the United States played a hand but rather from the very "culture" of Islam itself (Asad 2007; Mamdani 2004; Stockton 2009). Such an understanding of history does not mean that the United States was to blame for what happened on September 11, 2001, and I want to be very clear about this point. However, ignorance about the United States' role on the global stage allows many Americans to maintain a belief in this nation's "radical innocence" (Pease 2009)— a force promoting democracy and freedom across the world—obscuring its violent involvement with this (and other) regions. Thus, to the question asked repeatedly after 9/11, "Why do they hate us?" the only accessible answer for many Americans was one that depended on reading Islam as a (monolithic) culture that was fundamentally opposed to all for which the West in general, and the United States in particular, stood. Moreover, as Veena Das (2001) argues, by erasing particular histories and particular local conflicts, and by positioning the United States as the "privileged site of universal values," dominant political rhetoric reconfigured

> terrorism as a grand, single, global force that simultaneously cancels out other forms of terrorism and creates the enemy as a totality that has to be vanquished in the interests of universalism that is embodied in the American nation. (108–9)[12]

In the aftermath of September 11, 2001, dominant political discourses of liberal multicultural nationalism were mobilized in support of the United States' right to use its military power ostensibly in the service of democracy every-

---

11. Public opinion polls about Iraq, for example, showed that a majority of Americans believed there was some connection between Saddam Hussein's Iraq and al-Qaeda, and even after the invasion, a substantial minority maintained their belief that there were weapons of mass destruction in Iraq (Kull 2003).

12. Das (2001) points out that this political discourse mirrored discourse of the Taliban.

where, against the amorphous and omnipresent threat of radical Islamic "terror" (see also Kinsella 2007).

In tracking public discourses of liberal multicultural nationalism articulated in the post-9/11 moment, I have highlighted the work these discourses do in constructing a national imaginary that defined the United States in relation to values that are simultaneously positioned as deeply American and as universal: freedom, diversity, and tolerance. But I have also shown that this national imaginary is constructed in relationship to an imaginative geography of Otherness—to people who wish to "end our way of life." I have argued that the ability to imagine the United States as a nation that stands above history, as a beacon of universal democratic values worldwide, depends on hiding its contradictory role as an imperial power. I have elaborated these public political discourses because they tracked into educational spaces in different ways. As I show in detail in chapters 4 and 5, everyday nationalism shaped educators' beliefs about and relationships with Palestinian American youth at Regional High. However, in the remainder of this chapter, I turn my attention to how these discourses track into the curriculum.

Curricular Amnesia

The discursive framework of liberal nationalism, and the construction of Islam as this nation's nemesis, are deeply embedded in official school curriculum. As this was not a study of curriculum in action, I cannot comment meaningfully on how this official curriculum was enacted, or contested by teachers and students for a variety of reasons. The focal students were juniors and seniors enrolled in US history and government. However, in the classes we observed, the textbook was largely ignored, and curriculum was fragmented. None of our observations occurred during discussions of recent history—students reported that they never got far enough along in their chronological units to discuss recent events. The Middle East was never a topic of discussion in the US government and history classes that we did visit. Moreover, none of the focal students were in ninth grade—the year that students took world cultures—a subject that, according to their recollections, was mostly focused on ancient history.[13] Nevertheless, textbooks are critical

13. Students also reported little discussion of the Palestinian-Israeli conflict. Only three students in this study, none of whom attended Regional High, reported having an opportunity to present to their class on the Palestinian-Israeli conflict. All the other interviewees, including all of those at Regional High, reported no occasions for such study. The one classroom in which the Palestinian-Israeli conflict appeared to have been a more frequent topic was Khalida and Zayd's ninth-grade social studies class. According to their reports (and confirmed by their teacher,

sites through which normative discourses about the nation are produced and expressed (Schiffauer and Sunier 2004), and whether these textbooks merely reflected, or in fact constructed, narratives about the United States, the story these books told circulated widely.

The school district adopted *The American Vision* (2005) for its US history course.[14] Overall, the narrative paints a picture of the United States as a force for supporting and spreading democracy in the Middle East. At the same time, the text repeatedly emphasizes the idea that Middle Eastern states and Muslims in general have been angry with the United States for both its support of Israel and its desire to spread Western values, which putatively undermine Muslims' "traditional values" (2005, 1032). Nowhere does the text mention the United States' role in supporting repressive regimes or militarizing the region (Gregory 2004; R. Khalidi 2004; Mamdani 2004). Instead, it emphasizes the United States as a force for promoting democracy and human rights on the global stage. The book's discussion of Jimmy Carter's presidency offers an exemplar:

> A man of strong religious beliefs, Carter argued that the United States must try to be "right and honest and truthful and decent" in dealing with other nations. . . .
>
> **Morality in Foreign Policy**
>
> Carter had set the tone for his foreign policy in his inaugural speech, when he announced, "Our commitment to human rights must be absolute. . . . The powerful must not persecute the weak, and human dignity must be enhanced." With the help of his foreign policy team—including Andrew Young, the first African American ambassador to the United Nations—Carter strove to achieve these goals. (2005, 968)

The passage excerpted here sets up the goals of a US foreign policy that aspires to be just and moral, committed to upholding human rights and human dignity worldwide. It also implicitly suggests that President Carter had a commitment to racial equality at home, as demonstrated by his appointment of Andrew Young, the first African American ambassador to the United Nations. The passage subtly links two key elements of the United States' lib-

---

Anne Larson), Khalida and Zayd's ninth-grade social studies teacher, a US citizen, had fought in the Israeli army and appeared to discuss the current political strife without reference to the textbooks. These discussions reportedly ended in conflicts that resulted in some of the Palestinian students being sent to the disciplinary office. See chapter 5 for more details.

14. I refer to this edition of the textbook because it was the one in use during the years of intensive fieldwork in the classroom.

eral national imaginary: its role as a force for promoting universal human rights worldwide and its development as a multiracial democracy at home (Melamed 2006).

The main focus for the section on Carter's administration is the 1979 Iranian hostage crisis, in which, after the Islamic revolution in Iran, Iranians overran the US embassy and held US diplomats hostage for 444 days. The text does little to help students understand what led up to this crisis, or the depth of the US involvement in Iran prior to the Islamic revolution. The text states simply that the United States had supported the Shah because of strategic interests in oil, and in Iran as a "buffer against the Soviet Union." The Shah is described as having become "increasingly unpopular" because he "was a repressive ruler and had brought Westernizing reforms to Iranian society" (968–69).

This is the only context given to explain the Iranian revolution, the establishment of an Islamic state, and the ensuing hostage crisis. The text offers no way for a student to grasp the complex and controversial role that the United States played in Iran leading up to the revolution and the hostage crisis. There is no mention, for example, of the 1953 CIA-sponsored coup that deposed democratically elected Prime Minister Mossadeq. Along with many other left-leaning reforms, Mossadeq had nationalized Iran's oil resources, wresting control from British oil companies. Nor does it discuss the United States' role in supporting the repressive regime of Mohammad Reza Pahlavi, the king who was overthrown by the 1979 revolution. Rather, students are left with a picture of an unpleasant ruler who was, in part, unpopular because he was implementing "Westernizing reforms," and a United States caught off guard when religious militants (along with many other opposition forces) overthrew this ally. At risk of being read incorrectly as supportive of the hostage taking, I want to be clear about what I am saying here. Without an honest discussion of the role that the United States played in first imposing and then supporting a brutal dictator, which helps to explain the anger that the revolutionaries expressed at US diplomats, Iranians—Muslim Iranians, in particular—are rendered irrational, primarily driven by religious opposition to a Western way of life. This narrative obscures the ways the United States had leveraged its imperial power, underwriting the Shah's economic, military, and political power prior to the revolution—a history that contextualizes the conflict between the United States and the current Iranian regime.

Moreover, the narrative sets up an opposition between the United States' liberal values and Islamic norms. In a passage explaining "The Islamic State," all manner of political Islam is collapsed into an ahistorical description of the rise of a variety of Islamist movements:

> [An Islamic] state [is one] in which the codes and beliefs of Islam guide politics and thus direct nearly every aspect of life. Mullahs, or Islamic religious leaders, became political leaders as well, which allowed them to impose Islamic codes on Iranian citizens. In a religious state, religious practices are not a matter of choice but the law of the land. Politics and religion have joined forces in other parts of the Islamic world as well. In 1996, a group known as the Taliban transformed Afghanistan into an Islamic state. From insisting that men grow beards to forbidding women to work outside the home, Afghanistan's leaders enforced a social order based on an interpretation of Islam. What long-held American principle does the creation of a religious state violate? (2005, 969)

Although the passage concedes that an Islamic state represents "an interpretation of Islam," the reader is left with a picture of Islam as a monolithic religion guided by a set of principles that are, at their heart, in conflict with a fundamental "American" principle. This develops a view of Islam as frozen in time, clinging to a set of unchanging principles, rather than understanding political Islam as one aspect of modern Islam, which is itself an outcome of a multitude of historic and political forces that evolved from local and international processes (Mamdani 2004).

Moreover, in tying the Iranian revolutionaries to the Taliban, the passage does nothing to help students think about the differences between these regimes, or the ways that both of these states rose in relation to Cold War–era policies of the United States and the USSR in the region. In fact, as the story moves forward to September 11, 2001, the text continues to build this picture of terrorism as an outgrowth of *Muslims'* opposition to Western influence in the Middle East. The section that follows directly upon the description of the September 11, 2001, attacks is entitled "Middle East Terrorism," and begins with a statement that Middle Eastern terrorists have been responsible for the majority of terrorist attacks on Americans since World War II. The text develops a generalized picture of Muslims that emphasizes their opposition to "Western values" and their hostility toward the United States, all in an effort to explain terrorism. The emphasis on a generic Muslim public fails to address the diverse political, religious, social, and economic realities of the Middle East. Ultimately, this textbook sets up Islam as problematic for democracy, echoing dominant discourses that purport a fundamental "clash of civilizations" (Huntington 1996; B. Lewis 2002).

The discussion of the rise of al-Qaeda is remarkable for its colonial amnesia. The text states:

> In 1979, the Soviet Union invaded Afghanistan. In response, Muslims from across the Middle East headed to Afghanistan to join the struggle against the Soviets. Among them was a 22-year old Muslim named Osama bin Laden. . . .

Bin Laden's experience in Afghanistan convinced him that superpowers could
be beaten. He also believed that Western ideas had contaminated Muslim
society. He was outraged when Saudi Arabia allowed American troops on
Saudi soil after Iraq invaded Kuwait.

Readers are completely sheltered from the knowledge of the role that the
United States played in supporting and arming the mujahedeen in Afghanistan as a bulwark against the Soviet Union, and thus, the rise of political Islam is ripped out of its context (Mamdani 2004). The reference to "Muslims
from across the Middle East" risks collapsing Muslims in general with the
mujahedeen. Students (and their teachers) are likely to walk away from these
passages describing the buildup to September 11, 2001, with a generic picture
of Muslims as terrorists who are threatened by Western ideas and values.

Thus, the official social studies curriculum adopted by the city in which
I conducted this research offered students and teachers little in the way of
understanding the complex historic and political contexts of the conflicts in
the Middle East and South Asia. Instead, it articulated the dominant liberal
national imaginary, setting up the United States as a beacon of democracy and
freedom in the world against the irrational forces of fundamentalist Islam.
The official curriculum reinforced dominant narratives of liberal nationalism
that position the United States as a benign force in the world, rendering its
imperial power invisible under the mantle of the good fight to eradicate terrorism and establish democracy everywhere.

Silencing Alternate Views

The official curriculum left little room for students (or their teachers) to develop nuanced or critical perspectives on the United States and its role in
the world. However, what happened on the ground in the school district was
more complicated. The one attempt made by the office of curriculum to help
students deliberate about the United States' impending invasion of Iraq and
develop a more complex understanding of the "war on terror" was derailed
by the question of Palestine, and the parallel association of Palestinians with
a culture that breeds terrorism, and Israel with democratic, liberal values
shared by the United States. This tight association of Palestine with terrorism,
and of Israel with US democratic values, was one that, as I show in chapter 5,
also followed the Palestinian American youth in their schools.

May Liu, one of the school district's curriculum officers responsible for
social studies and multiculturalism, was troubled that in the immediate aftermath of September 11, 2001, no curriculum was developed to help teachers

educate students about the politics and history surrounding the attacks. In the aftermath of September 11, 2001, the district had offered some workshops for teachers that were psychological in nature, intended to help teachers process their feelings about the event. However, according to Ms. Liu, the district did not prepare materials to help teachers understand historical and political contexts as the war in Afghanistan unfolded.[15] Teachers at Regional High confirmed that they received no in-service or curriculum materials educating them about the issues.

In mid-March 2003, as the United States was building up to the invasion of Iraq, Ms. Liu was determined that this time the curriculum office would handle things differently, and provide teachers with resources for addressing this second war. Ms. Liu and her colleagues in the district's office of curriculum developed a supplement on the Middle East that it intended to distribute to principals and teachers in all of the city schools. In a letter that accompanied the curriculum, they referenced three primary goals for the supplement: to provide students with basic knowledge about the region in order to help them "make meaning of this international dilemma"; to offer "coping tips" for teachers and parents with a particular focus on families with active-duty service members; and to remind teachers to address the issues at hand with "sensitivity, impartiality, and respect for all students and families." It had taken two years, and a second war, before the district developed materials that addressed basic information, and even then, they dealt with only one of the two regions in which the United States had gone to war.

The curriculum contained a variety of materials. There were two documents from the National Association of School Psychologists: one that focused on supporting children in "unsettling times," and another that addressed the needs of children with parents called up for active duty. The former was written for the context of the "war on terror." It suggested that teachers be able to identify "vulnerable" populations. Among the groups listed were children who "are of non-US origin and may feel threatened by intolerance or racism." Interestingly, this characterization failed to acknowledge either the particular groups that would be racially targeted in the context of this war or that many US-born students were also being targeted by virtue of being, or being assumed to be, Muslim. Both these documents were aimed at maintaining a climate of safety and routine for children while also facing squarely the reality that children of parents in the military had real reason to be fearful for their parents. There was no mention that some children might

15. I was unable to confirm this fact independently. However, no teachers or students I met recalled any such curriculum.

have family members in the countries that were being invaded and thus might be feeling vulnerable in ways similar to the children of military families.

As important as these documents were for addressing the psychological health of children and for giving educators a vocabulary for establishing emotionally safe school environments, these documents also assumed a ready distinction between legitimate war and terrorism. In the document for "unsettling times," teachers and parents were told:

> Differentiate between war and terrorism. The conflict in the Gulf will be a highly visible event. . . . You can distinguish between the two types of actions. Acts of war involve attacks on military targets and are, in effect government-to-government actions linked to official foreign policy objectives. Terrorism targets innocent individuals with the goal of inflicting harm and terror.

And:

> Stick to the facts. Answer children's questions factually and include a positive element to the answer. . . . "Yes we may go to war, but our troops will keep us safe."

While aiming to reassure children about their safety, this document subtly supports dominant political narratives that draw a clear distinction between "war," presumably carried out by the United States for legitimate foreign policy reasons, using American soldiers to "keep us safe" and attacking only military installations, and "terrorism," which targets innocent people.

The curriculum materials for classrooms, however, also included a more nuanced approach to the impending war. In addition to maps that labeled the countries of North Africa, the Middle East, and Western Asia, and basic biographical materials about the key players in the conflict (e.g., George W. Bush, Saddam Hussein, Kofi Anan, and Hans Blix), the packet included short statements from a variety of conflicting viewpoints (the US and Iraqi governments, United Nations Security Council, and peace activists). Teachers were offered suggestions for helping students to critically analyze the various perspectives on whether or not the United States should invade Iraq.

Importantly, May Liu, who wrote the majority of the curriculum, included several activities that sought to have students break down the dichotomy between self and Other. One activity suggested teachers bring pictures of young people from Iraq and from the United States in order to highlight the similarities between Iraqi and US children.

A second lesson, entitled "Peacemaker Role Play," asked students to construct a "peaceful solution to the crisis." The students were to be given different roles (e.g., UN secretary-general and representatives of the British, Iraqi, and US governments) and asked to negotiate an outcome that would avoid the invasion of Iraq. Although this lesson was unlikely to teach students much about negotiating such a complex political situation, it represented an attempt to shake up dominant political narratives that simply divided the world between good and evil, and made war seem an inevitable outcome of that division.

Although she was a rare voice in the school district's central office, May Liu tried to educate teachers and students to be more knowledgeable about, and also more critical of, the domestic and foreign policies that had unfolded in the wake of September 11, 2001. Speaking of her rationale for the supplement, May Liu argued that the curriculum aimed to "help kids respond to stuff. But my own personal goal was to have some lift up, critical thinking, and critical inquiry on the part of students and alternative perspectives than what they were getting." May Liu was not shy about her political convictions. Describing herself as a progressive, she saw the curriculum office as a place from which to "fly under the radar and . . . talk about US imperialism, anticolonial struggles." She argued that immediately after 9/11, she worried about "the rise of fascist thinking," and was particularly concerned about "racial profiling" of Muslim students. She also worried that the post-9/11 patriotic fervor would result in an "entire xenophobic response toward immigrant kids in general." May Liu never hid her political convictions, but she was careful to develop a curriculum that presented multiple perspectives on the impending war in Iraq. With this curriculum supplement, two and a half years after September 11, 2001, the school district finally had some materials that teachers could use at the very least to help students become more knowledgeable about the second war that was unfolding, and at best to develop critical perspectives on dominant nationalist discourses that carved the world simplistically into the lovers and haters of freedom.

As it turned out, this curriculum supplement never made it into classrooms in the school district because of vehement opposition from pro-Israeli lobbying groups. The trouble came in the form of a twelve-page chapter, published in 1999 by the Center for Contemporary Arab Studies at Georgetown University (Tamari 1999). This chapter, entitled "Who Are the Arabs?" was part of a module developed for grade school teachers. The document's opening paragraph sets the tone for the piece:

What is the Arab world? Who are the Arabs? In an age where movie images and news from political flashpoints dominate American perceptions of the world, the Arabs are, at best, little understood. The stereotypical images of the wealthy shaykh, the exotic bellydancer, and the hooded terrorist do not reflect the diversity of contemporary Arab society and the richness of Arab history.

In what follows, the chapter emphasizes the richness and diversity embedded throughout Arab history, language, and culture. The document briefly summarized the origins of Arabs and the rise of Islam. Its description of Arab history focuses on the Arab world's relationship with the West. The author explicitly counters the belief that "Westerners, including Americans, often assume there is a deep division between Arab and Islamic culture, on the one hand, and European and Christian culture, on the other" (Tamari 1999, 3). In a brief three paragraphs, he proceeds to discuss the Judeo-Christian-Muslim cultural renaissance in Andalusia; at the same time, he acknowledges conflicts that emerged at specific periods in European history; and finally he rests the roots of contemporary misunderstandings between the Arab world and the West in the legacy of European colonialism and imperialism in the Arab world, as well as the "United States' preeminent role in the Middle East following the denouement of the British and French empires after World War II" (Tamari 1999, 4).

Tamari's description of the contemporary Arab world focuses on the economic, social, cultural, and religious diversity of the region, and argues that social and economic differences have led to civil strife in many countries. At the same time, the chapter acknowledges that the unresolved Palestinian-Israeli conflict and the US-led first Gulf War have stoked the sentiments of Arab nationalism. The chapter ends with two paragraphs about Arab Americans, followed by three stories and poems, and brief sketches of everyday people living in different parts of the Arab world. This short chapter presents a picture of an Arab world that, while not without its conflicts and struggles, is diverse, dynamic, and richly hued. It offers a much different and more complex narrative about the Middle East than the one represented in *The American Vision* (2005); Tamari's chapter focuses on the diversity of the region, and contextualizes conflicts between Western countries and Middle Eastern ones within specific histories and power relations.

It was the inclusion of this chapter that led to a swift attack on the distribution of the curriculum supplement. To read and hear the complainants, one would imagine the chapter had been entirely focused on the Palestinian-Israeli conflict. A coalition that included the extreme right-wing Zionists of America along with the American Jewish Committee and the Anti-Defamation League organized a petition, wrote to the school superintendent, and spoke at a public meeting of the district's state-appointed school committee, demanding that the curriculum be withdrawn from the schools. These groups objected to three references to the Palestinian-Israeli conflict that appeared in this chapter: the claim that with military and financial support from the United States, "Israel continues to deny Palestinian demands for statehood with violent results for both people" (Tamari 1999, 6); a reference to the conditions in the West Bank as "a Military Occupation"; and the inclusion of a poem by Mahmood Darwish, perhaps Palestine's most famous poet.

Public testimony at the state-appointed school committee meeting illustrates the tone of the opposition to this curriculum. Larry Gerson,[16] the president of a local chapter of the Zionists of America, began by attacking the credibility of the Georgetown center:

> It's a unit that was published by the Center for Contemporary Arab Studies at Georgetown University . . . nothing more than a forum of Palestinian Arab propaganda. The material is *anti-American; it's anti-Israel*; and it's unbalanced.

The question to ask is: why and how does criticism of Israel get framed as simultaneously anti-Israeli *and* anti-American? Post-9/11 political discourses strengthened the analogy drawn between the United States and Israel—bearers of shared liberal democratic values—both standing firm against the antidemocratic forces of terror (Gregory 2004; R. Khalidi 2013).

Gerson went on to object to the curriculum's inclusion of "Identity Card," a famous poem by Mahmood Darwish (1964) written in response to the experiences he and his family had as Palestinians living inside the Green Line after 1948, witnessing the destruction of Palestinian villages, being subject to military rule, and suffering the loss of a country and a way of life. His poem offers both an indictment of Israeli policies toward Palestinians and a declaration of existence and identity. One stanza offers a flavor of the poem.

> Write down!
> I am an Arab
> I have a name without a title
> Patient in a country
> Where people are enraged
> My roots
> Were entrenched before the birth of time
> And before the opening of the eras
> Before the pines, and the olive trees
> And before the grass grew

16. Although the meetings of the School Reform Commission are a matter of public record, I have changed the names of the participants in order to maintain anonymity of the school district.

Darwish's (1964) poem chronicles experiences of injustice, of a people stripped of their homeland and identities. He warns of the danger of injustice gone unattended. His poem ends:

> Therefore!
> Write down on the top of the first page:
> I do not hate people
> Nor do I encroach
> But if I become hungry
> The usurper's flesh will be my food
> Beware.
> Beware.
> Of my hunger
> And my anger!

The symbolic and emotional measure of a poet's art was completely lost in Gerson's testimony. He was particularly upset by a suggestion for an activity that children write a poem of their own in a similar tone and style, "from a nationalist perspective (Arab, American, or other)" (Tamari 1999, 12). Gerson viewed this as "an insidious manipulation to have the children analyze, internalize, and unconsciously identify with Palestinian violence and, in doing so, justifies the terror and cannibalism." In one sweeping sentence, Gerson collapsed Darwish's symbolic cry for recognition and remembrance into a trope of Palestinian barbarism—as nothing more than terror, violence, and *cannibalism*.

Jonathan Mintz of the local American Jewish Committee was equally condemnatory in his attack on the curriculum. He argued:

> This particular item is a modern Trojan horse, a politically motivated and biased piece of propaganda disguised as a teaching module. Its distribution and its use throughout the school system risks an educational catastrophe. In our view, the piece is subtly anti-American, overtly anti-Israel, and it contains rhetoric and buzzwords of hatred, prejudice, and even terror.

Using hyperbolic language—the curriculum as a "Trojan horse" that bodes "educational catastrophe"—Mintz, like Gerson, makes a direct connection linking the United States and Israel on one side, as forces that implicitly stand in opposition to "hatred, prejudice, and even terror."

The outcome of this campaign against the curriculum was that school district principals were warned to "use discretion" in distributing the materials, effectively keeping them out of the hands of the district's teachers. The district subsequently constituted a new task force, that of community partners (including myself, a professor of Middle East history, the heads of both the local Arab American development organization and the Arab American arts association, and members of the Anti-Defamation League and B'nai B'rith), to create materials on the Middle East. At the first task force meeting, two members of the Anti-Defamation League argued that the district should avoid all teaching about the Israeli-Palestinian conflict because, as one stated, it was "too confusing for teachers to figure out" and teachers could not be expected to be knowledgeable enough to assess unrepresentative "extremist perspectives." Instead, they advocated that the goals of such a task force should be to help teachers teach students to be tolerant of one another. As several of us at the meeting remarked at the time, this approach would effectively maintain status quo knowledge about the Middle East conflict and foreclose critical public deliberation about a complex, multifaceted issue. Nonetheless, as a result of the Anti-Defamation League's position, this task force never met again and no curriculum materials were developed to help educators teach about the Middle East. Tolerance—as an educational and national norm— would, as I show in the following chapters, prove a weak tool for addressing conflict, rendering subordinate perspectives on the Palestinian-Israeli conflict and the "war on terror" inaudible, often with serious consequences for Palestinian American youth who were associated with an imagined Palestinian geography of violence and terror.

Two years into the US war in Iraq, the school district had removed all materials about the Middle East from its official curriculum. The school district's director of curriculum, who had, two years earlier, signed the original letter encouraging teachers to make use of the supplement, admitted to a local Jewish newspaper that the school district had provided "questionable materials" in that original supplement, and no longer included the Middle East in its curriculum planning.

"Your Eyes See Only What They Want to See"

Despite the lack of an official curriculum that could help students and their teachers engage in complex and critical discussions about, for example, Afghanistan, Iraq, and the Palestinian-Israeli conflict in their school, the Palestinian American youth spoke up, finding opportunities to engage peers and teachers in critical discussions that offered alternatives to dominant perspectives on the wars and the United States' role in the region. However, as I show here and in the following chapters, these alternate perspectives had been rendered virtually incomprehensible by the dominant political discourses of nationalism that imagined the United States to be unassailable in its commitments to liberal democratic norms and values, and constructed shadowy landscapes of Muslim Otherness.

Sana Shukri was one of the few Palestinian American youth at Regional High who planned to, and later did, attend a four-year university. She was the only student in our after-school club who was in the school's honors track. Sana was a writer and a poet, eager to share her words and opinions with anyone who cared to listen. During her senior year of high school, Sana published a poem in the Regional High student newspaper. This poem challenged the unilateral characterization of Palestinian violent resistance as terrorism while ignoring the violence of the Israeli occupation of Palestine. Charging that "your eyes see only what they want to see," Sana's words called upon those who dismiss Palestinians as terrorists to consider the circumstances of the lives of ordinary Palestinians. Entitled "Terrorists?" the poem (excerpted here) read:

> Your eyes see only what they want to see. You claim we are the terrorists because we stand up for what we believe in no matter the cost. You say we are murderers yet millions die everyday in our country from the hands of your people. . . . You look at us with hatred as we weep for the child who is lying on the ground with blood all around him. . . . We are the women who cry as we see our children being shot as they are playing outside who fear the death of their husbands who are trying to make a living. We are the men who risk their lives for the hope that one day our families will live in peace.

With the heightened vigor of adolescent political passion, Sana decried the invisibility of the violence that Palestinians face daily, and argued for the rights of Palestinians to fight for their independence. The Palestinian American youth were fully cognizant of the fact that, particularly after September 11, 2001, the complex historic, political, and social context of the Palestinian-Israeli conflict was often invisible to a majority of Americans, reduced to a singular view that equated Palestinians with terrorism. In many different ways, from conversations to school reports to public statements such as Sana's poem, Palestinian American youth sought opportunities to interrupt dominant political characterizations of the Palestinian independence movement that often rendered the daily violence and injustices of the occupation invisible.

The publication of Sana's poem, largely misread as a justification for the 9/11 attacks, created a quite a stir at Regional High. All but one of the responses to the poem missed the context of the Palestinian-Israeli conflict completely. The newspaper staff was called to defend their decision to publish it, and Mira Rubin, the faculty adviser (and one of the sponsors of the Arab after-school club that year) had to weather a storm of criticism about her wisdom in allowing its publication. Nevertheless, with the backing of the principal, the newspaper staff was able to defend Sana's right to publish. In the subsequent issue, the editors wrote:

> We are lucky enough to find ourselves in a diverse school, made up of people of all races, nationalities, religions, and ethnicities who speak many different languages. At the same time, we realize that to live in this setting we all have to recognize that we may see the world in different ways and from different points of view. We encourage any of you who would like to express your feelings or opinions to write for the paper. Only through the exchange of these ideas will we begin to understand each other, even if we don't always agree.

Thus, the editorial staff drew on an ideal of this national imaginary—a nation characterized by diversity and freedom of expression—to remind the community of the value of public deliberation of conflicting perspectives. They argued that through engagement with these diverse perspectives, understanding might evolve. This editorial response reflected an important—if unfortunately all too rare—moment in which the ideals of liberal multiculturalism were leveraged to try to open up dialogue.

The responses to Sana's poem, however, illustrated how quickly these very same nationalist ideals (of liberty, diversity, tolerance) were mobilized to excoriate Sana for her political expression. In one response, the author began by echoing Sana's opening line:

> You must be blind. We are the soldiers liberating *your brainwashed nations* from their oppressor . . . while you live here, with *freedom*, at the expense of blue-collar taxpayers. . . . You live here where your treasonous poem gets published because of the *freedoms of the press and of speech* which we *instinctively* share with you. . . . So next time someone calls you a terrorist, just put your head down in shame for defending the real terrorists. *Consider it a small price to pay to live in the best country in the world.* (emphasis added)

This response, like Sana's poem, has all the markings of adolescent passion and hyperbole. However, unlike Sana's poem, which locates itself in the particularities of a specific political conflict, this author drew on generalized beliefs about US democracy—as a beacon to the world for universal values of freedom—to upbraid Sana as an ungrateful immigrant who should bow her head in shame for expressing her opinion. Never mind that Sana was born, and had grown up, in the United States. For this author, she belongs elsewhere—positioned as a member of "your brainwashed nations" and a defender of "terrorists." This writer views the US role on the global stage through the lens of "radical innocence" (Pease 2009). The deep and complex historic and contemporary role the United States has played as an imperial power remains invisible, hidden under a mantle of colonial amnesia. Instead, against the brainwashed masses of the oppressed Muslim nations, this young man posits Americans' *"instinctive"* commitment to freedom.

In a second response to Sana, one of the newspaper editors wrote:

> Your eyes see what they're told to see. . . . One life is much too precious to give up unless it is for *freedom and liberty* . . . . They are the soldiers that fight so that the people of this foreign country will not be tortured any longer. They are the soldiers of America. They travel through this country with no prejudice, but are aware of who are around them. They give out candy to the children who are starving now, but soon may see a better future. . . . Here in America, there are people from each country in the world living in the same place. . . . We give them the same rights.

Just as the other author did, this young man also expressed the taken-for-granted ideals embedded in dominant discourses of liberal nationalism. This nation is imagined to be a force for freedom, not only at home but also abroad. The national imaginary celebrates diversity, uniting people from all countries under one nation, and guaranteeing everyone the same rights. Again, the tenacity of this discourse of liberal nationalism obscures the less benign aspect of US power. Years after the revelations, for example, about the Abu Ghraib prison torture, and the absence of weapons of mass destruction in Iraq, this young man continued to argue that the US military's invasions of other countries were purely to bring democracy and freedom, and to end torture in those nations. US power and violence are made invisible as this young man imagines the United States as a benevolent force for good—its military "travel[ing] with no prejudice" through other countries distributing candy to starving children. Freedom, diversity, and tolerance at home translate seamlessly to a vision of America's role as the bearer of democracy and liberty everywhere.

These were just two of the many responses to Sana's poem, all equally laudatory of the United States and derisive of Sana's perspective, which was universally viewed as a blanket defense of "terrorism." Sana's poem and the responses it engendered were all expressions of nationalist sentiments. However, these nationalisms are grounded by different kinds of claims. Sana made a *particular* political claim for justice for Palestinians, and for the right to fight in a specific historic context—one that is, of course, decidedly uncomplicated and rife with exaggeration and hyperbole. However, in a move that required no small courage in the post-9/11 environment of the United States, Sana attempted to open up a debate about the definition of "terrorism" that is only applied to certain kinds of violence and not others.

Sana's detractors never addressed the specific content of her claims. Rather, in their responses, the authors drew on the discourse of liberal nationalism—a nationalism that posits American values as universal ones to be spread worldwide, and constructs the nation's "radical innocence," obscuring its colonial legacy and contemporary imperial projects (Gregory 2004; Pease 2009). Four years into the "war on terror," these young people appeared to have no questions about the United States and its military might as a force for breeding democracy and freedom in the world. In "civilization's fight," our "instinctive" love of freedom, our tolerance, and our democratic values muted any possible critique of the easy division made between the defenders and enemies of freedom, and promoted a view of American soldiers as the world's liberators. This narrative of the United States as a benevolent force for good was delivered with angry passion directed at Sana, who was positioned as an outsider who should hang her head in shame for daring to raise political questions that challenged the simple dichotomy of good and evil.

Liberal Multicultural Nationalism and States of War

The line that runs from former president George W. Bush's speeches to the angry letters written in response to Sana's poem tracks the norms and boundaries of the dominant national imaginary constructed in broadly circulating public discourses. The norms of the dominant discourse of liberal multicultural nationalism—a discourse that emerged in the wake of World War II and was rearticulated in the post-9/11 moment—bound the United States' commitments to freedom, diversity, and tolerance at home to its mission as the beacon for democratic values worldwide (Brown 2006; Melamed 2006). Critically, the discourse of liberal multicultural nationalism cocreates the American national imaginary *and* an imaginative geography of Other places and peoples—a geography of illiberality, oppression, violence, and terror that have come to be associated with Islam and the "Muslim world" (Abu-Lughod 2013; Gregory 2004; Said 1978).

In using former president Bush's speeches as touchstones for illustrating the central tenets of liberal multicultural nationalism, there is a risk of associating this discourse with conservative political thought. However, the construction of the US national imaginary as grounded in freedom, diversity, and tolerance represents the dominant (if not the only) discourse of nationalism—one that runs through the speeches of Democratic and Republican politicians alike, as it also does through popular media, films, and our textbooks. There are different flavors to this nationalism that vary with political party, but the fundamental beliefs that this nation stands on the side of freedom, diversity, and tolerance span a wide gamut of cultural and political discourses. For example, on June 4, 2009, President Obama gave a major speech in Cairo, Egypt. Importantly, in this speech he acknowledged histories of colonialism as a source of tension with many Muslims, and he argued that Islam and the United States shared "common principles—principles of justice and progress; tolerance and the dignity of all human beings." However, he also echoed, albeit with different emphases, much of former president Bush's vision of the United States. He argued:

> The United States has been one of the greatest sources of progress that the world has ever known. We were born out of revolution against an empire. We were founded upon the ideal that all are created equal, and we have shed blood and struggled for centuries to give meaning to those words—within our borders, and around the world. We are shaped by every culture, drawn from every end of the Earth, and dedicated to a simple concept: *e pluribus unum.* "Out of many, one."

President Obama went on to describe democracy as a universal ideal that America would support everywhere. Thus, the discourse of liberal multicultural nationalism may take somewhat different forms, but certain core beliefs about this nation remain steadfast across a range of political party affiliations. I want to be clear that I am not arguing that liberal multicultural nationalism is the only form of nationalism available in the United States. Certainly, there are explicitly racist forms of nationalism deployed, for example, by white supremacist groups. Moreover, there are also oppositional voices critical of this nationalism, represented by courageous educators such as May Liu. However, it is this dominant form of nationalism that shapes mainstream political discourses, popular media, and most school curricula.

In this chapter, and in the chapters that follow, I focus on liberal multicultural nationalism because it plays such a fundamental role in the processes of racialization through which Arab and Muslim[17] people are positioned as suspect members of the nation, and invisible or dangerous subjects of Other places. The norms and values imagined to make the United States both what it is and an example to all nations are juxtaposed with Other places and Other people whose cultures are inimical to "our way of life." For the Palestinian American youth with whom I worked, this juxtaposition framed them as out-

---

17. See the introduction for an explanation of why I use this terminology to demarcate these widely diverse and incommensurate groups of people.

siders to the United States—as individuals incapable of, or unschooled in, the values and norms of this nation.

The "war on terror" highlighted this juxtaposition and sharpened the boundaries of exclusion for the Palestinian American youth and other Arab and Muslim communities. States of war heighten nationalism's ugly underbelly, solidifying distinctions between insider and outsider, and narrowing the scope of acceptable deliberation (Benei 2008; Ben-Porath 2006; Calhoun 2007). However, this hardening of boundaries draws on embodied nationalism that is always already there (Benei 2008), forged, often silently, in the unnoticed, but constant, drip of everyday discourses and practices. Discourses of liberal multicultural nationalism—discourses that imagined the United States as the model of freedom, diversity, and tolerance, and mobilized a fundamental "clash" between the liberal West and the illiberal "culture" of Islam—were strongly entrenched well before September 11, 2001. I have traced these broadly circulating discourses of liberal multicultural nationalism here because, as I illustrate in the next two chapters, they showed up in everyday discourse and practice at Regional High, positioning the Palestinian American youth as outsiders, members of imaginative geographies and cultures of illiberality and violence (Gregory 2004). I suggest that if we are to understand the processes by which these communities are racialized and excluded, we must focus careful attention on nationalism as a key mechanism of contemporary global racial formations.

4

"The Beauty of America Is It's a Salad Bowl": Everyday Nationalism at Regional High

> I think it's important that first of all, that [im/migrant students] come in contact with other people, because the one thing that you can say about America: it is a quilt, if you will. It's the one thing I say about what makes this country different from other countries. I mean there are no Americans. And so it's important, I think public education has a real responsibility, because it's a chance for people to work with other people that they're going to be living with, while at the same time respecting their identity. Because I don't think it's like at the turn of the century when they used to have people throw in their flags and take out an American flag, and you were supposed to become this homogenized thing. I think we understand that that's just ridiculous. So I don't think that's our job, but I think it is to educate children about getting along with other people.
> — LAUREN HEANEY, Regional High English teacher

Lauren Heaney's words tell a story about America and about American public education—a story that was told and retold at Regional High. It is a story about the uniqueness of this country and about the changing image of what it means to be American, the melting pot yielding to a patchwork of many peoples joining together while retaining their unique identities. It's also a story about American public schools as spaces for teaching "children about getting along with other people." I would hear many variations of this story over my years of fieldwork at Regional High.

I heard a version of this story the very first time I visited the school. Two months after September 11, 2001, I was invited to attend an evening meeting at Regional High. The leader of a local Arab American community organization had asked the school to host an open event for Arab American students, parents, and community members to discuss how the school was addressing the post-9/11 climate for Arab American students. Throughout the event, both administrators and parents emphasized again and again the notion that "we are all Americans." It was at this meeting that I would first hear the phrase "zero tolerance for intolerance," which emerged as Regional High's dominant mantra for describing the school climate. In response to one parent's story about his daughter's hijab being pulled off by another student, one of the administrators responded, "These are issues that come up with all cultures. Teenagers are part of it—fear of the unknown. The more familiar people become with people who are different, the more comfortable they are with difference. The more you interact with others, the more accepting they become. You go beyond skin, beyond clothes." Throughout the evening, Arab American parents and students raised questions and concerns about the school climate in the aftermath of 9/11. In response, administrators repeatedly emphasized that Regional High was a place where people generally got along, that the "issues" the school had faced after 9/11 were minimal—the product of "teenagers doing stupid things." Moreover, they insisted that the school's "zero tolerance for intolerance" policy offered a surefire guarantee that students' cultures and identities would be respected. The evening's dominant refrain, against which there were only a few naysayers, portrayed the school as a microcosm of American society—a place where diversity was valued and intolerance was a rare outcome of misguided individuals whose behaviors and attitudes would be quickly sanctioned.

This story and its variations are familiar ones narrated throughout US schools, as they are in US society—a reflection of the liberal multicultural national imaginary described in chapter 3. This portrait of America—painted in miniature form in local schools—trumpets a song of a peaceable kingdom in which, as a rule, all people learn at least to tolerate and at best to respect all people and their cultural diversity. This story is on display inside schools in many versions. From multicultural fairs and signs that greet visitors in different languages to school conduct policies and the formal adoption of multicultural curricular goals, images of a multicultural America have, in many educational institutions, come to refigure the rusty melting pot into a multicultural "salad bowl." The United States is currently fashioned as a multicultural haven—a model for freedom, diversity, and tolerance worldwide (Brown 2006; Melamed 2006; Moallem and Boal 1999).

The stories educators told about America and American education, and the educational practices these stories engendered, are expressions of *everyday nationalism*. Everyday nationalism references the implicit and explicit ways in which broader discourses of nationalism circulate in everyday life through talk and action, drawing upon, and in turn constructing, the national imaginary (Calhoun 2007; see also Abu El-Haj 2010; Benei 2008; Billig 1995). Through a careful analysis of the stories educators told—their words, images, metaphors, and explications—I illustrate how they implicitly drew upon the discourses of liberal multicultural nationalism, fashioning Regional High as a microcosm of the larger national imaginary. The stories we tell ourselves, the images and metaphors they produce, express who we believe we are, what we believe in, and what the norms are by which we expect to live and interact (Taylor 2002). Imagining Regional High as a space ruled by the fundamental and interwoven "American" values of individual freedom, diversity, and tolerance, educators viewed public education as the forum for inculcating those values in the nation's newest subjects and assimilating im/migrant youth to the norms of American society.

The stories educators narrated about Regional High as a place in which all students, but especially newcomers, learned to become Americans—to take up the values and norms of liberal multicultural nationalism—also structured their assumptions about, and interactions with, the Palestinian American youth. The stories we tell about who we are contain within them stories about who we are not. As teachers and administrators at Regional High narrated the school as a space in which each person was treated as an equal individual, each person's culture was respected, and tolerance was the reigning value, they (often implicitly) positioned Palestinians and Muslims as illiberal subjects of Other places in need of liberation from or discipline for these illiberal tendencies. The normative discourse of liberal multicultural nationalism tenaciously maintained the fiction that Regional High, like the United States as a whole, was a place where the democratic values of individual liberty, diversity, and tolerance were the rule for everyone, blinding most educators to the ways that liberal multicultural nationalism co-constructed belonging for some and exclusion for others.

Critically, in this chapter and the next I show that the invocation of national boundaries that excluded Palestinian American Muslim youth were not only manifest in moments of conflict and tension, as was evidenced, for example, in the confrontation described in the introduction to part 2 between Samira Khateeb's computer teacher and the Muslim girls in his class. In fact, exclusion from the national imaginary was often signaled through more benign interactions, such as the community meeting I described above highlighting the school as a haven of cultural pluralism and tolerance. In this chapter and the next, I draw attention to the connections between the kind of "hot" nationalism of Samira's substitute teacher and the more liberal sentiments of multicultural nationalism expressed in other, seemingly banal, interactions. I argue that both banal and hostile interactions emerge from and reproduce liberal multicultural nationalism in ways that make certain kinds of Palestinian and Muslim identifications impossible to include in the American national imaginary. Through this exploration in these two chapters, I consider how the processes of social inclusion for im/migrant communities must be understood in relation not only to processes that draw newcomers into the United States' racial hierarchy but also to the production of a national imaginary related to global racial formations and the nation's role as an imperial power (Abu El-Haj 2010; Cainkar 2008, 2009; Naber 2008; Maira 2009; Rana 2011; Winant 2004).

In what follows in this chapter, I explore the ways that principles of liberal multicultural nationalism informed educators' beliefs about Palestinian American Muslim youth, and about the role public education plays as a vehicle for assimilating these young people into American society (see also Buck and Silver 2012; Ghaffar-Kucher 2014). I analyze the interviews my research assistant and I conducted with the focal students' teachers, as well as other key school administrators, carefully tracking the language, images, metaphors, and turns of phrase through which they express their ideas about America, the Arab and "Muslim world,"[1] public education, and its role in incorporating youth from im/migrant communities. My focus here is on the strong thematic threads that resonated across all these interviews. My analysis of educators' discourse, then, is not an assessment of them as teachers. The teachers that my research assistant and I observed as we shadowed the focal students ranged from energetic and engaged to lackluster and uninspired. Most were generous in their interactions with their students, although a few were not. What was remarkable was the discourse they shared as they talked about America, American education, and Arab/Muslim youth. Thus, I pay careful analytic attention to language—to discourse—as text through which we can discern the normative assumptions, beliefs, and values through which the national imaginary is expressed and operates in everyday practice, for, as I show, these assumptions shaped assumptions about, and relationships and interactions with, the Palestinian American students.

Salad Bowls and the United Nations: On Individualism, Diversity, and Tolerance

The themes of individual freedom, diversity, and tolerance as key characteristics of this national imaginary reverberated throughout everyday discourse and practice at Regional High. Educators believed that Regional High was a place where each student was treated as an individual, cultural diversity was lauded as the rich hues and textures against which each individual stood out, and the democratic commitment to tolerance was the glue that allowed this vast diversity to flourish.

At the core of liberal multicultural nationalism remains a commitment to treat each individual as a free and equal member of society—a commitment

1. See n. 9 in the introduction.

to the primacy of the individual over group membership (Banks 2008; Brown 2006). Educators expressed this commitment through post–civil rights era color-blind discourse, insisting that they did not see difference and that all students were treated equally. For example, Tom Blackburn, the social studies department chair, who identified himself as of German ancestry, said, "When I see kids, I see kids. I don't see colors. I don't see anything." Other statements, such as "I tend to look at all students as just people" and "I try to deal with all my students on the same level," reflected teachers' deeply held beliefs that their interactions with students were shaped primarily by a commitment to seeing each person as an individual. Talking about their roles as teachers of im/migrant students, educators often emphasized the need to care for new-comers individually. When asked what advice she would give to new teach-ers of im/migrant students, Alexandra Borofsky, Adam Mattar's ESL teacher, who identified herself as a Russian immigrant, said, "To make them feel wel-come. To care about them. To respond to them. To treat them *very individu-ally* [emphasis added], to try to relate to them." Claudia Tomaselli, another of Adam's ESL teachers, who identified herself as Italian American, described her approach to teaching: "I think all students need understanding. So really I transcend, or at least I try to in my teaching, those differences per se. So, I'm not really aware of the Arab students as a community." Critically, this insistence on not seeing students as members of communities was at odds with the central role that group membership played in shaping the lives of the Palestinian American youth. Without seeing the Palestinian Americans as fundamentally grounded within a Palestinian community, teachers were blind to the ways that these young people had fashioned multifaceted social, cultural, religious, *and* political commitments through their experiences with group membership.

Moreover, these and other similar statements reflect the ubiquity of color-blind discourse in US schools that insists that this nation is indifferent to racial and ethnic differences (A. E. Lewis 2005; Pollock 2004). Color-blind discourse has been resoundingly critiqued for being one of the primary means through which US schools depoliticize structural inequalities and the con-flicts that ensue from these inequalities (A. E. Lewis 2005; Pollock 2004; see also Bonilla-Silva 2006). Color-blind discourse maintains status quo beliefs that US schools are meritocratic, and that the reasons for the persistent edu-cational underachievement and economic struggles of marginalized groups rest with children and youth and their families and communities, rather than with systemic processes of oppression and exclusion. This discourse of color blindness, and the racial regime that it supports, must also be understood as entwined with the production of a national imaginary. The diffuse circulation of the dominant discourse of liberal nationalism trumpets the almost unshakable creed that the United States is a nation in which all people are treated as equal individuals.

In what might appear to be paradoxical, this national ideal—that people are treated as individuals—rested comfortably next to another ideal celebrating the rich diversity of the United States. Teachers used many metaphors to describe the United States as a nation committed to cultural diversity. Bill Andrews, Samira Khateeb's and Khalida Saba's English teacher, who identified himself as African American, referenced the proverbial "salad bowl," stating:

> See, the beauty of America is not that it's a melting pot like they used to say. It's not. It's a salad bowl. But when you have a salad bowl, when you put the lettuce in, it retains its own identity. When you put all the elements of the salad in, it retains its own identity, but it's so good together. And that's what America is. It's not a melting pot. Everybody's not going to blend. Everybody's going to be who they are. But we're all in that salad bowl called America.

Lauren Heaney, Sana Shukri's English teacher, who identified herself as Irish American, explained:

> It's really important that kids see that America and—There is no way of defining that word because everybody in the room is an American. And they bring to that whatever—I like—I mean, I realize people would say a stew or whatever, a melting pot. I think of it as a salad. Each thing you put in a salad retains a distinctive flavor, but when you put them all together, it makes a fabulous meal.

The salad bowl was the most common metaphor educators used to describe US society. Other metaphors—for example, those of a "quilt" and the "United Nations"—invoked similar images of a nation resplendent in its diversity, one respectful of the variety of colors and flavors of its distinctive cultures. Not surprisingly, teachers' talk reflected the discursive shift that occurred during the course of the twentieth century as the metaphor of the United States as a melting pot gave way to one of a colorful salad. Heaney's claim that "everybody in the room is an American" and Andrews's claim that "that's what America is" suggest an imagined nation that is infinitely accommodating of cultural diversity. Unfortunately, as I show in what follows, there were constraints on the flavor of diversity that was allowed to spice up this American salad. The deep-seated commitments to transnational citizenship and belonging that the Palestinian Americans had developed found little purchase in this American patchwork.

These changing metaphors for the national imaginary track with the social and political changes that have occurred since the 1950s, as the United States outlawed legal segregation, changed its immigration policies to end explicit racial exclusion, and positioned itself as the beacon of freedom and democracy on the global stage (see Melamed 2006; Omi and Winant 1986; Moallem and Boal 1999). Without dislodging the centrality of individual freedom, multicultural diversity joined the pantheon of critical American values (Melamed 2006; Moallem and Boal 1999). The new images of an American society resplendent with distinct cultural flavors served to manage diversity within the nation without challenging the structured power relations (Melamed 2006; Moallem and Boal 1999). At the same time, this liberal multicultural national imaginary positioned the United States as the beacon of democratic values worldwide. Against ethnic and religious conflict in "other" places, the United States projected itself as a model for modern democratic multicultural harmony (Brown 2006; Melamed 2006; Moallem and Boal 1999).

If cultural diversity characterizes the landscape of this new "American" quilt, it is tolerance that stitches together the otherwise rough edges, allowing for understanding and harmony. Teachers and administrators argued that one of the primary purposes of schooling was to promote respect and tolerance in this national context of increasing diversity. Mr. Andrews described Regional High: "[There are] fifty-nine different languages in this building. So what is this but the world's microcosm?" holding out the hope that "if you can come into a circumstance like this and give everybody's culture respect, let everybody have their say about their country, their ethnicity and all like that, then everybody begins to understand." Teachers described US education, particularly in relation to youth from im/migrant communities, as a force for taming intolerance and for engendering understanding of and respect for others. As Vice Principal Diane Lawrence, who described herself as Italian American, put it:

> *Becoming acculturated and American means that there's tolerance* [emphasis added]. There's an acceptance. I think it's [that] hopefully we're seen more as individuals, as human beings, rather than as this type, that type, the other type.

Ms. Lawrence's words suggest two critical and interwoven ideas about the relationship between becoming American and learning tolerance. First, tolerance is appropriated as a piece of the American cultural fabric. By implication, if this is a value that is learned through acculturation, then it is one that im/migrants are presumed not to have before the acculturation process. Second, as Ms. Lawrence's words suggest, learning tolerance marks the moment of, in a sense, deculturing the other—turning those whom we identify as different from ourselves from group members into *individuals*, and *human beings*. This idea that learning tolerance entailed seeing other people as individuals apart from their racial, ethnic, and linguistic group was a consistent refrain throughout educators' talk. The strain of individualism runs deep, as evidenced by the tight relationship Ms. Lawrence's words draw between being seen as an individual and as a human being. For these teachers, becoming American is most critically about the process of individuating from one's group and coming to see others—and to be seen—as individuals. Diversity may be central to the nation, but it is to be worn lightly, an aspect of identity we tolerate or celebrate but one that never trumps our interactions as individuals. This formulation of the relationship between the individual and her or his community is at odds with the more intimately braided sense of self and community that Palestinian American youth experienced.

This idealized image of the United States as a diverse and tolerant nation was projected against both implicit and explicit images of Arabs and Muslims (and the places from which they came) as hostile and aggressive, particularly toward the United States. Reflecting on his experiences with Arab youth, Principal Jack Moore, who self-identified as European American, argued that on arrival in the United States,

> [there] was often an aggressive posture by the Middle Eastern and, in particular, the Palestinian kids. Now I don't know if that had to do with the fact that they were raised where they were raised and then they're coming here and they may have had preconceived notions as it relates toward Americans. I always felt it was aggressive and kind of irreverent.

His assumption that Arab students were generally hostile to the United States and its citizens was one that many teachers expressed in their interviews. Mr. Moore suggested that an "aggressive posture" and "irreverent" attitudes toward the United States were traits cultivated on Middle Eastern, particularly Palestinian, soil, where the students had developed "preconceived notions . . . toward Americans." As I discuss in more detail below, Mr. Moore drew on an imaginative geography of the Middle East as a space hostile to the United States and its values. Moreover, his curious emphasis on the Palestinian students as "irreverent" suggests that im/migrant youth should feel "reverence" toward this nation.

Over time, however, through the processes of schooling and acculturation, Principal Moore proposed that many Arab youth dropped their hostile and irreverent attitudes. He offered the following example of a young Lebanese student, Amir Khalid.

I have come to understand that maybe if they viewed Americans as the enemy . . . if this is what was basically professed where they were before . . . then coming here and having lived here for x number of years, I've definitely seen an assimilation. [For example,] Amir Khalid was an angry, angry man when he came here. You know, he drew pictures of planes and bombs and guns and all kinds of stuff. I worked closely with him and his father. . . . I saw, little by little, he was venturing out from his group and he was involved in the Asian club. It was Asian break-dancers. It looked like break dancing and they were Asian kids plus Amir.

Mr. Moore argued that "venturing out from [one's] group" through the process of assimilation tamed the earlier grip of aggressive, anti-American sentiment. He presumed that many Arab youth "viewed Americans as the enemy." However, Mr. Moore suggested that the "hostile" and "irreverent" attitudes that he believed Amir (and other Arab, and particularly Palestinian, youth) brought to the United States melted away as Amir abandoned an angry, Lebanese identity in favor of joining in new, hybridized cultural forms.[2] In a refrain echoing Ms. Lawrence's words quoted above, the process of acculturation is one that entails breaking away from rigid group boundaries to create more fluid relationships with others. In Mr. Moore's eyes, Amir becomes less aggressive and more tolerant as he draws on the diverse cultural milieu to make choices that reflect individual interests rather than group allegiances.

Cultural diversity plays a critical role in constructing a harmonious national imaginary. Without the rich diversity of this multicultural national quilt upon which he could fashion himself anew, Amir might have remained locked into his anger and aggression. Here I want to draw attention to the way that diversity is imagined in fairly thin terms. This is diversity that is extraneous to who we "truly" are as individuals. This is the cultural diversity of the private realm—customs and values that are to spice up, but not weigh down, our public interactions in democratic states. This is the stuff of dominant practices of multiculturalism in schools: food fairs and festivals in which we celebrate together our rich, "colorful" cultural diversity. Teachers often pointed to Regional High's annual multicultural fair as a symbol of its united nations. As an institution for promoting acculturation, school is imagined as a place where we can all learn to get along only once we come to interact as individuals separate from our group commitments. These thin applications

---

2. It is interesting to consider how the fact that Amir joined the Asian students—the presumptive "model minority" group—might have factored into Mr. Moore's perspective that he was assimilating to American norms.

of diversity in educational settings have been resoundingly critiqued for a failure to address power and oppression (Abu El-Haj 2006; McCarthy 1990, 1993; McLaren 1994; Mohanty 1989–90). I suggest, however, that we must also focus on how these discourses about diversity intimate a national imaginary. Regional High, as a symbolic microcosm of the United States, was imagined as a peaceable kingdom where diverse peoples come to learn and live together in respect and tolerance. Discourses of liberal multicultural nationalism offer this image of the United States as a culturally diverse democracy and a model for the rest of the world.

This attention to diversity as a variety of cultural flavors that we can easily share, adopt, or shed silences powerful political experiences, conflicts, and critiques that smudged the glossy portrait of the liberal multicultural national imaginary. While I cannot attribute meaning to the particular drawings of guns, bombs, and planes made by Amir, a child of war-torn Lebanon, my point is that Mr. Moore sees Amir's adoption of Asian break dancing as a kind of resolution to his former preoccupation with the violent, political realm. Mr. Moore never queried the significance and meaning of Amir's depiction of armed conflict; instead, he assumed the drawings represented aggression against the United States.[3] Moreover, Mr. Moore never considered the possibility that Amir's experiences with conflict and war might have led him to forge legitimate political perspectives that might have confronted the United States' image of itself as the world's peacemaker. Rather, as I show in detail in the following chapter, Palestinian American students' conflicting political perspectives—perspectives they developed through their transnational experiences—were repeatedly silenced. Nothing was allowed to challenge the doctrine that, at Regional High (as in the nation in general), everyone could get along if they all learned to venture out of their disparate groups and adopt tolerant views of others. In a sense, Amir's multicultural break dancing "performs" the nation—a space in which everyone can just get along.

Tolerance was also instantiated in official school policy. Regional High had adopted a policy of "zero tolerance for intolerance" that explicitly tied the value of tolerance to democratic society. This policy was a constant reference point for the principal and other administrators, who insisted that it set the tone for the school climate. It began:

3. The experiences that Amir and many of the Palestinian American youth had with war and conflict were not discussed as possible indicators of trauma that might have influenced their behaviors. In a national context in which all kinds of behaviors are interpreted through the lens of trauma and PTSD, it is interesting to consider why I never heard anyone in the school use the lens of trauma to make sense of the behaviors of many of these young people who had been directly affected by war and conflict.

As members of *a diverse community in a democratic society*, we are obligated to provide a safe and secure environment for all of our students. Our entire school community must embrace this responsibility in order to create schools and classrooms where students can learn and grow in an environment free from intimidation. *Regardless of our personal feelings or individual biases, our actions should be socially appropriate and reflect tolerance for each member of our Regional High community.* In accordance with the School District policies, *we have established a zero tolerance policy toward the language and behavior of intolerance.* This includes verbal as well as physical harassment. (emphasis added)

In its opening words, the policy echoes the discourse of contemporary liberal multicultural nationalism, weaving together diversity and democracy. The school's zero-tolerance policy reflects the tensions inherent in the discourse of tolerance. Hailed as a hallmark of a democratic society, tolerance is offered as a path for individuals to work together regardless of "personal feelings or individual biases." Tolerance policies often position conflicts (particularly those that arise between social groups) squarely in the domain of individual thought and behaviors. Brown (2006) argues that tolerance is a political practice for managing diversity that depoliticizes conflicts and inequalities by substituting emotional and behavioral remedies in the place of justice. Tolerance, as a discourse and practice, does not resolve or even engage political conflicts. Rather, as I illustrate in the next chapter, it serves to hide conflicts, and in doing so, makes room for excluding and expelling those who are defined as intolerant and those who adopt "the language and behavior of intolerance."

Educators invoked an image of Regional High as a tolerant space even in the face of clear examples of intolerance. For example, describing the stance he took to protect Arab American students after 9/11, Mr. Moore told me:

I took the approach that again nobody in this building had anything to do with the events of September 11th. And I asked for everybody's help. *I also told them that I wouldn't tolerate any negative, mean-spirited behaviors or anything like that on the heels of this event* [emphasis added]. And the issues we had here [after 9/11] were, in my mind, really minimal issues.

Moore invoked tolerance as the prime value guiding the school's climate; he let it be known that he would not "tolerate" bigoted behavior. It is important, however, to pay attention to the assumptions he made here in comparison to those he made about Arab youth earlier. Whereas he attributed Arab hostility and aggression toward the United States to beliefs and attitudes these youth were presumed to have absorbed on Middle Eastern soil, he cast evidence of American intolerance as the "negative, mean-spirited behavior" of *individuals.* The "minimal issues" to which he referred were not viewed in that light by the Palestinian students subjected to routine harassment for years following September 11, 2001. Ranging in severity, these "minimal issues" included: constant taunts of "terrorist"; girls having their scarves torn from their heads; boys in physical fights resulting from ongoing verbal and physical harassment; and hostile comments and unwarranted disciplinary sanctions from teachers. Presuming that tolerance was the primary value on which the school and, by extension, the United States operated, Mr. Moore glossed over aggressions that Arab Americans experienced after 9/11 as "minimal," located in individual acts, and not endemic to the American landscape. Moreover, as far as I and the Palestinian American students were aware, the school's zero-tolerance policy was never used to punish the intolerant behaviors that their non-Muslim or non-Arab peers and teachers directed at them. At the same time, as I show in the next chapter, this discourse of tolerance constructed an opposition between American tolerance and Muslim intolerance, and served, at times, to discipline the putative intolerance of Palestinian American youth.

One way to understand Mr. Moore's continual insistence, in spite of evidence to the contrary, that Regional High was a space ruled by tolerance is to see his position as a reflection of the institutional silences around racial oppression pervading US schools—as a practice of whiteness (Fine 2004). Tolerance policies maintain the status quo by substituting individual behavioral remedies in place of systemic approaches to structural oppression (Brown 2006). However, to see it only in this light is to miss the critical part that tolerance plays in the discursive construction of the national imaginary. The unshakable creed that tolerance was the reigning value at Regional High is part and parcel of the fabric of American liberal multicultural nationalism in these times (Brown 2006)—the glue that holds together this nation of diverse individuals.

Educators at Regional High narrated many versions of the imagined nation. These stories were all variations on a theme—the tale of Regional High as the nation writ small, a place in which individual students were treated equally, diversity was celebrated, and tolerance was the rule of law. At Regional High, the discourses and practices of everyday nationalism constructed a normative understanding of who Americans are, and the values for which the nation stands. In much the same way that the United States as a whole is imagined in its "radical innocence" (Pease 2009)—as a beacon for multicultural democracy worldwide—Regional High is constructed as a (neutral) haven that invites newcomers to join in the values and practices of this tolerant, diverse nation.

The National Imaginary and the Imaginary of Other Places, Other Peoples

Multicultural liberal nationalism, however, constructs the nation in relation to Other places and Other people. If the national imaginary reflects the normative assumptions people make about who they are, what values they hold, and how they act together, it also creates a boundary between self and the imagined Other, between inside and outside, here and there. Teachers' talk reflected not only their assumptions about America and Americans, but also presumptions about the places from which the Palestinian American youth had emigrated. Not surprisingly, in the post-9/11 world, those geographies were often fashioned as spaces ruled by enmity toward the United States (Gregory 2004) and an imaginative geography of the Middle East shaped by Orientalist discourses (Said 1978).

As noted above, Mr. Moore believed that Palestinian and other Arab students had learned their reputed hostile feelings toward the United States in the places they were raised before coming to this country. Ms. Heaney described how her feelings had changed after 9/11 as she came to understand that there are "people who really, really hate this country." Hani, Adam's younger cousin, recalled that when a friend told their teacher he was considering visiting Palestine, "she told him not to because he'll grow up to do bad things to the world." Hani's teacher appeared to construct Palestine as a dangerous, radicalizing space that inevitably leads young people astray, presumably to commit violent acts in the world. In a similar way, Claudia Tomaselli told me that after being informed by a colleague that Palestinians who lived in the Middle East celebrate suicide bombings with candy, she then recalled that several of the Palestinian American girls at Regional High had shared candy on 9/11; she retrospectively interpreted their actions as being supportive of the attacks.[4] Ms. Tomaselli reread the girls' exchange through a lens that placed these youth squarely within the borders of Other territories—territories that were viewed monochromatically as violent and hostile spaces. My point here is that the geographies of enmity (Gregory 2004) that some educators imagined reigned in the Middle East were, at times, folded seamlessly into how they interpreted their Palestinian American students' words and actions, and how they constructed these youth as racialized Others—a point I illustrate in more detail in chapter 5.

Educators also expressed ideas about the Arab and "Muslim world" that while not necessarily driven by a presumption of enmity and hostility, never-

---

4. The girls I knew shared candy and gum on a regular basis, and none of the students ever expressed anything but horror for what had been done in the name of Islam.

theless constructed an opposition between "here" and "there," and "us" and "them." Several educators explicitly invoked the popular political argument that the culture of Islam and the Arab world is incompatible with democracy. Discussing skepticism that the United States government's stated goal of bringing democracy to the Middle East would succeed, Mr. Blackburn, the social studies chair, argued, "Does [democracy] mix with the culture? Are they ready for democracy? You can say democracy, but you see what's going on in Iraq. You've got Iraqis killing Iraqis." This idea that the "Muslim world" is culturally mismatched with democracy subtly reinforces a belief that democracy is the domain of the United States and the West. His words also intimate that the Middle East remains, to a large extent, backward—a territory not yet "ready" for democracy, for reasons of culture and internecine strife.

Recounting an experience about a time when a Palestinian student expressed the belief that Osama bin Laden was not responsible for the September 11, 2001, attacks, Ms. Borofsky (Adam's ESL teacher) said:

> So all of a sudden, [the student] said, "Bin Laden didn't do it, because if he had done it, he wouldn't be afraid to admit it like he admitted it in '93." And then he said to me, "Am I in trouble for saying that?" So I said, "What would have happened in Saudi Arabia if you had expressed that?" He said, "I would have gone to jail." I said, "Well the beauty of this country is you can express your opinion and nothing is going to happen to you." I told him, "It makes me sad that you have views like that. But there is no way you're going to be punished." I said, "This is the beauty, that's the freedoms we fought for, and that's what we have."

In this interchange, Ms. Borofsky set up an opposition between the democratic freedoms of the United States—ones that "we fought for"—and the autocratic state of Saudi Arabia. It is important to ask why a teacher's response to her student's contentious political belief was to draw Saudi Arabia into the conversation as a foil for illuminating the "beauty" of America. (Ms. Borofsky's claim that there was "no way" that a student would be punished for contrarian political views was not true, as I show in chapter 5.) Her words make sense, however, as an everyday expression of liberal multicultural nationalism—language and imagery that set up an opposition between the benevolence of American democracy manifest in her liberal American classroom and the illiberality of Other places associated generally with Islam and Arabs, as epitomized by Saudi Arabia. In the process, Ms. Borofsky asked her student to imagine himself, and in doing so, she implicitly placed him, in that illiberal space, beyond the protections of a liberal America. As discussed in depth in chapter 3, normative discourses of liberal multicultural nationalism draw on the thesis that democracy is a Western tradition that is incompatible with Islamic "culture" (Mamdani 2004). The thwarted aspirations of people across the Middle East for democracy and the history of Western involvement that has often played a crucial role in derailing those aspirations (R. Khalidi 2004, 2013; Mamdani 2004)—including the United States' staunch support for the current Saudi regime—are rendered invisible by a hegemonic discourse that positions Islam as culturally incompatible with democracy (Brown 2006; Mamdani 2004).

If educators typically expressed the belief that the "Muslim world" was a different kind of place, ruled by norms and values that were fundamentally opposed to guiding principles of the United States, they also imagined that the people belonging to those places embodied those different norms and values. Teachers echoed broader political discourses about Muslims, viewing them as members of nations, cultures, and families that restricted individual freedom and choice (see also Ghaffar-Kucher 2014). Thus, educators often constructed Arabs and Muslims as living according to different rules and sensibilities than those required of citizens of a democratic state.[5]

A key tenet of liberal multicultural nationalism posits an ideal citizen who is free and capable of acting out of individual conscience and conviction, not from predetermined group allegiance. Currently, this image of the free, agentic American citizen[6] is projected against a dominant view of Arabs and Muslims as captive to cultural beliefs and practices (Abu-Lughod 2002, 2013; Brown 2006; Mamdani 2004). Whereas Americans are purported to act out of individual choice and conscience, Arabs and Muslims are viewed as simply following the conventional mores dictated by their cultural and religious community. Importantly, the "war on terror" has mobilized this opposition between American individualism and Muslims' imagined cultural

5. I hope it is clear I do not hold the dominant values and assumptions that guide many democratic societies to represent some universal ideal. In fact, many communities have substantive disagreements with these values and assumptions (see Asad 2003; Mahmood 2005). My point is twofold. First, the dominant public perception that democracy and Islam are at odds blinds many Americans to democratic governance and movements in the "Muslim world" and to the ways that US foreign policy has been instrumental in thwarting democracy in much of the region. Second, this perception led teachers to read the Palestinian American students (and other youth from Muslim communities) and their families as lacking in, or hostile to, democratic values and commitments.

6. This ideal, which has been characterized as an expression of the "American creed," holds that the United States is a land where individuals from all over the world can come to remake themselves through the opportunities afforded by the nation's political commitments to equality and liberty of all people (Gerstle 2001; Smith 1988).

captivity, particularly in relation to women's oppression in Arab and Muslim[7] societies and regarding the United States' potential role as their liberator, here and abroad (Abu-Lughod 2002, 2013; Brown 2006; Jarmakani 2008).

Educators at Regional High bought into this opposition between an *American* commitment to individual freedom and choice, and the religious and cultural practices they believed limited individual freedom in Arab and Muslim countries and, by extension, in Arab and Muslim im/migrant families. Contrasting American and Arab families, Diane Lawrence argued:

> Americans are also taught, we teach our children to be very independent in their thought, to be independent in their decisions as they get older. . . . They should do things to please themselves more than to please their families. That's probably not as true in Arab families. There is more of an emphasis on family honor.

Personal liberty—independence—positioned as an American value was set against the restrictions that Arab families were presumed to impose on Arab youth. That is, Americans are free and agentic subjects *in contrast to* Arabs, who, constrained by religious and cultural practices and beliefs, are expected to act in accordance with expectations for group membership in their families.

Arab and Muslim women are seen as particularly vulnerable to these cultural constraints on individual freedom (Abu-Lughod 2002, 2013; Brown 2006; Haddad, Smith, and Moore 2006; Jarmakani 2008; Zine 2006). Dominant political narratives about Islam frame gender relations among Muslims as primarily repressive and regressive—the products of outmoded cultural traditions. These discourses co-construct Arab Muslim women as silent, passive, invisible, and victimized, and American women as free subjects, who are the agents of their destinies. In interview after interview, teachers frequently drew on dominant images of Arab and Muslim women's oppression, stating, for example, that they "are subservient," "are viewed as male property," "walk three steps behind their husbands," and "have no freedom." Talking about the Muslim girls he had taught, Aaron Silverman, a social studies teacher who self-identified as Jewish, said:

> Their father said, "Oh, you must wear this. Oh, you have to do that and that." And where I'm from, I come from the perspective that's your choice. It should be your choice if you want to do that or not. I think that's too broad, because

---

7. See the introduction for an explanation of why I use this terminology to demarcate these widely diverse and incommensurate groups of people.

you know what, even in America our parents say you must do this. You must do that. And I say, yeah, you have to listen to your parents but you have to make choices and take the consequences of those choices. But I think that with Arabs or with Muslims, it's more dictated by religion.

Mr. Silverman laid claim to individual choice and agency as an American characteristic in opposition to the restrictive religious demands of Islam. While nodding to parental authority "even in America," he suggested that American youth must make choices and face the consequences of those choices, whereas Arabs and Muslims are "dictated" to by their religion. In a sense, he claimed, *we* are free agents and *they* are not.

The Islam he describes is reified as a monolithic culture, one that teachers most often described as inherently fundamentalist and deeply constraining of its followers' lifestyles (Abu-Lughod 2013; Brown 2006; Mamdani 2004). Lauren Heaney, for example, expressed this blanket view of Islam. She described her feelings about the Muslim community as follows: "I guess I feel about Muslims the way I feel about right-wing Christians, that there's no room, there's no room at the inn for me." Whereas she qualified the Christians she was speaking about (right-wing Christians), she made no distinctions about Muslims, treating all Muslims as similar to fundamentalist Christians. Islam, in her view, made "no room" for diverse—read democratic—perspectives and practices.

Even more sympathetic views of Muslims and their putative gender relations reinforced this idea that individual freedom is America's domain. Ms. Lawrence had spent time in a majority-Muslim country when she was in college. She felt that many Americans misunderstood gender relations in the Middle East.

> I think maybe Americans see males—Arab or Palestinian or Iranian or Middle Eastern men—as not respecting women, but I think perhaps they don't understand. It's that they are trying to protect them and out of sort of a culture that says that it's unsafe for a woman to be by herself. It's unsafe for women to do many things in the countries which they come from and hence, we're looking at it as sort of stifling. We see it as stifling. They're stifling their rights, their freedoms of women. It's not so much that as a protective mechanism that needs to be discussed and it needs—people adapt. I mean every generation immigrants have changed. The Arabs will be no different. The Palestinians will be no different. They will change.

Ms. Lawrence reframed the dominant perspective that Middle Eastern men do not respect women, a view that a majority of the other teachers expressed explicitly in their interviews. She suggested instead that gender norms in the

Middle East reflected *cultural* norms aimed at protecting women in what she perceived as "unsafe" societies. However, in suggesting that "we" should not necessarily view this as "stifling their rights, their freedoms," she implicitly located individual freedom and rights squarely in the domain of the United States. Moreover, she argued that the process of assimilation—of becoming American—would lead inevitably to the adoption of US norms and presumably to the liberation of women.

The United States' role as a liberator of oppressed people was implied throughout teachers' talk about Muslim and Arab communities. Educators described residence in the United States in general, and American education in particular, as potential liberation sites for loosening the grip of Muslim and Arab culture and Americanizing im/migrant youth. Education was viewed as a path toward individual freedom, particularly for girls. On one of my first visits to the school, Mr. Moore confidently informed me that Arab girls and women are silent and never assert themselves, believing that "it's a cultural thing." Moore also expressed his hope that the Arab student after-school club would offer girls the confidence to break their perceived silence and, in his words, "have a voice." His description of Arab girls did not match the lively, outspoken, at times verbally combative young women I came to know. Nevertheless, Mr. Moore and other educators frequently spoke about Palestinian girls as subjects in need of liberation.

The hijab—to Western eyes the most visible evidence of Muslim women's oppression—was a topic of discussion among teachers, as it so often is in the media. Describing what she believed to be true about Muslim women, Ms. Heaney said:

> You know, they're viewed as male property. You know, the whole covering of the hair. And I know there are other reasons for that, but it can come down to that, that there's some kind of special defined way that a woman is supposed to be. And, I know that some women choose this and say it's very freeing. *But it rankles me and I guess it's because I'm born an American* and it just bothers me that somebody's taught to cover up. I do respect somebody's desire to do that, as long as they're really choosing to. . . . *It's just that I like the freedom to be who I want to be and I guess I feel everybody should have that right.* Every woman should have that right. (emphasis added)

Even as she tried to construct some latitude for women who might actually have chosen to wear headscarves, Ms. Heaney ultimately could not let go of her gut sense of their oppressive nature "because I'm born an American." This affective dimension—the feeling of what is right that comes from being "born American"—is a critical aspect of how nationalism works. Nationalism gets embodied; it becomes an inextricable part of our emotional registers (Benei 2008). Thus, Heaney expressed that it is her national identity—the condition of *being American*—that rankles at the sight of this (putative) lack of freedom and rights. Her words also illustrate how Muslim women are always already outside the national imaginary, as their headscarves simultaneously signal their putative oppression and the condition of not being "born an American" (Cainkar 2008). If being American were the condition from which flowed the freedom to "be who I want to be," then Muslim women's presumed lack of freedom (manifest in their headscarves) played counterpoint to American women's putative liberty to choose their dress. Only certain kinds of actions count as "choices" in this national imaginary.

Importantly, teachers saw the Arab Muslim girls as active agents in their lives only when they conformed to American standards and expectations: not wearing a hijab was seen as a choice Muslim girls made, whereas wearing one was viewed as an imposition. However, as described in chapter 1, the Palestinian girls—both those who wore and did not wear the hijab—frequently engaged in lively debates about the choices[8] they were making to be visibly Muslim or not. Yet these complex debates among the teenagers were inaudible to a majority of the teachers, who appeared to unquestioningly adopt broadly circulating political discourses that equated Islam with women's oppression, and that denied the possibility that Muslim women might be active agents in the decision to adopt a hijab.

These political discourses about Muslim women's oppression were manifested in everyday practices that demarcated the borders of inclusion and exclusion in the imagined national community. Palestinian girls who did cover their hair often found themselves positioned as outsiders subjected to outright hostility or strange curiosity. Samira's encounter with the substitute teacher, described at the beginning of part 2, clearly signaled the image of Muslim women's oppression that many teachers and students held. Suleima, Samira's sister, recalled that a teacher, speaking of her headscarf, told her that she looked "like a disgrace in that thing." Several girls reported having peers try to tear their scarves off their heads. Many of the youth told me stories about their and their female relatives' hostile encounters in public spaces, including verbal abuse and refusal of service.

If the girls often encountered hostility among teachers, peers, and com-

---

8. Of course, the very notion of "choice"—and its relationship to *freedom*—is problematic, a central concern of feminist literature (see Abu-Lughod 2013; Brown 2006; Hirshman 2003; Mahmood 2007).

munity members regarding the hijab, some also confronted teachers' lack of knowledge about the headscarf. In an interview, Haneen Haddad, a Palestinian American senior who grew up in the United States and Jordan, told the following story about a conversation in which Ms. Borofsky talked with Haneen about her headscarf and expressed a curiosity to see her hair.

> That lady, she was going on [about the hijab] and I even showed my hair to her. She was like, "How it looks like?" I worried she was going to think something is going on with my hair. And I was like, "You know what? You're a woman and I can show you my hair, but would you do me a favor?" And she was like, "What?" "Could you close the door? I don't want anyone to see me." She's like, "Fine." And she was also surprised and she was like, "You look more girl now." And I was like, "Do I look like a girl?"

Ms. Borofsky's interest in Haneen's hair reveals how the Western obsession with the hijab, and with the oppression it is presumed to represent, contains normative assumptions about femininity, sexuality, and women's agency that render Muslim girls—especially those who cover their hair—invisible. Haneen did not "look like a girl" until she removed her scarf. For Western eyes, it is only in this moment of uncovering that the Muslim woman is offered agency, visibility, and individuality.

The pervasive discourse that Muslim women were oppressed and needed to be rescued from their own community (Abu-Lughod 2002, 2013)—a discourse embodied, for example, in the school principal's belief that our after-school club would give girls their voices—shaped many daily interactions between Palestinian students and their teachers. Thus, contrasting definitions of Americans as free individuals and Arabs as cultural captives shaped an educational project of liberation, especially for Muslim girls, a project symbolically represented by that moment of showing one's hair.

The discourses of liberal multicultural nationalism co-construct self and Other, and the imagined communities of the United States and the "Muslim world," in oppositional terms. In this construction, Palestinian and other Arab American youth were imagined to belong to those Other places and cultures, and to be ruled by norms and values fundamentally different from those embraced within this liberal multicultural national imaginary. Whereas the United States and Americans were taken to value individual freedom, diversity, and tolerance, the "Muslim world" and its people were positioned as unlikely subjects of the nation, unprepared to practice the values of democratic citizenship. Critically, educators' beliefs in the differences between American and Muslim values and norms illustrate the limits of liberal multicultural nationalism. Despite the claim to valuing diversity and tolerance, only certain choices, expressions of cultural differences, and political beliefs could be tolerated as compatible with liberal multicultural nationalism.

Education as a Force for Making Liberal Subjects

Informed by the normative discourses of liberal multicultural nationalism, educators imagined Regional High as a kind of experiment in American democracy—a space for cultivating the norms and values of the nation.[9] In the post-9/11 context, many believed that education had a particularly important role to play as a force for calming the passions and the presumed intolerance and hostility that they believed their Arab and Muslim students felt toward the United States. How did teachers think that American education could teach norms of liberal multicultural nationalism? First, as described above, many educators argued that with time, im/migrant youth would assimilate organically to American norms and feel free to make choices about their own lifestyles that were different from the cultural norms of their families. Second, many teachers suggested that the act of being *educated* together in a kind of model United Nations leads young people inexorably to expand their cultural horizons, assimilate to American values, and interact peaceably with people who are different from themselves. (This was the case, for example, with Mr. Moore's description of Amir.) Finally, they also believed that their classrooms could serve as a neutral zone in which youth might learn to deliberate dispassionately, in the presence of an objective teacher; through this kind of moderated dialogue, teachers hoped the seeds of understanding and peace might develop. For many teachers, teaching young people to listen to and tolerate divergent ideas seems particularly weighty in the context of the "war on terror." Unfortunately, as I show in chapter 5, the normative assumptions of liberal multicultural nationalism that implicitly drove these efforts left unchallenged the boundaries that had been created between insider and outsider, and often silenced alternate perspectives on Regional High as a haven for multicultural diversity and coexistence.

Many educators believed that education had a critical role to play in the face of international conflict. For example, Ms. Heaney expressed her distress when, after September 11, she realized that "there are people who really,

---

9. See the volume edited by Schiffauer et al. (2004) for a portrait of how schools in four European countries educate teenagers from im/migrant communities into the "civil culture" of those nation-states.

really hate this country." She argued that an American education might prove a healing balm for these animosities:

> I think [the hatred against the United States] points out how even more important it is—it's incredibly important that children are educated. That's why I think this school's wonderful. It's the one place I've seen where it's not all segregated. I mean, you have kids—I mean my two classes are little UNs. You have kids from all over, and just the fact that they would have the experience of being in class together, you see the person as a real person. Even if you have to hear some prejudices and whatever baggage you're carrying around, if you're sitting next to each other, you see that person, as opposed to being segregated off where you never meet people and you don't ever have to realize that they're real people.

Portrayed through the pervasive symbol of a miniature United Nations, she positioned the school as a space in which youth from all over the world, by virtue of simply getting to know one another, come to see others as "real people." Her words convey the power of liberal multicultural nationalism's focus on individuals; the "prejudices" and "baggage" that people carry with them from segregated spaces simply fall away as people get to know one another. This is an idealized United Nations, imagined without vested interests and enduring conflicts. Moreover, particularly in a time of war in the face of "people who really, really hate this country," education becomes a vital experiment for the cultivation of tolerance and peaceful interaction among diverse groups of people. This is, critically, an *American* education she describes—an imagined integrated (rather than "segregated") space that brings together people from all over the world.[10] The fruits of education in a multicultural democracy are imagined to lead to a more peaceful world.

Mary Malone, an ESL teacher who described herself as Irish American, recalled that soon after 9/11, she sent several Palestinian boys to the disciplinary office because they drew pictures of planes approaching buildings (as had, I must note, many children across the country). The boys were suspended from school. Speaking of this incident in retrospect, Ms. Malone regretted her decision to report the boys to the disciplinary office.

> What I would do now is just try to—not that I could do this as one person— but just, maybe, *appeal to them as human beings* [emphasis added]. Like, I understand their situation and how they could, you know, I could understand

10. The notion of Regional High as an integrated space masks the racial/ethnic tracking that—similar to schools across the nation—filled low-track classes with newcomer youth and students from racially/ethnically marginalized communities.

like if someone's a suicide bomber, to me, that would just mean they feel so strongly about their position. They're not sane and I'm not saying that would be the right way to go. But just to get them to see that maybe there could be another way to solve conflict. It doesn't have to be through, you know, death and planes going through buildings. I wouldn't rush out to get them in trouble, because I think they may still feel that's the right thing to do and they would hide that feeling rather than bringing it out and maybe having more of a dialogue.

In thinking critically about her earlier response to these students' actions, Ms. Malone imagined that educational dialogue—rather than discipline and exclusion—might prove more effective in quelling the strong feelings that lead to violence. However, this educative dialogue that she imagined was premised on a particular view of these young men. In shifting seamlessly from understanding the boys' "situation" to understanding "if someone's a suicide bomber," she conflated her particular students with the diffuse and dominating images of Islamic terrorism in the contemporary US political discourses—images that position both the suicide bombers and her young students as enemy aliens. In contrast, she carved out her own stance as one of liberal tolerance. She sought to understand the positions she assumed that both the boys and the imagined suicide bombers shared, and, in doing so, she tolerated intolerable ideas. Moreover, she considered *education* and *dialogue* as ways to "appeal to them as human beings," to eschew violence and find other ways to solve conflicts. For Ms. Malone, American education offered a path for rescuing these young men from the clutches of a culture that is presumed to breed intolerance and revere violence. Although Ms. Malone rethought her disciplinary response to the young Palestinian men, she did not question the assumptions she had made at the time and continued to make, when we spoke several years later, about the reasons for the students' drawings. She never questioned her assumption that the boys drew the pictures because they supported the attacks.[11] If Muslim girls were believed to be in need of liberation from their religious oppression, Muslim boys were often imagined to require pacification—to be returned to the fold of humanity through the educative dialogue promoted by American education. With US government policy fashioning the nation as the police force for the global "war on terror," American education could position itself in a supporting role, working to turn young Muslim men away from the presumed lures of radical Islam.

Although many teachers expressed the conviction that simply living in

11. As I said earlier, none of the Palestinian American youth I met ever expressed anything other than horror at what had been done in the name of Islam.

the diverse American salad bowl would ameliorate prejudice and hatred, they also spoke of classrooms as spaces for actively teaching tolerance and mutual understanding. In this endeavor, many teachers hoped to foster the civic skills of dialogue and dispassionate deliberation—skills they felt were critical to realizing racial, ethnic, and religious tolerance, or better harmony and understanding. Although a majority of the teachers interviewed described this as their goal, my research assistant and I saw no evidence of these kinds of discussions in any of the classrooms we visited. However, in interview after interview, teachers described their classrooms as sites for calming passions, and for promoting respect and tolerance for diversity. Bill Andrews explained his classroom philosophy:

> It's important to me for everybody to understand everybody. And not be afraid to talk about the things that you have in terms [of difference]. Now everybody's not going to necessarily agree. And there are still going to be people who point fingers and things like that, but at least we open the forum in here for the discussion, the *multicultural* discussion. (emphasis added)

In his curious reference to a *multicultural* discussion, Mr. Andrews implicitly invoked the radical possibilities of cultural diversity to foster deliberation and tolerance, if not actual agreement, across cultural groups.

Mr. Andrews continued:

> And if you look at my desk, you'll see that I have words written down from other languages, you know, because I want to be able to, you know, I want to be able to say what I have to say in [other languages]. And I can give everybody's culture their own respect and dignity and that kind of thing. So like when the Arab students come in, I look at them, go, "*al-salām ʿalaykum*." They go, "*ʿalaykum al-salām*." Because I want them to understand that, while 9/11 upset me like it upset everybody, I know they're not at fault. This is larger than them, much larger than them, and it goes back thousands of years. You know, it's a geopolitical thing that we can't solve in here by, you know, hating or disliking, but if we understand, at least that's a step in the right direction.

Mr. Andrews argues that as a teacher, he can signal respect for the dignity of each student's particular *culture*, represented here by greeting them in Arabic. In referencing his own feelings about 9/11, he makes the case for focusing on culture as a means to create distance from the anti-Muslim, anti-Arab passions that followed those attacks. Cultural understanding, developed through public education in this liberal, multicultural democracy, might not be able to "solve" geopolitical conflicts that Mr. Andrews argues are too large to resolve and have been brewing for "thousands of years," but it can move people away from the passions of hatred. The "multicultural discussion," then, aims to foster cultural tolerance, even as it glosses and silences discussion of broader political conflicts, such as those that engendered, and were engendered by, 9/11.

Moreover, as he speaks, Mr. Andrews makes two important, if implicit, moves. Unlike some of his colleagues, he did not associate his Arab students with the 9/11 attacks; he knows "they're not at fault" and this is "much larger than them." At the same time, his reference to seemingly intractable conflicts that have been centuries in the making—that "go back thousands of years"—invoked the clash of civilizations hypothesis (Huntington 1996; B. Lewis 2002). Unfortunately, attributing disputes with and within the "Muslim world" to unyielding, incompatible, ancient conflicts, rather than to more recent political processes (Gregory 2004; R. Khalidi 2004; Mamdani 2004), *and* placing these conflicts outside of the classroom and the nation—as something much "larger" than the lives of his students—left little room for a "multipolitical" discussion. This subtle and pervasive educational practice eschewing political dialogue for cultural remedies had serious consequences for the ability of Palestinian American students to be full participants in their classroom and school communities. For many of the Palestinian American and other im/migrant youth, these geopolitical conflicts had long affected their families and communities directly, yet they were expected to take a backseat to cultural remedies for intergroup relations. As I show in the following chapter, a focus on culture silenced more difficult dialogue as Palestinian American youth raised diverse and contentious political perspectives that challenged dominant perspectives on the United States as a beacon for liberal democracy at home and in the world.

Mr. Andrews was not naïve about divergent political perspectives present among Arab Americans. Continuing from above, he turned his attention to the feelings and emotions of the "Arab community" in the United States, arguing:

> And then there's the anger in the Arab community too. I mean there is an anger that is like, right below the surface. And if you don't address that concern, if you don't address that anger, then it could explode. So I like to address it. So we, like I said, we cut across the cultures. Say what you have to say. You know but angry people are angry people you know. And I think because I have Jewish students in class, and I have Arab students in class, and they really do get along. Kids in this school get along really, really well. But I think it's my responsibility to help them get along. To help them talk. To help them discuss these things. You know and to be the moderator. And I don't stand on the right and wrong point of view. I stand at a moderate point of view. . . . And I think it helps.

From Mr. Andrews's perspective, Arab anger threatens to explode unless education can be leveraged to help people talk *across* cultures. This education is conducted by a neutral (American) teacher who is the self-proclaimed "moderate," mediating religious conflicts between Jews and Arabs, in which there is no "right [or] wrong point of view." Importantly, this "Arab community" is imagined as monolithic,[12] characterized by anger, but also implicitly presumed to be Muslim. Mr. Andrews's belief about this looming anger in the Arab community echoes widespread fears across Western countries that Muslim residents are at increasing risk of being drawn to terrorism, rather than to allegiance to the nations in which they reside. Education is viewed as a potential site for integration of youth from these Muslim communities.

Moreover, Mr. Andrews's words also invoked the fantasy that I heard teachers describe again and again: Regional High was a public space where students from wildly different cultural backgrounds all "really do get along." I heard teachers and the school principal repeatedly insist this was the case, even as they lamented the fact that students seemed to hang out almost exclusively with their racial/ethnic peers. Multiple interracial/interethnic conflicts ripped through the school periodically each year; during my first two years in the school, some of the Palestinian American youth were involved in serious physical fights with Russian Jewish and Colombian youth. These conflicts were never treated as opportunities to address racism and interracial conflict. Mr. Moore was particularly insistent that these incidents were nothing more than typical teenage behavior, silly fights over basketball or other trivial issues that morphed into intergroup conflicts that had no deeper meaning. Chinks in the armor of Regional High's mantle of multicultural tolerance left little lasting impression.

However, in the midst of a deafening silence about anti-Muslim, anti-Arab, or—for that matter—any other racism at Regional High, Bill Andrews was one of the few teachers to acknowledge any evidence of misguided anger directed at Arab and Muslim communities in the wake of 9/11. Mr. Andrews's description of how he intervened against this prejudice is instructive.

> And I try to tell the kids you know, all bad people aren't black and all black people aren't bad. All white people aren't good and all good people aren't white. Just trying to make them understand it's a human thing, it's an individual thing. And just like the majority of the kids in this school, whether they're red, yellow, white, black, or brown, the majority of the kids in this

12. Research on Arab Americans shows wide variability in their political opinions on both domestic and foreign policy (with the exception of the Palestinian-Israeli conflict) (Stockton 2009).

school will do and want to do the right thing. They don't want any trouble, they don't want any problems. It's a very small minority of people that do the wrong thing. And it's the same way I would believe in the Arab community. I mean, the average Palestinian is not a terrorist; their families are not terrorists. They want to live in peace like everybody else wants to live in peace.

Against dominating stereotypical images—of black people as bad, white people as good, and Palestinians as terrorists—Mr. Andrews tries to educate his students to see all groups of people as the same. Whether they are "red, yellow, white, black or brown," most people are essentially good.

Mr. Andrews continued, bringing in his own experience as a black man:

So you've got to be angry about that [stereotyping], you know. And then you have people saying things, again, the minority in the school, saying things that create that kind of thing. You know, so I understand why they're angry, I mean, I get it. From my own perspective, I've lived it. So you know, it's not hard for me as a person of color to look over and see where is this coming from. You know, and I understand why white Americans are angry about 9/11 too. You know? And their anger is either on the surface or right below the surface too. So if we don't delve into this and we don't talk about this, and we don't get some kind of understanding in this, the microcosm we call the classroom, then there may never ever be understanding. But if we can get understanding here, then we may be like that proverbial pebble in the pond, you know, one ripple, another ripple, another ripple, another ripple, another ripple. And that's all I try to do, that's all I can do, is that one class at a time, one person at a time, one group at a time, and hope that it like filters out, that people will begin to understand. And we get along really well in here. I mean, I'm really, really happy being here. I wouldn't want to be anywhere else. And when the kids get upset about things I say, I picked this, I wanted to be here, now, though we don't always agree we should respect everyone's right to disagree.

In this passage, Mr. Andrews stakes out a complex position from which to advocate for educating youth for multicultural understanding. He argues that, as a person of color, he has "lived it" and thus understands the feelings that Palestinians have in the face of prejudice against their community. He distances himself from anti-Arab prejudice, but he also claims to "understand why white Americans are angry about 9/11." Interestingly, these words implicitly construct the international conflict as one between Arabs/Muslims and white Americans, the latter of whom are implicitly positioned as the presumptive national citizens. Thus, Mr. Andrews's words intimate the fault lines in the national imaginary—the realities of a racial regime that separates him from the normative (white) national citizen.

At the same time, Mr. Andrews leans on the principles of liberal multicultural nationalism to propose an education for understanding. Invoking the radical potential of a color-blind America in which no matter one's "hue," we are all individuals—human beings mostly trying to do the right thing—Mr. Andrews argues that, while the anger of prejudice may be understandable, it must be overcome through education. Classrooms must operate as "microcosms" of the world we desire, fostering understanding while also respecting others' *right* to disagree. Creating one classroom at a time in the image of the multicultural kingdom we might hope to engender, Mr. Andrews launches that "proverbial pebble" into the world's pond.

Again and again, teachers described the classroom and the school as a space for promoting rational, deliberative discussions that could engender understanding across differences, particularly in relation to emotionally charged topics. Claudia Tomaselli argued that schools had an important role in helping students learn to discuss hot topics rationally:

> I think schools should promote discussion. They should promote subjects where reasoning is involved. Philosophy, ideas like this so that students can talk about things but be reasonable about them.

Learning to listen without passion was seen as key to this kind of rational deliberation.

Bill Andrews also argued for the educative power of rational debate:

> I've never in the five years I've been here had a heated argument. We've had divergent views, but never a heated argument. . . . It has to be respectful. We have to be respectful. Everyone has his or her own opinions, whether you agree with it or not, but it must be kept on a respectful level.

Similarly, Lauren Heaney was convinced that dispassionate, rational deliberation was critical to education, even if it seemed difficult to realize. Speaking of the passions engendered in discussions of the Palestinian-Israeli conflict, she said:

> And I do believe there is an answer, because I think people can work together if they can just not scream all the time. But it just happens that almost any discussion becomes screaming, and they're not listening.

Thus, being able to work together, coming to an understanding—tolerating different perspectives and peoples—depends on taming passions. The conceit here is that individuals can (and should) step back from their passions and discuss conflicts calmly. In interview after interview, teachers insisted that calm dispositions must be the rule in these deliberations; they often interpreted calm as signaling respect. The "multicultural discussion"—the symbol of an education in liberal multicultural nationalism—must be a dispassionate one.

And in the midst of students' irrational passions, teachers continually imagined themselves as neutral brokers. Mr. Andrews, quoted above, fashioned himself as standing "not on the right or wrong" but "on the moderate point of view." Alexandra Borofsky described her stance when students discussed Middle East politics in her classroom:

> I become very neutral and I say, you know, if I see it's getting like very heated then I just stop it and I say, you know, I try to be objective.

Ms. Borofsky fashioned herself as the objective peacemaker, quelling the political passions of her partisan students. It is important to pay attention here, and elsewhere, to the number of times that teachers proclaimed that their position was one of dispassionate, balanced neutrality holding out against extremes, claiming an objective, apolitical high ground. These beliefs that Regional High was a haven for cross-cultural understanding, and that teachers were neutral brokers of peaceable interactions, reverberate with the broader dominant political narratives of the United States' role as a disinterested bearer of universal norms and values of democratic citizenship worldwide (discussed in detail in chapter 3). Just as the United States was imagined to be capable of bringing peace to a world in the grips of terrible internecine conflicts, American schools, with their increasing international diversity, could educate youth in the skills needed for building a harmonious global community.

Implicitly, this insistence that an American education in respectful and dispassionate dialogue—one that brings people together in a diverse classroom and school community—could promote peace and understanding imagines an Other who must be taught to stand back from the passions that engender violence and hatred. Bill Andrews fantasized about Arab anger bursting out from under the surface if education failed to develop understanding. Lauren Heaney watched in despair as discussions of the Palestinian-Israeli conflict devolved into "screaming." Ms. Malone hoped that dialogue would displace her students' affiliation with suicide bombers. In none of these descriptions did teachers imagine that their own passions were somehow also engaged.

In being critical of the ways that teachers imagined American education's potential to foster cross-cultural understanding simply by modeling multicultural community and actively promoting dialogue and dispassionate deliberation in classrooms, I am not arguing against educational practices that bring together youth from diverse communities or pedagogical strategies that engage these students in critical dialogue with one another. In truth, I believe that public schools should teach students to deliberate, and to consider others' ideas and commitments carefully (Abowitz and Harnish 2006; Gutmann 1987; Hess 2009; Parker 2006; Parker and Hess 2001; Rubin 2012). And I certainly believe that we should be committed to creating schools where people from diverse backgrounds can learn from and live with one another in meaningful and growth-inducing ways. However, I am trying to show here how these educational commitments must also be analyzed critically in relation to the political practices of everyday nationalism.[13] Unquestioned presumptions of liberal multicultural nationalism shaped educators' commonsense feeling that, at its core, the school and their classrooms embodied American commitments to individual liberty, diversity, and tolerance. These normative beliefs made it difficult for them to consider how certain kinds of identities, and certain kinds of critical, political conversations—identities and critical perspectives that Palestinian American youth had forged—were rendered invisible and silent by the discourses of everyday nationalism. Instead, most educators maintained a belief in the United States as an innocent beacon of democratic values worldwide—fundamentally committed to individual freedom, diversity, and tolerance—and in Regional High as an embodiment of these American ideals.

Imagining the Nation through Everyday Practice

At Regional High, the stories told about what America stands for and the norms and values that guide American society co-constructed belonging to and exclusion from the imagined national community. The norms of liberal multicultural nationalism that educators believed guided their practices (and the nation as a whole) are, at this historic moment, fashioned in relation to an imaginative geopolitical geography of Otherness in which illiberal Islam plays a starring role (Abu-Lughod 2013; Gregory 2004; Mamdani 2004). Palestinian and other Muslim and Arab youth were often read through the (deeply gendered) lenses of this imaginative geography, and interpreted as illiberal subjects in need of assimilation, liberation, and pacification (see also Ghaffar-Kucher 2014). Thus, the discourse of liberal multicultural nationalism, expressed in everyday practice, does work on the ground, articulating the boundaries of belonging to this nation and creating norms for participation—boundaries and norms that made it difficult for these Palestinian American students to be full participants in their school community.

13. Sunier (2004) documents argumentation strategies taught in four European states as part of a broader study of "civil enculturation" that educates young people from im/migrant communities into each country's civic culture.

Coda: Civilized Discussions and the Politics of Neutrality

Adam Mattar had only one goal for his senior year: graduation. He had
watched his brother and several of his Palestinian male peers disciplined or
expelled from Regional High for reasons that often seemed to him to have
more to do with their ethnicity/nationality than with their offenses. Adam
expressed no interest in continuing on to college after high school; he wanted
to get a real estate license in order to build a business that would support his
family here and in Palestine. Nevertheless, he had resolved to graduate from
Regional High with a high school diploma.

Adam approached most of his classes with a determination to be help-
ful to his teachers, do as much as it would take to pass his classes, and find
ways to socialize with his cousins and other Palestinian friends. It was only
in Ms. Borofsky's class that Adam's role as a genial and compliant student
unraveled. The tension between Adam and Ms. Borofsky was always palpable. One day in May, Adam purposefully arrived late, knowing that this
would set off his teacher, who, as expected, yelled at him as he entered. For
her lesson that day, Ms. Borofsky played a brief movie as a precursor to a
class discussion about immigration. She introduced the clip stating, "We're
watching a report on illegal immigrants." The clip was from a television news
documentary entitled *American Identities for Sale*. The host investigated the
black market for identity papers that undocumented Mexican workers buy
in order to find employment. After the clip, Ms. Borofsky opened the floor
to discussion, saying, "I would like to start with giving the opinion of His-
panics on illegal immigration." One of Adam's Latino friends, Hector, was
enraged, telling his teacher that he found the movie "racist." Ms. Borofsky's
response was "It's not racist; plus, you're not even Mexican." When Adam
began to support Hector's position, she immediately interrupted him to ask,
"Are you here legally?" to which Adam quickly retorted, "I have an American
passport." A second Latino student, Fernando, claimed that the movie "isn't
racist; it's reality." Hector, however, was undeterred by both his teacher and
his peer. He tried to articulate his sense of what was wrong with the movie's
political position, stating that undocumented im/migrants buy these black
market papers because "they don't got no option." Adam made another attempt to support Hector's position, but Ms. Borofsky cut him off once again,
saying, "You cannot interrupt. It's a civilized discussion." As the discussion
continued in this vein, Adam had had enough and got up to leave with the
excuse that he needed to go get his phone from a friend. Ms. Borofsky tried
to convince him to stay, pointing her finger at him and stating, "You're making me nervous. You stay in the seat." After this, Adam appeared to be on a

mission to annoy or frighten his teacher, and he kept popping up and down until the end of class.

Adam's typical stance as a quiet, compliant student fell apart in this space where the parameters of inclusion and exclusion were so palpably contested. Ms. Borofsky's direct challenge to Adam's citizenship status and her refusal to let him interrupt because the conversation was "civilized" reflected a politically charged classroom climate in which Adam and other im/migrant students' right to belong was challenged. Although, as quoted earlier in this chapter, Ms. Borofsky believed that she became "objective" in the face of controversial discussions, this was clearly not the case. Her conceit of neutrality broke down in the face of a challenge to dominant constructions of undocumented people as "illegal," and an attempt to open up a conversation about racial oppression. Ms. Borofsky's obvious nervousness around Adam resonated with other incidents in the school in which teachers and peers seemed to fear that the Palestinian American male students were threatening and potentially violent. Ms. Borofsky's response to Adam's friend Hector indicated that Adam was not the only im/migrant student to face her hostility. The accusation of being undocumented sweeps up many im/migrants who do not fit the dominant image of "Americans." At this historic moment, there is, for Muslims, an additional layer to the accusation of being undocumented, since a generalized fear of Muslims as sleeper terrorist cells has gripped the nation since 9/11, justifying mass detentions and deportations. A challenge to Adam's legal status inevitably called up this context, and Adam's insistence on his citizenship was never far away from his fear—one that he spoke of with me—that the United States might one day deport all the Arabs. Ms. Borofsky's reference to the "civilized" nature of the discussion also silently, unconsciously invoked the historic confrontation between the "West" and its civilizing mission in relation to the non-Christian world (Rana 2011). This small moment in one classroom illustrates the daily acts through which the national imaginary (and the parameters of belonging and exclusion) are continually constructed within intimate, local spaces, such as Regional High.

It might be tempting to dismiss this interaction as a sign of one teacher's weak pedagogical skill, coupled with her strong political views. However, this example illustrates a moment in which an education in liberal multiculturalism breaks down quickly in the face of challenges to a certain construction of the nation. As I show in the next chapter, this incident in Ms. Borofsky's classroom was not simply aberrant. When Palestinian American youth challenged the dominant perspectives of liberal multicultural nationalism, this liberal nationalism often shifted into more explicitly exclusionary forms of nationalism, slamming shut the figurative borders of the country.

5

"Are You or Are You Not an American?": The Politics of Belonging in Everyday Life

It was morning assembly for seniors, and the students were gathered in the cavernous auditorium. As some students appeared to be sleeping, others sat quietly, while still others ignored the presentations on the stage, chatting idly with their friends. Ms. Jones, one of the school's vice-principals, asked the students to donate to a "bunny hop-a-thon" to support children with muscular dystrophy. As trays were passed around to collect money, a group of small children from the school's day care center proceeded to the stage, decked out with bunny ears and tails, hopping along to some jaunty music. Next, the school's college counselor took the stage to encourage seniors who had not yet done so to come by the office. He warned them that taking time off after graduating from high school often led to being swept up in the exigencies of adult life, with "jobs," "car payments," and "babies" leading them away from pursuing higher education. As the assembly dragged on, students became less and less attentive. Despite Ms. Jones's repeated admonitions to the students to be quiet—which ended with her telling them to "shut up" and threatening to take away their prom tickets—the din grew steadily louder. Midway through the assembly, the vice-principal announced that they would now salute the flag. Suddenly, a majority of the students were called to attention, rose, placed their hands over their hearts, and recited the Pledge of Allegiance. Then the school band struck up the national anthem. During this routine exercise in what Billig (1995) calls "banal nationalism"—the everyday rituals through which the nation is flagged, imaginatively constructed, and reconstructed in daily practice—Adam, Zena, Zayd, Leila, Samira, and Mai (a girl whose Muslim faith was visible because she wore a hijab) stood alongside their peers. Leila was the only one who also recited the pledge. Khalida, however, remained seated, as did a handful of other students scattered across the auditorium.

The Palestinian American students had various and complex reasons for their decisions to stand or not stand during this daily nationalist ritual. Some, such as Zayd and Samira, believed that standing for the pledge offered the broader community a symbolic gesture they hoped would counter dominant images of Palestinians, Arabs, and Muslims as enemy aliens. Earlier in the year, Mai had been threatened by a vice-principal with disciplinary action for refusing to pledge allegiance to the flag. Fearing that he might actually carry out his threat, Mai had decided to comply with his demand. Even Anne Larson, the sponsor of our after-school club, who stood but did not pledge the flag for religious reasons, had been called into the principal's office for her silence. She recalled that Mr. Moore told her she should be saying the pledge in order to set an example for the students. As she reminded him, however, she and the students had a constitutional right to silence.

It was much harder for students to withstand the pressure to pledge allegiance to the United States; however, Khalida Saba was determined to exercise this right. Khalida explained how she initially came to the decision not to stand for the pledge or the national anthem.

> There was a day we were in the auditorium. There was an assembly, and the teacher told us to stand up for the Pledge of Allegiance. And that day I was really feeling lazy and not wanting to. And the teacher comes up to me, she says, "OK, you need to stand up for the Pledge of Allegiance." I told her I didn't want to. She was like, well, she was like, "Are you American or are you not American?" I was like, "Yes, I'm living in America." She was like, "Exactly. You are living in America, so you have to stand up for the Pledge of Allegiance." And I refused to. And since that day, it was in December of 2002 when it happened. And after that, I never stood up for the Pledge of Allegiance.

What began for Khalida as, perhaps, a simple act of adolescent ennui quickly turned into a more charged political confrontation about her status as an American. In Khalida's narrative, she responded to the teacher's challenge as to whether or not she was "American" with a slight, but critical shift in nuance: "I'm living in America." Khalida claimed the United States as a space, rather than an identity, that she inhabited. As described in chapters 1 and 2, Khalida's sense of being first and foremost Palestinian grew from her long residence in Palestine as a child and early adolescent. At the same time, her experiences as Palestinian, Arab, and Muslim in the post-9/11 United States had engendered an awareness of the racialization of her community that led her to feel less than fully part of the imagined American national community. What to her teacher might have appeared a simple question about national allegiance—are you or are you not an American—was, for Khalida, neither straightforward nor stable. This teacher's one-dimensional perspective, which demanded simple adherence to performing this daily rite of national loyalty, glossed the complex realities of Khalida's sense of belonging. Moreover, the teacher showed no curiosity to understand, and perhaps even learn from, this young woman's life experiences.

The range of responses that Palestinian American youth had to this mundane ritual practice of banal nationalism reflected the multifaceted ways they positioned themselves and were positioned in relation to Palestinian and American imagined national communities (Chun 2013). As chapters 1 and 2 illustrated, Palestinian American youth fashioned a complex and multifaceted sense of belonging and citizenship across transnational fields. These experiences led them to a variety of political actions in response to the daily symbolic call for loyalty to the United States. Some protested. Others tried to symbolically signal their membership in this multicultural nation, seeding images of themselves as "good Muslims" (Mamdani 2004)—loyal citizens of the United States. As I show in this chapter, these political gestures were tied to perspectives they had developed on a range of issues, including the politics of Palestine, the US claims of democratic equality, and the nation's foreign policy.

However, these complex political perspectives and actions were inaudible to many educators who were unable to hear the stories and experiences that shaped the Palestinian American youths' lives and political perspectives. A general tide of belligerent nationalism (Ben-Porath 2006), expressed in times of war, narrowed the scope of public deliberation and dissent across the country, demanding uncritical patriotism and loyalty to the United States. As an example, in the state where Regional High was located, one of the first legislative acts after September 11, 2001, required all schools (public and private) to have students recite the Pledge of Allegiance every day—an act that was subsequently stayed through court order. For Palestinian American youth, the demands of belligerent citizenship were paradoxical. On the one hand, they faced constant challenges to prove themselves loyal and patriotic US citizens. At the same time, as I illustrated in the previous chapter, they were already prefigured as people who belonged to Other places—places that were imagined as hostile to the United States and inimical to its values. As a consequence, it was difficult (and often impossible) for the Palestinian Americans to be recognized and accepted as full citizens. The complexities of these young people's political and cultural identifications and perspectives were rendered invisible as a majority of their teachers and peers read them through lenses shaped by long-developing Orientalist and Cold War ideologies, and the more recent construct of the "war on terror" (described in the previous two chapters). The political critiques Palestinian American youth had developed and the symbols of Palestinian nationalism that they often displayed were all conflated with tropes of terrorism, disloyalty, and intolerance.

This chapter focuses attention on the politics of belonging as they unfolded on the ground in everyday life at Regional High. The politics of belonging (Yuval-Davis 2011) involves the political projects that establish the boundaries of imagined communities, drawing distinctions between "us" and "them." They involve both hegemonic constructions of belonging and their contestation by those positioned outside the boundaries of belonging. Looking at particular sites of conflict that emerged between Palestinian American youth on the one hand, and their teachers and peers on the other, I examine the Palestinian American youths' everyday bids for citizenship, by which I mean the ways in which these young people made claims for belonging and worked for equality, justice, and inclusion (see also DeJaeghere and McCleary 2010; García-Sánchez 2013; Sánchez 2007; Seif 2011).[1] Unfortunately, as I show, these bids for citizenship gained little traction and were often met with practices of silencing and discipline at Regional High. This chapter illustrates how Palestinian American youths' bids for citizenship—demands for full participation, membership, and equality in school and society—were constrained by the practices of everyday nationalism that constructed them as outsiders to this national imaginary.

Living as Enemy Aliens

One cold February afternoon in 2004, the Arab American After School Club gathered in Anne Larson's social studies classroom for our weekly meeting. There was a large group this day, and for the first fifteen minutes the room felt noisy and chaotic as students greeted one another and screeched metal chairs along the scuffed linoleum floor, pulling them into a circle. Eventually, we all settled into our seats, and the room quieted as the youth got ready for our day's activity. The plan for this day—one that was generated by Khalida Saba and Zayd Taher—was to continue a discussion of the dominant representations of their community in public discourse, create symbolic images of these representations, and find ways to break the bonds of these racialized

---

1. The young Palestinian Americans were deeply concerned with questions of justice. Although from Cairo to Hong Kong, Tunis to Ferguson, to all the Occupy movements and beyond, we have, in recent years, witnessed people—especially young people—organize and demand more just and inclusive policies and governments, bids for citizenship are not always antioppressive in orientation. (See, for one discussion of this, Christou and Ioannidou 2014.)

FIGURE 1

images. Responding to the question "What do others think about Arabs?" the students generated the following list: strict, they hate us, terrorists, evil, monsters, they're afraid of us. The group agreed that they wanted to figure out how to symbolically represent and respond to the image of Palestinians and Arabs as terrorists. Before bringing out the cameras, the students launched into an intense conversation about their sense that the school police officers were particularly harsh on the Arab boys. They described one officer in particular who routinely cursed at, and sometimes shoved, the boys in the group. This sense of being unfairly targeted by police generated an image they wished to capture on film. One of the young men wrapped his head and face in a black-and-white checkered kafiyyeh, leaving only his eyes visible (see fig. 1). Another student bound his hands behind his back (see fig. 2). One student took a series of photographs that began with the boy's covered face, turned to the image of him as a bound prisoner, and ended with a young woman cutting the bonds (see fig. 3), which the youth described as liberating themselves from this dominating image of the Palestinian, Arab, Muslim male as terrorist.

This was not the first or last time that students in the after-school club would talk about, and seek ways to respond to, the dominant and oppressive images that depicted their community. In the wake of 9/11, Palestinian Americans at Regional High were often construed as the local face of terror. On a few occasions, this overt racism actually came from their teachers. The

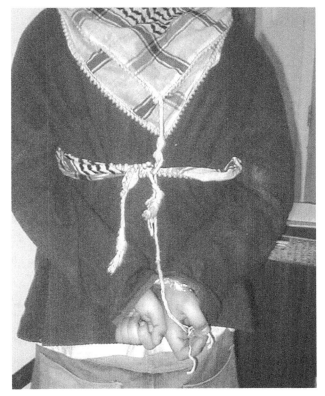

FIGURE 2

story that opens this book of the teacher who demanded the principal "round up" all the Palestinian students on September 11, 2001, was perhaps the most egregious example. Unfortunately, this was not the only example. After the start of the US war in Iraq, Lamia Baroudi, a member of the after-school club, witnessed a teacher yell at an Iraqi boy, "Go back to where you came from." Sometimes the challenges took the form of a "joke"; Nadia Khabbaz reported a teacher who would teasingly refer to her as "Osama bin Laden's niece." This type of "joke" was not unusual, and Palestinian American youth told numerous stories of friends and neighbors making similar wisecracks about familial relations to bin Laden. Adam Mattar recalled that one of his ESL teachers refused to let his friend Majed take a picture of their class. She jested that she could not be sure he had not hidden a bomb in the camera. Although after Adam discussed the comment with her, he said she apologized to Majed, the boys did not feel this was a laughing matter.

Whereas overtly racist incidents involving teachers were, fortunately, rare, the Palestinian American youth recounted myriad stories about their peers.

FIGURE 3

FIGURE 4

Students described the climate immediately after 9/11 as being particularly harsh. Zayd, for example, recalled his peers' responses in the following way:

> [They would say,] "Oh, you wanna, oh you come to this school, you come to school thinking, oh that's it, like that's over. You're gonna bomb the towers and then sit? Get the hell out of this school. Dirty animals." And then that would start a fight.

Zayd reported that some of the most overt harassment that followed immediately on the heels of 9/11 was ameliorated after Mr. Moore, the principal, announced over the school loudspeaker that there would be zero tolerance for such incidents. Nevertheless, for years after September 11, 2001, Palestinian American youth reported repeatedly encountering harassment from peers who construed them as "terrorists."

Some of this harassment continued to take the form of "jest." Hasan Hamadi reported peers who would quip, "Run for the hills, there's an Arab coming," as he passed by. Zayna Sha'ban recalled being asked by a peer more than three years after 9/11, "Did you know that your uncle was going to bomb the World Trade Center when he did?" After his friends teased, "Do you have a bomb in your backpack?" Majed was searched by one of the school's nonteaching assistants, who took their words at face value. As painful as these "jokes" were, they paled in comparison to the more vicious taunts that sometimes led to serious conflicts. Although the Palestinian American youth often tried to ignore or educate their peers and their teachers, at times they found themselves drawn into verbal and physical conflicts. Again and again, young men told me stories of how being called "terrorist" quickly escalated into physical fights, which landed them in trouble with the disciplinary office. However, it was not only young men who had this experience. Khalida told the following story:

> Some students would be telling me to my face, "I think all Arabs are terrorists after 9/11." I was like you're really being ignorant just saying it to my face. So I don't even want to hear it. Actually I had a pink [disciplinary] slip once. I almost got suspended for having a fight about something like that. Some girl actually threatened me; that's why I didn't get suspended [in the end]. She called me an Arabian whore. Me and her got into a fight because she was like, "Oh, you Arabic people marry your cousins and what not." Then she was like, "What are you going to shoot me? Are you going to throw a grenade?" I was like, where is this coming from? She's like, "You are Palestinian."

The pervasive associations of Palestinians with violence, terrorism, and a presumptive "backwardness" implied in the quip about marriage between cousins[2] followed the Palestinian American youth through their schools and into their communities.

This association of Arabs with "backwardness" also made appearances in less obviously politically charged situations. In one observation of Adam's social studies class, his teacher, describing Native American Indian communities as "primitive," discussed how the United States government developed policies to eradicate polygamy in indigenous communities. The teacher stated that under these policies, Native American Indians would be allowed to have "one wife, not four," and then, pointing directly at Adam, he said, "No, that's you. They [Native American Indians] had more wives than that." This short interchange hints at the weight of colonial legacies across time—indigenous nations and Muslims are both configured as racialized Others whose practices are characterized as "primitive" and problematic.

Given the racialized, and explicitly racist, discourses that circulate broadly in the public sphere, it is no wonder that the Palestinian American youth at Regional High (and similarly at other local schools) were often confronted with naïve at best—and racist at worst—images of their community. However, the fact that there was no attempt on the part of the institution to systematically address either the general lack of knowledge or the specific racist discourses about Muslims or Arabs left the Palestinian American youth vulnerable to the ongoing misconduct of their peers, leading some to feel betrayed by their teachers and the administration. The youth with whom I worked told me many stories of peers' inappropriate or racist comments being simply ignored by their teachers. Hasan described a time when, after enduring ongoing harassment from a peer, he finally snapped.

> There was this one kid in particular who was Irish, of Irish descent. And he would just like say things like every day, on a daily basis. . . . In class, he would always say racist things and then kid [about it]. And it just built up. I did feel it, like at the end, when I felt it build up, that's when it really hit me that this stuff can be hurtful. And then finally I retaliated and I said something racist. I kind of regretted it. I said something about the Irish. I said like go drink something, you Irish something. . . . And this was in the middle of class. It was an argument and he said numerous things about me being Arab and how I'm a terrorist and everything like that. And [the teacher] didn't care. And as soon as I said something about him being Irish, she said, "Hasan, I'm Irish too!" And then I flipped. I said, "I don't give a fuck if you're Irish. I don't give a fuck if he's Irish. He was saying all this crap about me being Arab.". . . I was

---

2. Marriage among cousins is not atypical in many countries, including Palestine.

like you're supposed to be the supervisor. You're supposed to be in charge of us, keeping the peace. . . . He said all this crap about me being Arab. I say one Irish joke and you go apeshit on me? And then [the teacher] was stunned and said, "Wow, Hasan, I didn't know you felt that way." It was overwhelming that basically it was the first time I was truly defending myself, that I felt it's my right to defend myself when somebody says something racist. . . . And later the teacher said, "I'll stop it next time it happens."

After enduring daily taunts from his peer, Hasan finally lost his cool. It was, however, his teacher's response that pushed him over the line, leading him to yell and curse at her. Hasan was particularly upset by his teacher, whom he saw as having repeatedly abdicated her responsibility to educate against racism and discrimination. Fortunately for Hasan, his outburst ended up educating this one teacher, and she promised to take a more active stance in the future.

Palestinian American youths' recurring encounters with dominant images of their community illustrate the link between reflexive racism and xenophobia triggered by national and international events—racism that does boundary maintenance work setting the terms for national inclusion and exclusion. The charged moments in which the Palestinian American students found themselves positioned as enemy aliens were the visible traces of a nationalist politics of belonging that continually constructed them as outsiders in the American national imaginary. These encounters illuminate the ways that the national imaginary is constructed in relation to global racial formations. Palestinian American youth were continually positioned as belonging to Other imaginative geographies that were viewed as hostile and threatening to the United States.

The Question of Palestine[3]

In the American public imagination, Palestinians have played a distinct role in these discursive constructions of Otherness, often symbolically embodying the quintessential image of a terrorist. In dominant political discourses in the United States, the Palestinian struggle for self-determination has often been reduced to a question of terrorism. The multifaceted processes through which Palestinians have struggled for independence (for example, the grassroots development of self-sufficient economic ventures, as well as many nonviolent resistance strategies) have been all but invisible in the American media. More-

3. I borrow this title from Edward Said's 1979 book.

over, the hypervisibility of the terrorist and the suicide bomber as the face of
the Palestinian resistance movement has often rendered critical discussions of
Israeli state-sponsored violence mute, cast simply as a legitimate response to
security concerns (R. Khalidi 2013). The long-standing, tight alliance between
the United States and Israel was further fortified after September 11, 2001, as
American and Israeli politicians highlighted the parallels between, on the one
hand, the United States and Israel (and their affinity as democratic states), and
on the other, the Palestinian independence movement and al-Qaeda (Gregory
2004; R. Khalidi 2013).

As a result of the broader cultural politics that conflate Palestine and ter-
rorism into an imaginative geography (Gregory 2004) of illegitimate violence,
the question of Palestine was ever present in the lives of young Palestinian
American students inside their schools. Palestinian American students found
that 9/11 reinforced the image of their community as the public face of terror.
The story of the Regional High teacher who asked Mr. Moore to round up the
Palestinian students is emblematic of this problem. In a school that served
Arab im/migrant students from a number of countries, it was the Palestinians
that the teacher singled out for his detention fantasy, imagining them as some
kind of threat to the nation.

Long considered a controversial issue in US schools and university settings, education about the Palestinian-Israeli conflict often struggled to gain
ground even before September 11, 2001. After September 11, 2001, the space
for deliberation about the conflict narrowed considerably in public political
discourses that often elided Palestinians' aspirations for independence, with
al-Qaeda's attack on the United States, and that made both Israeli and US
state-sponsored violence virtually invisible (Asad 2007). From one perspective, it is possible to argue that space for debates about the Palestinian-Israeli
conflict has widened over the past few decades, particularly in institutions of
higher education. For example, social activists on college and university cam-
puses have been organizing against the occupation, particularly by advocating
a boycott, divestment, and sanctions (BDS) campaign similar to that launched
in response to South African apartheid; the BDS has been endorsed by both
the Association for Asian American Studies and the American Studies Association. In December 2013, the Swarthmore College chapter of Hillel broke
from the national organization, rejecting its restrictions on speaking engagements and collaborations with critics of Israel (Goodstein 2013).

Nevertheless, several high-profile incidents also illustrate the political
climate of silencing around this issue. For example, in 2007, there was a successful media campaign to oust a New York City principal who had been ap-
pointed to design and head up a new bilingual Arabic-English public school,

the Khalil Gibran Academy. The principal, Debbie Al-Montaser, a Yemeni American, had been photographed wearing a T-shirt with "Intifada NYC" written on it, promoting an Arab women's arts organization that ran youth programs. Despite her attempts to explain that intifada references "shaking off" oppression, and that the organization was using the term to signal the ways that young women could claim a place for themselves as active citizens of New York, the board of education forced her to resign before she could take the helm of the new school. In 2010, eleven Muslim University of California–Irvine students were arrested and ten were subsequently convicted on misdemeanor charges after they staged a political protest against a speech by the Israeli ambassador to the United States because of his support for the recent Israeli invasion of Gaza. The university also took disciplinary action against the campus Muslim Students Association, shutting it down for six months. In 2012, the California legislature passed a resolution asking institutions of higher education to condemn acts of anti-Semitism, defined in relation to a broad range of activities including certain (undefined) criticisms of Israel, and the calls for sanctions and boycott of Israel (California House Resolution 35, August 22, 2012). As discussed in chapter 3, the local school district's attempt to create a curriculum that would help teachers address the US invasion of Iraq was shut down because of references to the Palestinian-Israeli conflict. These incidents suggest that critical debate about Palestine has often been cast as intolerable speech—speech that is conflated with anti-Semitism—that must be barred from the academy rather than used as an opportunity to open up deliberation and discussion of this complex political conflict.

At Regional High, the "question of Palestine" proved highly flammable, deeply affecting how the Palestinian American youth with whom I worked experienced their lives in the school. The dominant school culture attempted to silence discussions of Palestine and critical perspectives on Israel. Anne Larson, the teacher who sponsored our after-school club, was a longtime peace activist who supported the rights of Palestinians to an independent state. When she, in her role as a citizen, wrote a letter to the local city paper criticizing the policies of the Israeli occupation, colleagues anonymously posted it in the faculty lounge and mail room with "anti-Semite" written across it, and several staff members asked the school principal to discipline her for the letter. Mr. Moore called her into his office to discuss the letter with her, but given that she was not writing as a representative of the school, in the end he supported her right to speak her mind in the public sphere. Anne was often confronted by colleagues, for example, who objected to her support for the Arab after-school club, one of whom told her it was "the equivalent of starting a KKK chapter"; another claimed that Palestinians "really do just raise them all up to be suicide bombers." In this climate, Anne could only imagine the pressure that the Palestinian students must have felt, and she was committed to being an adult ally for them in her role as a teacher and as the sponsor of the after-school club.

Anne had reason to be concerned. Palestinian American youth often faced serious consequences for expressing their feelings about and political affiliation with Palestine. After 9/11, symbols of the Palestinian movement were immediately flagged as signs of support for terrorism. Teachers complained to the administration that students should not be allowed to sport backpacks or clothing with the acronym *PLO*[4] on them because it was, from their perspectives, a terrorist organization. At least one student was subsequently written up for carrying a backpack with a PLO patch displayed. Kafiyyehs, the black-and-white checkered scarves that have come to symbolize the independence movement, were also banned on and off in the years following 9/11. This stricture was evident in other local school communities: a young woman who attended one of the city's premier magnet high schools received twenty-seven detentions for wearing her kafiyyeh and was threatened with not being allowed to graduate. The Palestinian flag was a particular flashpoint for conflict, as I show below. In a nearby high school, immediately after 9/11, two white students burned a Palestinian flag that hung in the cafeteria amid a display of flags from all the places from which the school's im/migrant families hailed. For Palestinian youth, the symbols of Palestine expressed their affective connection with a place and a dream. However, within the US political landscape, the many meanings and experiences they brought to these symbols were invisible, reduced to the simple, hegemonic narrative of Palestinian terrorism.

In the politics of the Palestinian-Israeli conflict, the word *Palestine* is itself often a source of struggle. The political power of naming played out in significant ways in the everyday lives of the Palestinian American students at Regional High. Lamia Baroudi, a regular member of the after-school club, had moved to the United States in middle school. One afternoon during her junior year, she arrived at the after-school club visibly upset. She told us that she had been sent to the disciplinary office earlier that day after an argument with her teacher over a map of Asia, in which the western half of the continent was missing. Lamia recalled:

4. It is important to remember that with the Oslo Accords (brokered by the United States), Israel recognized the PLO as the legitimate representative of the Palestinian people and its partner for negotiating peace.

I look at [the map] and asked him, "What happened to Palestine?" He said, "Palestine is not a thing." So I felt mad like. So I told him, "What do you mean it's not a thing?" He said, "It's not a thing, so I don't want to hear anything about it." I looked behind him and saw a big map on the wall. I said, "Why don't you point out on the map where it says Palestine?" I thought he was going to say Israel, but he didn't say Israel. So I just gave him a chance to say something. Just that it exists. Not even a thing! So he ignored me. I said, "You want me to get up there and show you?" He said, "No, forget about it. I said it's not a thing and that's it." I said, "Look, I came from Palestine, and you're saying it's not a thing. Then you need to tell me, where did I come from?"

This interaction—one that was similar to other stories that students reported to me over the years—reflects the discursive power of language in political conflict. Lamia's outburst—"Look I came from Palestine and you're saying it's not a thing. Then you need to tell me, where did I come from?"—symbolizes a central experience in the lives of Palestinians: the contradiction between the absence of a recognized state and the experience of belonging to a national imaginary. It echoes Musa Baladi's lament, quoted in chapter 1, that being Palestinian meant "having an identity without a place in the world." This argument between Lamia and her teacher represents the politics of naming, writ small, in which Palestinians and Israelis have been engaged for more than sixty years. This battle over names has taken place repeatedly since 1948: Arab names for villages and towns within the Green Line (the 1949 armistice line) were written off the maps; many Arab villages were destroyed, while others were renamed with Hebrew names. Many Israelis insist on referring to the occupied Palestinian West Bank as "Judea and Samaria," and maps in the Arab world are printed with "Occupied Palestine" identifying the land of historic Palestine. The power to name contains within it the very possibility of existence. And, for young people such as Lamia, the affective impact of this naming and not naming developed from the lived experiences they had with a particular place, and with particular people. In confronting her teacher about a standard map that did not recognize her homeland, Lamia was making a political claim—one that grew from her lived experiences—taking back the right to name the land from which she came Palestine. Unfortunately for Lamia, her teacher wrote her up and sent her to the disciplinary office for disruptive behavior, silencing rather than engaging this opportunity for educative dialogue and deliberation about divergent political perspectives.

Ibtisam Sabri had immigrated to the United States in middle school. After her parents and three younger siblings had gotten their green cards and moved to the United States, she and her older brother stayed in their village in the West Bank awaiting their papers. By the time she was a freshman at Regional High, she was no stranger to the political controversy that was embedded in calling her homeland Palestine. She told the following story about a middle school teacher who asked her,

> "Where are you from?" So I was like "Palestine." He *know* where I'm from, he just want to ask. Then he didn't say anything. The next time he saw me in the hallway, he's like "Oh are you from Palestine?" And I was like "Yeah." He was like, "Oh you're not from Israel are you?" I was like, "It's Palestine," and he started saying Israel. When I told him it's Palestine, so every time he sees me in the hallway he's like, "There's the girl who's from Israel who's coming in here."

It is difficult to imagine—especially given that this was a recurring incident—that this teacher did not know full well the political implications of telling a Palestinian student that she was from Israel. Rather than acknowledge, engage with, and perhaps even learn from, Ibtisam's experiences and her perspectives on Palestine, this teacher silenced any possible dialogue with her.

A Palestinian American student who attended a different high school told me that her computer teacher put a screen saver of Israeli flags on the computer she was assigned in the lab; none of the other students had similar screen savers. Whereas many students directly confronted their teachers' political stances, others had learned to avoid controversy by staying silent. Anne Larson told the following story:

> I mean, the beginning of the year, one of the girls I had, who's a ninth grader, she was—and I just have them do some "who are you" stuff—and she wrote she was from Israel, and I knew she was from Irdas because I had taught two of her other sisters. And I wrote back, I said, "You can write Palestine, it's OK." And now when she writes, she'll often pick news articles to show me and stuff. So, but that told me that somewhere along the line she was told she couldn't do that, or she was afraid to do it. But I think this whole thing of being able to identify as a people is important, because being told, whether it was told you don't exist or then told we can't say that word.

Naming—oneself, one's country—is, as Anne points out, about existence. Anne believed that this kind of naming is connected to the United Nations Declaration of Human Rights, which insists that everyone has a right to a nationality, and to the United Nations charter, which declares that people have a right to self-determination.

Palestinian students reported other incidents in which teachers seemed to explicitly bait them. Several students at Regional High independently told me about one of their social studies teachers, who taught their world cultures class in the 2001–2 academic year. From their perspectives, he appeared to almost seek out conflict with them about Palestine and Israel. (He was gone by the time I began working in the school, but Ms. Larson confirmed the students' perspective on this teacher, recalling similar encounters she had with him.) In a conversation with this teacher about the Israeli-Palestinian conflict, Zayd described, "He just started saying, 'All the Palestinians deserve to die,' and 'They're all dogs.' . . . 'They're like animals.'"

Speaking of the same teacher, Khalida reported on a conversation following 9/11:

> [Palestine] came up from the day we came back. We had half a day [off because of] 9/11. Then we came back. And we were discussing about terrorism and what we think about what happened. So, I don't know exactly how but it all came up to the issue of Palestine and Israel. [The teacher] said kinds of things like Palestine will never be free and it's Israel. He said Palestine doesn't exist. And he's trying to stuff it in our face that there's no more Palestine. It's Israel. So, we had [an argument].

In speaking with Khalida, and also with Zayd, about this particular class period, it was not possible for me to reconstruct how a discussion about September 11, 2001, devolved into a political debate about Palestine. However, the fact that the first class discussion after 9/11 turned into a debate about the Palestinian-Israeli conflict suggests that the question of Palestine is often conflated with, or reduced to, the subject of terrorism. And, at least in this one classroom, the pedagogical ideal—expressed by so many Regional High teachers quoted in chapter 4—that teachers should serve as neutral brokers of rational deliberation, promoting mutual tolerance, was missing in action.

Palestinian American youth sometimes faced serious consequences for expressing their political perspectives on the Palestinian-Israeli conflict. Lamia, as noted above, ended up in the disciplinary dean's office when she insisted on the right to call her homeland Palestine. Lamia's strong sense of belonging to a national imaginary was denied, her political perspective regulated and silenced as a sign of individual misbehavior in need of disciplinary action. In the spring of 2003, Regional High's annual event to celebrate cultural diversity ended with two Palestinian American boys being suspended and transferred to a disciplinary school over a verbal argument they had with the students staffing the Israel table. The backdrop to this argument was a multicultural event earlier in the year that was sponsored by the school's ESL program. In response to pressure from several vocal teachers on the faculty, Palestinian youth had been banned from displaying their flag during a dance performance because it was perceived to be too controversial—a symbol "of violence," as one teacher told me. The Palestinian students were informed that in order to be fair to everyone, all flags (with the exception of the US flag) would be banned at public events at the school.

Palestinian students arrived at the all-school multicultural event in May to find an array of national flags, including the Israeli flag, on display. Many Palestinian students were upset, not just because of the unfair and exclusionary treatment of the Palestinian flag, but also because earlier in the spring Zayd approached the coordinator of the multicultural fair to sign up a group of Palestinian students who wanted to participate. The coordinator had told him there were no plans for such an event. The Palestinian students were caught off guard by the event and by the presence of the flags. In the course of the fair, two Palestinian boys got into an argument with the girls staffing the Israel table. Their disciplinary reports—which curiously used identical quotations for both students—stated that the boys, referencing the map on display at the table, argued, "Fuck. That's not Israel. That's Palestine." The disciplinary dean, with the backing of the principal, suspended the boys and recommended them for transfers to disciplinary schools on the grounds of racial/ethnic harassment. Invoking the school's "zero tolerance for intolerance" policy as a justification for disciplinary action, the dean subsumed the politics of the Israeli-Palestinian conflict to a unilateral interpretation of the argument as evidence of anti-Semitism directed at individuals and, thus, as intolerable speech. In its decision to invoke its "zero tolerance for intolerance" policy, the school refused to use the argument as an opportunity for all of the students involved to discuss together the complex, contentious political perspectives they held—perspectives that, at least for the two Palestinian youth, developed from their lived experiences with the occupation.

Symbols of Palestine and its resistance movement (flags, maps, and kafiyyehs) were constant flashpoints for conflict at Regional High. As described earlier, it was not unusual for Palestinian students to be disciplined for wearing kafiyyehs or writing *PLO* on their backpacks, or even for stating that they came from Palestine. Rather than treating political disagreements or the symbolic markers of Palestinian national identity as opportunities for engagement and educative dialogue about conflicting perspectives on Middle East politics, too often teachers and administrators reacted to these symbols as evidence of Palestinian intolerance and advocacy of terrorism that could be justifiably expelled from the school community, particularly because of the context of the "war on terror." Ms. Tomaselli, the ESL teacher, for example, justified the school's ban on Palestinian flags, explaining her support for the ban as follows: "I guess with Americans, with any country, whatever, you know—I guess I feel particularly sensitive because of the Twin Towers, because of 9/11. And it may not be rational, but that's how I feel about it."

Ms. Tomaselli's words illustrate the relationship between the affective dimensions of nationalism—it may not be rational, but she just feels that way—and a geopolitical imaginary that constructs a kind of generic terrorist threat. Palestinians may have had nothing to do with 9/11, but it just feels right to ban the Palestinian flag. Moreover, she justified this by drawing a national boundary line. This sensitivity rests with "Americans" (or any other nation); the language positions the Palestinian American youth outside of the imagined community of Americans.

I want to pay careful attention here to the role that a discourse of tolerance played in disciplining Palestinian American students' political expression. As discussed in chapters 3 and 4, tolerance is one of the tropes of US liberal multicultural nationalism. Educators believed that Regional High (and American schools in general) offered an education in tolerance, supporting young people to become accepting and peaceful human beings. At public meetings with parents and students, and in every conversation I ever had with him, Mr. Moore pointed to the school's "zero tolerance for intolerance" policy as the glue that held this multicultural haven together.

Brown (2006) insightfully argues that we must understand tolerance not simply as a personal value but, more important, as a political practice that simultaneously manages diversity at home and acts as "a civilizational discourse that identifies tolerance and the tolerable with the West, marking nonliberal societies and practices as candidates for an intolerable barbarism that is itself signaled by the putative intolerance ruling these societies" (6; see also Wemyss 2009). In relation to policies such as the one adopted by Regional High, tolerance depoliticizes conflicts and inequalities, thus subsuming them in favor of individual actions and behavioral remedies. The administrative response to the argument at the multicultural fair and to the symbolic displays of the nation that Palestinian youth wore on their clothing and backpacks illustrates how this depoliticization works: political conflict was erased, and individuals were disciplined for their misbehavior. At the same time, these responses illustrate how the project of tolerance is connected to the United States' role as an imperial power. Associated with an imaginative geography of Palestine—a place conceptualized as violent and illiberal—these words and symbols could be justifiably exiled as intolerable speech.

Pledging Allegiance

The Palestinian American youth with whom I worked were continually reminded that as Muslims, Arabs, and Palestinians, they were considered outsiders, never full members of the US national imaginary. The consistent silencing of Palestinian American youth perspectives and the refusal to ask about or listen to their stories and lived experiences engendered pain and anger that often left many of these young people frustrated and alienated from the larger school community. However, this alienation made many of the youth even more committed to everyday bids for citizenship through which—in both self-conscious and implicit ways—they critiqued the status quo and made demands for inclusion and justice. They were outspoken about the racism they faced in school, as well as within the broader community. They were frustrated with the silencing they encountered when they tried to initiate public conversations about Palestine, yet they persisted. Many of the young women were particularly incensed by the dominant belief that they were oppressed, living under the thumb of their male relatives, and they routinely combated that perspective. It is with this notion of bids for citizenship in mind that I return to a discussion of these young people's varied responses to the recitation of the Pledge of Allegiance (see also Chun 2013). While for many of their teachers and school administrators the daily ritual appeared to be a straightforward affair—an unproblematic flagging of loyalty to the nation—it was anything but simple for the Palestinian American youth.

As described at the beginning of this chapter, Khalida's decision one day to stay seated during the Pledge of Allegiance precipitated a confrontation with her teacher about whether or not she was an American. Khalida did not originally conceive of her refusal to stand for the Pledge of Allegiance as a sign of political critique. She described "feeling really lazy" the day she first decided not to stand for the Pledge of Allegiance. However, following the confrontation with her teacher over this refusal, Khalida had substantive political reasons for continuing her protest of this ritual act of banal nationalism. Khalida explained:

> Well, there's a lot of things in the Pledge of Allegiance that, like, for example, "with liberty and justice for all," there isn't always justice for everybody. That's like one thing the United States don't have, is justice.

Khalida did not buy into the claims of liberal nationalism that the Pledge of Allegiance symbolically saluted. Asked to explain how she came to this perspective on the United States, Khalida began by offering the example of a fight between Arab and Russian boys that occurred in the spring of 2002. This was not, as I was told, the first time that Palestinian Muslim and Russian Jewish boys in the school had gotten into physical conflicts. Khalida described the aftermath of the fight as follows:

For example, the fight that happened between the Russian group . . . here at Regional High and the Arab group at Regional High. Well, it was between both of them. They both got into the fight, but the only ones that had to pay were the Arab students. I don't know if [the administration] did that because they are Arab or not. But I know three [Arab] students got expelled, two students got arrested, and one got suspended. And the students from the Russian group, nothing happened to them. So that's really unjustified. There's no justice whatsoever. Because they were in the fight. There wasn't anyone else who was in the fight, and they threw punches; they hit each other's cars; and they did all this kind of thing, but they [the Russians] . . . didn't serve any time for being—not meaning jail, but they didn't get no detentions, no suspensions, nothing.

Khalida read the school's response to a violent physical fight that had occurred between Arab and Russian boys—a fight that students reported arose from tensions between these groups—as partisan and unjust. In this fight, several students on both sides had been injured, but one of the Russian boys was hurt severely enough to require hospitalization. The school suspended the Palestinian boys after determining that they were responsible for his hospitalization. The school did not, however, also address the feeling among some Arab students that justice should be meted out equitably and that several of the Russian boys should also have faced some disciplinary action. Moreover, although the fight had been between Russian Jewish and Palestinian Muslim im/migrant students, the school refused to see this as an outcome of racial/ethnic and religious tensions that needed to be addressed more systemically for all of the students involved. Administrators repeatedly spoke of this and other similar conflicts between these two communities—conflicts that had occurred on more than one occasion over a couple of years—as being simply the outcome of, in the words of Mr. Moore, a "few bad (teenage) apples."[5] The school's failure to address the underlying and ongoing conflicts between these communities left many of the Palestinian students with a feeling that their community was unjustly and unilaterally punished in these fights, and it did nothing to offer students the tools to address the interethnic/interreligious conflicts by more productive means. Through incidents such as this fight, Khalida had come to believe that the Pledge of Allegiance's claim that the United States provides "liberty and justice for all" was belied by the facts on

5. In the aftermath of this fight, I was asked by community leaders to attend a meeting with parents and the students involved. The administrators present refused to listen to students who tried to talk about the tensions between the groups, or to parents who felt there was more to the conflict than had been acknowledged. The administrators' party line was that this was the outcome of an argument over basketball getting out of hand.

the ground that she and her community of peers had experienced, especially in the wake of 9/11.

The incident Khalida described above was not the only reason she had to feel that the disciplinary system at the school was unfair. She was upset by other experiences in which she had been the butt of peer harassment, or witnessed other students being harassed with no consequences to the perpetrator. It was, unfortunately, impossible to assess whether, in fact, this sense that Arab students were disproportionately disciplined was borne out by the actual numbers because the district follows federal guidelines classifying Arabs as whites. As a consequence, it was not possible to get a statistical measure of disciplinary actions against Arab students. However, over the years I spent at Regional High, there were enough incidents in which Arab students had been treated as the sole aggressors, or were disciplined for questionable offenses, that I had little trouble imagining how Khalida and many of her peers developed the sense that injustice was being perpetrated. Palestinian American students had been written up for a variety of reasons, including the drawings of the planes described in the previous chapter; as noted above, carrying a backpack with *PLO* written on it or wearing a kafiyyeh across one's shoulders; repeatedly saying the word *terrorist* (in fact, the student had been trying to pronounce *tourist*); wearing a T-shirt with an image the teacher believed to be Osama bin Laden (it turned out to be a picture of Bob Marley). As a consequence of these kinds of disciplinary incidents, Khalida developed a principled reason for her refusal to stand for the Pledge of Allegiance that challenged foundational myths of liberal multicultural nationalism that this is a nation in which people are treated as equal individuals, diversity is respected, and tolerance is the norm.

Although a majority of the youth with whom I worked expressed critical perspectives on the US racial regime, not all of them responded to the pledge in the same way that Khalida did. Many of the Palestinian American students chose instead to stand for the pledge out of "respect." They wanted to plant images of Arabs and Muslims that would serve as alternatives to those they believed were held by a majority of Americans. Zayd, for example, adopted a leadership role among the Arab students, urging them to stand during the ritual.

> I make sure that when I'm there, [the Arabs] stand during the Pledge of Allegiance. If you don't want to say it, don't say it. But stand out of respect. We are Arabs, and it's after 2001, after September 11th. Just stand up or they are going to talk against us. It's better for us. They are going to say, "OK. We're the better people." Unlike a lot of other people that are just too lazy to get up. We get up. We just stand through the thing, but we're not going to salute it.

Zayd viewed standing for the Pledge of Allegiance as an important public act through which Arab students could show respect for Americans and improve the image of Arabs in the larger school community. Although his sentiment seems similar to the one expressed by Khalida's teacher—"stand out of respect"—his purpose in performing like a loyal citizen is different. Seeking to gain ground as "the better people," Zayd stood in order to challenge the exclusionary boundaries that had come to delineate Arabs as outsiders or enemies. Zayd was making a claim for inclusion (and safety). Despite the very different positions that Zayd and Khalida took, their actions in relation to the pledge reflect what I call everyday bids for citizenship—an active engagement with the complex political context of the post-9/11 United States.

As these young people made decisions about how to deal with the recitation of the Pledge of Allegiance, they wrestled with complex questions about the meanings of citizenship and belonging. Leila, Khalida's sister, also argued for standing as a sign of respect *and* as a mark of her connection to her US citizenship:

> You were born in America. You have an American passport. In the auditorium, when they get up to pledge allegiance to the flag, most of the Arab students they sit down. To me, that's rude, disrespectful to the American flag. Disrespectful to the country we're living in today. They stay sitting down like, "Oh, I'm not going to respect the American flag." Just get up. Stand up. Look at the flag. You don't have to say the pledge. You're just looking at the flag and having the respect toward the people that are standing. So, as for respecting the United States, it's a big thing. To me, I respect where I live. I'm glad to be Palestinian. And I'm proud to be Palestinian and a Muslim and an American citizen you could say.

For Leila, it is the country—in which she lives and of which she is a citizen—that is due respect. Leila named multiple sources of identification (being Palestinian, Muslim, *and* a US citizen) as reasons for pride, and so expressed less conflict than most of her peers about the relationship among them. Her words represented a moment in which her multiple sources of identification rested comfortably next to one another. At the same time, Leila's stance toward the pledge was complicated, rather than a straightforward allegiance to the nation. Though she stood out of respect and was one of the few Arabs who recited it, she also told me, "I say it even though I don't mean it from the heart." Leila's multiple sources of identification did not translate directly into a *feeling* "from the heart" of belonging to this nation.

Speaking about the pledge, Samira Khateeb also revealed a complex relationship to her citizenship identity:

> We're sitting in the auditorium full of Americans in the morning. When we get
> up and Americans look at us, and they're like, "Oh my God. She's wearing a
> *mandīl* (headscarf), and she's standing for our flag." Even though I'm not saying
> the Pledge of Allegiance, I stand up as a matter of respect toward those people.
> I love when they look at me, especially those teachers and they're like, "Look.
> She has respect toward herself and others because she's standing up for our flag."
> Even though it is my flag too, because I'm living in the United States of America.
> I don't feel that it's my flag, but the truth is, you're a US citizen, so it's your flag.

Samira imagined that other students and teachers viewed her as a visible outsider because she wore a *mandīl*. By standing for the pledge, she hoped to seed an image of Palestinian Muslims other than the one she believed those students and teachers were likely to hold. Fully aware of the position of Muslims in the United States at this historic moment, Samira, like Zayd, actively engaged in symbolic political action to assert a place for her community as members of the national imaginary. They were, in a sense, trying to stretch the boundaries of the national imaginary.

At the same time, Samira explored her insider/outsider status as a citizen: she was conflicted about her relationship to this flag that was hers by virtue of her citizenship, but that evoked no emotional connection for her. Samira, it should be recalled, was one of the few youth who had spent her entire life in the United States. However, as a Muslim and a Palestinian, she felt a tension and separation from "Americans"—a difference between residing in and belonging to the nation. Yuval-Davis, Anthias, and Kofman (2005) argue that belonging is a "thicker concept" than citizenship—it is a social connection that is created, to some extent, through experiences of inclusion or exclusion. For Samira and many of her peers, myriad school experiences with negative assumptions about their community contributed to the development of tension between their citizenship status and their sense of *not belonging* to, and actively being excluded from, the US national imaginary.

For Samira and other Palestinian students, the decision to stand but not to pledge was also related to global politics. Samira argued that standing for the pledge was a sign of respect for the "American people"; however, she feared that saying the pledge would indicate support for US foreign policy, such as the war in Iraq. She stated:

> I feel like they're pledging for—there are the American troops in Iraq killing
> Arabs. So when I think about it, it's like me praying for the troops to kill more
> Arabs. That's how I think of pledging to the flag.

Samira was deeply conflicted about whether pledging the flag was a sign of supporting the war in Iraq and, as such, condoning the killing of Arabs. Feeling connected to those Othered places and peoples, Samira was capable of an imaginative relationship that rejected the United States' military actions and ambitions.

Khalida also viewed US foreign policy as a large part of the reason for her actions. Khalida cited US support for the Israeli occupation as another critical reason that she did not want to pledge allegiance to this nation. Khalida told me that she felt confused about the implications of paying taxes in the United States, which might make her complicit with the occupation of Palestine, given the level of financial support the United States provides to Israel. There was often little room for Palestinian students to articulate and discuss the political disagreements that led them to be critical of expressions of US nationalism, or of US foreign policy. For example, Khalida described an incident in which Arab students in one of her classes refused to stand in a moment of silence for the victims of 9/11, followed by a recitation of the Pledge of Allegiance. As she told the story, they had argued "why no one— they only think about Americans when something bad happens to them, but they never think of others." The direct challenge to nationalism expressed here, similar to Samira's above—to valuing the lives of "one's own" over the lives of others (Robbins 2012)—grew out of young people's experiences living within transnational fields. These young people could imagine the lives of Others. However, rather than engage the Arab American youth in a discussion that might have directly addressed their anger at the invisibility of victims of violence elsewhere, the teacher sent them to the disciplinary office for insubordination. Thus, these symbolic performances of everyday nationalism—small moments of flagging the nation—shut down opportunities for nuanced discussions about a range of important topics worthy of educative discussion. From talk about discrimination to myths of equality, from arguments about state-sponsored versus non–state-sponsored violence, from discussion about national versus multinational belonging, students were met with silence rather than critical dialogue. The conflicted feelings that so many of the Palestinian American youth expressed about their experiences as US citizens in relation to US policies in the Middle East make palpable the lived experiences of youth from transnational communities that render the demand for allegiance to a single nation-state anachronistic in an world in which people often hold complex, multilayered senses of belonging.

The Politics of Dissent

Unfortunately, this multilayered sense of belonging was at odds with the belief that many teachers held that as outsiders, im/migrants should be grateful for the opportunities and rights they enjoyed in the United States, and therefore should not be critical of the state. For a number of the teachers, citizenship, particularly in a time of war, demanded unrelenting loyalty to the state (see Ben-Porath 2006). However, there was a politics of belonging at play that made the demand for unremitting loyalty from Arab and Muslim[6] im/migrants simultaneously more strenuous and impossible to achieve. In order to understand why teachers often failed to engage the Palestinian American students in discussions about their objections, for example, to standing for the Pledge of Allegiance, or engaging in a moment of silence—and sometimes disciplined them for their refusal—it is critical to analyze carefully teachers' arguments about the rights and responsibilities of citizens and im/migrants.

Bill Andrews, Khalida and Samira's English teacher, for example, argued:

> The United States was born on dissent. It continues to live on dissent. And as long as it's respectful dissent, I'm OK with it. . . . I think it's the Constitution or the Declaration, I forget. One of those documents says, you know, you have the duty to dissent.

However, Mr. Andrews set the limits of this "duty to dissent" within the boundaries of the national imaginary. Mr. Andrews continued:

> What disturbs me is when I go in the auditorium and they're going to do the salute to the flag that you [Arab students] won't stand up. I'm like, "Yo, you know that flag that you won't stand up for is symbolic of what gives you the right to, you know." See, the beauty of America is not that you will succeed but that you can succeed. You know? And it doesn't matter whether you're red, yellow, white, black, or brown. You know, you can succeed in this country. People have gone from abject poverty to multimillionaires or billionaires. So that's wide open. But the flag is symbolic of what allows you to do that. When you disrespect the flag, then you tend to start bringing out that anger from other people that doesn't need to be. If I'm in an Arab country and everybody stands up for the flag, I'm not going to sit there because I'm American and it's not my flag or whatever or I'm angry about 9/11 or whatever. I'm going to stand up *because I'm in your country*. (emphasis added)

This complex passage resonates with the discourse of liberal multicultural nationalism, and at the same time it positions Palestinian and other Arab youth as not belonging to this national imaginary, in spite of their status as legal citizens. Mr. Andrews argued that the right to dissent is not only fundamental to, but also a duty of, citizenship. However, he then implicitly circum-

---

6. See the introduction for an explanation of why I use this terminology to demarcate these widely diverse and incommensurate groups of people.

scribed this right for those who are defined as being outside the imagined national community. According to him, it is precisely the ostensibly color-blind liberties and opportunities this state is assumed to guarantee that demand unquestioning respect (and by implication allegiance) rather than critique. "The beauty of America"—its place as a land of equal opportunity for all—requires a kind of symbolic flag-waving. The flag—the hallmark of this nation—is its unassailable symbol. By giving the hypothetical counterexample that he would stand for an Arab flag even though he is American and "angry about 9/11" and "in *your* country," Andrews implied that the Arab American youth do not belong to this nation—they are implicitly in someone else's nation, and they should stand for its flag. Critically, Mr. Andrews talked about being in a generic "Arab country" that invokes his feelings of anger about 9/11. It is essential to note his use of pronouns here. Arab students are referred to as "you" throughout this passage, and are ultimately positioned as members of the hypothetical Arab country ("your country") in which Mr. Andrews claimed he would stand for the flag. This "you" signifies the foreign Other—the people who are not (yet) "we."

Bill Andrews's implication that dissent should be limited by an unassailable respect for the nation became even clearer later in his interview. When asked to say more about what he called "respectful dissent," he described his response to the African American Olympic athletes Tommie Smith and John Carlos, who in 1968 raised their fists during the awards ceremony, just when the US flag was hoisted and the national anthem was played.

> I thought that was respectful. It was not—it was a salute that acknowledged, but it was not the salute that people were used to. So if they had, for example, gotten on the podium and turned their backs, see to me, that's like a disrespectful kind of dissent. And this is only a personal opinion, you know, I mean to me that would have been disrespectful dissent. But they saluted it and they saluted it in a different way, you know, to draw attention to the plight of the African American in America.

In what I read as an interesting turn of phrase, Mr. Andrews reframed the Olympic athletes' actions as saluting the flag "in a different way," rather than as a political symbol of the Black Power movement, which, at the time, provoked considerable national outcry—a gesture that was read as deeply threatening and disloyal to the nation. Mr. Andrews argued that he would not have supported them "turn[ing] their backs" to the flag—an action that might be read as turning one's back on the nation. Mr. Andrews's use of the phrase "in a different way" indicates the shifting discourses of nationalism from the 1960s to the present day. He now incorporated the symbol of black nationalism within the new language of multiculturalism through which we can now celebrate our "different ways" of doing things.

One theme that emerged in the interviews with educators was the distinction between acceptable and unacceptable dissent that tracked the boundaries of the national imaginary. Unquestioning loyalty was demanded from people who did not belong to this national imaginary. For example, discussing limits on the appropriateness of Palestinian and other Arab students' criticisms of the US war in Iraq, Ms. Tomaselli had the following exchange with my research assistant:

TOMASELLI: In other words, if the person is taking from the system, which he is protesting, then to me it doesn't, I just won't take it seriously.
RESEARCH ASSISTANT: So, does the civil rights movement fall into that category? Like black people would be living here and working here, but—
TOMASELLI: They were. That's right. But being enslaved here, being denigrated here, I think that's a whole different ball game. *It's a different category, different problem.* (emphasis added)

For Ms. Tomaselli, then, the right to struggle for political and civil rights follows the imagined boundaries of national belonging. From her post–civil rights era perspective, because of their history of enslavement and oppression in the United States, African Americans had earned a right to protest[7] that Palestinian (and other new im/migrant) communities have not. By positioning African Americans as national insiders struggling to attain equal rights, Ms. Tomaselli constructs im/migrants as outsiders who are not accorded the same rights. It is important to pay attention to the role that African Americans play in both of these teachers' talk. Usually positioned as less than full and equal members of this national imaginary, here African Americans are drawn into the circle of belonging in relation to Palestinians, who are constructed as outsiders belonging to Other places. Although a "hierarchy of belonging" (Wemyss 2009, 133) to the US national imaginary never disappears, it shifts and changes over time, and after 9/11, some racially minoritized groups were drawn more closely into the fold of American identity, while Arabs and Muslims were pushed further outside (Volpp 2002).

This sense, expressed by both Ms. Tomaselli and Mr. Andrews, that

7. These two teachers' incorporation of African Americans as legitimate members of the national imaginary illustrates Jodi Melamed's (2006) point that the national imaginary shifted in the years after World War II to project this nation as a multiracial democracy that should be a model for the world.

im/migrants, particularly Arabs and Muslims, should be uncritical, loyal citizens of the United States was paradoxical, premised on a politics of belonging that had already excluded them from this citizenry. For Palestinian American youth, this politics of belonging also constructed them as particularly dangerous and threatening to the United States, which heightened demands that they perform as if they were loyal citizens and made dissent difficult or risky. As I have shown, some Palestinian American youth who expressed objections to symbols of US nationalism or to this nation's foreign policy faced disciplinary sanctions. Khalida's example of the boys who were disciplined for refusing to stand in silence for the victims of 9/11 was one such example. The vice-principal's threat that Mai would be disciplined if she did not recite the pledge was another. Thus, despite teachers' insistence that this nation was founded on commitments to individual liberty, diversity, and tolerance, the Palestinian Americans were often silenced and disciplined for expressing divergent and critical perspectives—perspectives that grew out of their positions as members of a transnational community and as a racially minoritized group.

The most serious incident of disciplining dissent resulted in a family having their house searched by the US Secret Service after the school district's central office had called in a report that Ibrahim, a seventeen-year-old Palestinian American student who was Adam's brother, had threatened to kill the president. According to Ibrahim, Adam, and other Arab students who were present, the alleged incident took place in an ESL class in the midst of an argument about the US occupation of Iraq. Some non-Arab students were discussing recent news reports about the Abu Ghraib prison torture and several kidnappings and assassinations of foreigners in Iraq. They mocked Arab students, suggesting that Arabs were partial to violence. The Arab students reported that Ibrahim (who was still struggling with English proficiency) responded by asking the group how they would feel if one of their important leaders were killed.

It was several days before the teacher contacted the dean's office. According to her, Ibrahim was quietly reading a newspaper in the back of her class when he called out that he would like to kill the president. In response to this belated report, the school suspended and later expelled Ibrahim and called the school district's central office, which then notified the Secret Service. Adam arrived home one day to find his frightened mother unable to fully comprehend what was happening as Secret Service agents rummaged through their house, demanding explanations of, for example, a picture of the Dome of the Rock with a Palestinian flag flying above it. Although the search was fruitless, the family's sense of security was rattled by the incident. After the family filed an appeal, a school district judge found credible Ibrahim's account of what happened. However, the judge did not overturn the expulsion because Ibrahim had publicly announced he would "get" the person who had snitched on him. The school called on its zero-tolerance disciplinary policy against verbal threats and transferred Ibrahim to a disciplinary school for his senior year. Thus, similar to the school's response to the argument at the multicultural fair, the tolerance policy was leveraged to exclude Others perceived as intolerant and thereby intolerable (Brown 2006).

Claudia Tomaselli, reflecting on her extensive discussions with the teacher involved in this incident, had strong feelings in relation to the limits of dissent. She argued that Ibrahim had "crossed a line" when he made the alleged comments about President George W. Bush. When asked about the line separating acceptable from unacceptable critique, she said:

> The line is just, you know, within me as a human being. It's just my personal feeling that if I'm living in a country and eating the food in this country. I'm working. I'm getting money here. Then to entirely say things to express myself in a way that doesn't show respect. That to me would be crossing the line. If you're living in a place, you're eating the food, you're working there, and then to be completely disrespectful of it in terms of not recognizing the country as a unit in some way.

The line is that which demarcates both the nation-state and the boundaries of the imagined national community. As Arab Muslim im/migrants, Ibrahim and his peers lived forever outside that boundary; they were perceived as living, eating, and earning in someone else's country, and this permanent guest status required respect for the sanctity of the national "unit," banishing critique as a sign of danger and disloyalty. Interestingly, this line rests with Ms. Tomaselli "as a human being"—a reminder of the ways that, as a white American, she occupies a universal, unmarked position (see chapter 4; Melamed 2006; Wemyss 2009). For Ms. Tomaselli and many of her colleagues, the limits to the fundamental rights guaranteed by democracy tracked the national imaginary. Although a few educators vigorously defended the rights of Arab students to express their opinions about US foreign policy, others felt that criticizing the US wars in Afghanistan and Iraq was unacceptable. Critique was disallowed, as one of the other ESL teachers, Ms. Borofsky, put it, "when Americans are dying." Paradoxically, although the US national imaginary was fundamentally defined by its commitments to individual freedom, diversity, and tolerance, in the eyes of many teachers, the exercise of democratic rights depended on inclusion within the folds of the imagined national community. Palestinian Americans were excluded from this national imaginary, read as threatening and dangerous outsiders who had no right to criticize this nation.

As illustrated by the experiences of Palestinian American students at Regional High, it is critical to understand how one fundamental tenet of US nationalism—tolerance—often played an important role in shutting down critical political perspectives that many of the Palestinian American youth brought to the table. Most of the time, this shutting down involved a refusal to consider the possibility that these alternate perspectives might be worth discussing or even have some validity. Rather than, for example, engaging students in conversations about why they refused to stand for the Pledge of Allegiance, or why they felt the war in Iraq was misguided, reports from both teachers and students illustrated an overwhelming tendency to refuse to have substantive discussions about these issues. In a few instances, as in the multicultural fair or Ibrahim's ESL class, Palestinian American youth were expelled from the school community under the guise of Regional High's zero-tolerance policy. On other occasions (as illustrated in chapter 4), the refrain of the notion of US tolerance was subtler in its expression, although equally unlikely to lead to real political conversation. In the political climate of the "war on terror," there was little space to maneuver in between unquestioning support for the United States and presumptive support for the terrorists. As shown throughout part 2, the Palestinian American Muslim youth were positioned as members of Other places imagined as illiberal and violent, and, as such, their critical perspectives were often read as intolerant—and thereby intolerable—speech to be disciplined and excluded, through the direct exercise of Regional High's official tolerance policy. Construed as the domain of liberal societies, tolerance is exercised within a civilizational discourse that aims to contain the Other (Brown 2006).

Dancing with Flags

It was one of those days in late May, the weather anticipating the sultry summer ahead and the students rumbling with the breakout energy of the end of the school year. I arrived early to join Anne Larson to go support the youth from our after-school club in the school's annual multicultural fair. Chaos reigned in the hallways leading to the school gym, where the fair was taking place. As I was pushed forward by what seemed like hundreds of students, I felt a moment of panic wondering what would happen in the event of a fire. Teachers were screaming at the students to no effect. Anne and I were stuck in the crush for a long time, unable to make our way through the surging students. When we finally got to the door, the woman monitoring the entry was quite strict about seeing my pass, and I worried she might make me head back to the office against the throngs of students still trying to get in.

Finally, I convinced her of my legitimacy and was allowed to enter. A horseshoe of tables representing different countries lined the walls of the cavernous gym. Anne and I quickly spotted Tala, one of the girls from our after-school club, staffing a table and waiting for other friends to join her in setting up the display. Tala had propped up a three-sided poster board describing the Arab world, and she had a steaming brass pot of *waraq dawāli* (stuffed grape leaves) and paper plates sitting on the table next to her, ready to be served to adventurous passersby.

Soon after the second-period bell had rung, one of the cofacilitators of the after-school club showed up carrying the fabulous mosaic design students had made, with individual tiles representing the members of the group. Khalida, Sana, Zayd, Adam, and a few other students arrived soon after and set to work decorating the wall behind their table. They prominently displayed many symbols of the Palestinian nationalist movement (a black-and-white kafiyyeh, a Palestinian flag, and the word *Palestine*) on the gym wall. The Israel table was nearby, sporting a large flag, so I suppose it was hard to deny the Palestinians the right to display their flag this year.

About ten minutes into the period, a series of performances began. My colleagues and I moved over to the bleachers to get a better view of the show. The Palestinian boys had been scheduled to dance *debke* (a popular type of folk dance) during that time. They disappeared to a corner of the gym to get ready. Suddenly, with the loud beats of Arabic music blaring from a boom box, the boys bounded onto the gym floor. They all wore kafiyyehs covering their heads and shoulders, and they carried a flag, passing it smoothly from person to person, and integrating it into the traditional folk dance. Energized and flushed, they seemed really proud to be able to display the flag and perform their dance. On the bleachers around me, students were clapping and stomping to the beat of Arabic music. After the show, the boys ran over to us, excited about their visibility and the positive reception they felt from their peers.

This event took place a year after the incident at the school's 2003 annual multicultural fair that had ended with the expulsion of two of the Palestinian American youth. The dual insults of first being excluded from participation in the fair and then having two students expelled for a political dispute galvanized the Palestinian American youth at Regional High to seek a club of their own in the following school year. From its very beginning, the youth in this club were determined that they would be a part of the 2004 multi-cultural fair.

The Palestinian American students' commitment to be included in the spring multicultural fair represents an everyday bid for citizenship—a claim for belonging and demand for equality. This particular bid for citizenship can be read in multiple ways. On the one hand, it is a bid that buys into the typical ways that multiculturalism frames inclusion. It is a cultural bid, promoting the value of diversity and making visible the United Nations of US society. It offers a display of food, clothing, music, and artwork—all cultural markers that, while typically belonging in the private sphere, can make their way into the public celebrations of this multicultural democracy. These Palestinian American youth had figured out a thing or two about belonging in the United States. They were claiming a place for themselves, as one of the many different cultures that made up the American salad bowl.

At the same time, these youth brought their transnational identities and politics in through the back door. The symbols of the Palestinian nationalist movement, which had been so often banned, were prominent and present. The identity tiles on the mosaic were replete with flags, the word *Palestine* (written in Arabic) was the centerpiece, and a sketch of the Dome of the Rock anchored one corner. (See fig. 4, p. 176.) The boys danced with the scarf of both the fellah (peasant) and the feday (freedom fighter) on their heads, and the national flag in their hands. There was a kind of symbolic triumph in their courage to show their faces with kafiyyehs wrapped around their heads and shoulders, flag in hand, given the ways that both of these symbols had been received as signs of support for terrorism. The boys symbolically recast the image of Palestinians as terrorists, putting a face to the shadowy figure, and claiming a place for their right to be seen as members of not only a cultural, but also a political, imaginary. The politics of Palestine were hidden in plain sight at this year's multicultural fair. On occasions such as this one, the young people were savvy to the ways that they needed to couch their bid for citizenship in cultural clothing, but they were not laying down their political arms in the struggle for Palestine. In many ways, this is how it had to be in the context of Regional High. The only permissible way to lay claim to their transnational citizenship was to shape it within forms of multicultural recognition. And although this multicultural framework had limited power to carve out a space in which they could fully express their sense of belonging and citizenship, the Palestinian American students had, at this event, for this moment, mobilized the liberal multicultural national imaginary to claim a place for themselves in their school's United Nations.

Nationalism in Times of War

Palestinian American students' bids for citizenship—their claims for social and cultural inclusion—laid bare a politics of belonging that was at play just as much in the intimacies of everyday life inside Regional High as it was on the national stage. Their struggles to be heard and included as full and equal members of their school community were related to a nationalist politics of belonging that positioned their community as impossible subjects of the US national imaginary. As discussed in detail in chapters 3 and 4, this politics of belonging constructed self and Other in relation to a liberal multicultural national imaginary, one that intimated the United States' role as an imperial power. Palestinians were imagined to belong to Other geographies construed as illiberal, and threatening to this country and its values and aspirations. As the Palestinian American students sought membership in their school community, and expressed their cultural and political commitments, they were often caught between an impossible demand that they perform as uncritical, loyal citizens of the United States, even as they had already been configured as dangerous and threatening Others—outsiders who could never belong. Thus, expressions of American nationalism in everyday practice—expressions of a politics of belonging (and not belonging)—often silenced the alternate perspectives voiced by Palestinian youth. This silencing was a reinforcing loop: without serious critique of the United States' internal racial regime, or its role as an imperial power, hegemonic ideas about the United States as a beacon of democratic values worldwide—of this nation's radical innocence—continued unchallenged. The experiences of these Palestinian American students illustrate the ways that everyday nationalism mediates belonging and exclusion *on the ground* inside American schools for youth from im/migrant (and other marginalized) communities (Abu El-Haj 2010; Ghaffar-Kucher 2014).

Certainly, the exclusionary climate that Palestinian American students faced must be understood in the context of the "war on terror." States of war often serve to constrain the exercise of democracy, restricting expression and rights for all people residing within the nation. Ben-Porath (2006) argues that in times of war, a "belligerent citizenship" (2) emerges. Belligerent citizenship shrinks the parameters of democratic citizenship, demanding compliance, patriotic unity, and restrictions on deliberation. However, the unity that is invoked comes at greater expense to those members of the state who are not part of the majority, particularly those construed as enemy aliens. The idea that Palestinian American students should not express opinions critical of the United States and its foreign policy was a consequence of this belligerent citizenship, and must be understood as part of a broader context in which there have been serious restrictions on the civil liberties of their communities; it was precisely these restrictions that led to the Secret Service's visit to Adam's home. In times of war, being positioned as outside the national imaginary has serious consequences for these communities.

However, this more belligerent or "hot" nationalism mobilized in the war-time context built on discourses of liberal multicultural nationalism that were constructed long before the "war on terror" began. Times of war make rigid and visible the lines of demarcation that have already cast some people as less than full members of the nation. This was certainly the case for Palestinian Americans. This is why, as I argue in the conclusion to this book, we must pay attention to everyday nationalism in our schools, and the terms along which it constructs self and Other, not only in times of war but also in times of (relative) peace. We must investigate the nation as a normative construction, one that simultaneously includes and excludes. We must see how the practices of everyday nationalism silently structure both educational opportunities and experiences for many young people.

Conclusion

These days, at least, nationalism is not so self-flaunting or loudly belligerent. On the contrary, it usually seems a quiet default setting that relishes an intermittent solidarity with fellow nationals, and wishes no harm to anyone. At the same time, however, it assumes, or is not quite ready to dispute, the principle that people far away don't matter as much as Americans do or don't matter as much as Americans do as long as Americans' survival is at stake. . . . The proper object of polemic or even reeducation on the parts of teachers, scholars, and other cultural workers: the indifference, the ignorance, the lazy habits of backing one's own and of not thinking too much about the other side that maintains a sort of perpetual rehearsal for future military actions while they also legitimate and enable ongoing ones.
— BRUCE ROBBINS (2012, 6)

When I first wrote this conclusion in the spring of 2014, the "war on terror" appeared to many living in the United States to belong to a different era. At that time, American "boots" had been "off the ground" in Iraq for several years, and the military seemed to be winding down its commitments in Afghanistan. Never mind that the United States had left enduring violence in the wake of its military invasions, the drone wars continued, and the United States played a role in conflicts raging from Libya to Egypt, Yemen, Syria, and Palestine, many people living in the United States felt curiously distant from these Other(ed) spaces, these geographies of war. In many ways, the American public had moved on, and a reinvigorated colonial amnesia had set in. However, the conflicts currently raging in Afghanistan, Pakistan, and the Middle East reentered US public consciousness in the summer of 2014 with a bang. The rapid rise of ISIS in Iraq and Syria hurtled the United States into renewed airstrikes in Iraq and new ones in Syria. Almost a decade and a half since September 11, 2001, the United States continues to position itself as the world's peacemaker and beacon for global democracy.

Many Americans (and members of other Western nations) remain anxious and fearful, not only about threats to Americans abroad but also about enemies they imagine to be hidden within the national gates. The wars abroad move in and out of most Americans' direct line of sight, but Arab and Muslim[1]

1. See the introduction for an explanation of why I use this terminology to demarcate these widely diverse and incommensurate groups of people.

communities remain firmly positioned as dangerous outsiders, members of imaginative geographies of illiberality and violence. Inevitably, these fears and anxieties have been inexorably heightened in the face of violent attacks close to "home" such as the bombings at the Boston Marathon in 2013, and in the subways in London in 2005 and the trains in Madrid in 2004. Unfortunately, I believe that the public soul-searching that ensues in the aftermath of these tragedies focuses on the wrong questions, asking about the problematic status of Muslim Others within the democratic body politic rather than about the intractable problem of violence committed by a few in the name of many. This reality struck me full force in a conversation I had with a neighbor in the sleepy Vermont town where I spend most of my summers. Approaching me at a local community event, my white Christian neighbor opened with the statement that of all the people he knew, I was best suited to comment on Islam, and he proceeded to ask me, "What were those two young men thinking at the Boston Marathon?" After a moment or two of incoherent fumbling, attempting to communicate that this was no version of Islam my deeply religious grandmother would have recognized, I retorted, "I don't generally understand people who commit violence. I wonder, what was Timothy McVeigh thinking?" This response may have been quick and glib. However, my point here is that my neighbor's question reflected a set of assumptions about Muslims in general, and their inexplicable connection to violent political actions—assumptions that he would never have made about people who appear to share much in common with McVeigh. Rather than seeking an explanation for particular individuals or groups that become radicalized to commit horrifying violent acts, my neighbor wanted me to speak for and explain this behavior of "Muslims." I am not prepared, nor is this book, to answer the question of why some people (of all types) turn to violence. What I have addressed in this book, however, are the processes that make my neighbor's question seem a reasonable one for him to ask—*and* how and why these processes are consequential for education today. Although the "war on terror" slips into and out of many people's immediate consciousness, the positioning of Arabs and Muslims in Western nations has not changed significantly. They remain a "suspect" group in the eyes of much of the public—people who are not seen as members of this national imaginary.

As multicultural states become more and more the norm, practitioners and researchers who care about justice and inclusion cannot afford to become complacent about nationalism. National imaginaries that construct insiders and outsiders become calcified during times of war, but they are constructed in times of (relative) peace. The racialized Othering of the Palestinian American youth with whom I worked began long before September 11,

2001, and it continues well after the moniker "war on terror" was retired by the Obama administration. Moreover, Arabs and Muslims are not the only groups constructed as outsiders to this national imaginary. Political debates about immigration, which focus primarily on Latinos, turn on similar constructions of a national imaginary that position Latinos as foreign intruders and potential threats to the nation's economy, society, and politics. Now is a critical time for educational researchers and practitioners to pay careful attention and track how communities become Other, not only in the public media but also through *the micropolitics of everyday nationalist discourses and practices inside our schools.*

Even as we need to keep on eye on these exclusionary mechanisms, I hope I have also shown we have much to learn from the young people with whom I worked, and many other communities like them, about developing citizenship education that is flexible and looks beyond the nation-state. Palestinian Americans drew on the experiences they had and the knowledge that they had developed in transnational social fields to craft bids for citizenship that demand inclusion and justice within the United States and beyond. As I argue in what follows, they offer a hopeful response to the Othering discourses— one that is echoed in the ways that many young people across the world today are calling for justice that crosses borders, and one that can inform our formal efforts at citizenship education.

Tracking the Consequences of Nationalism in Education

One critical question I have been concerned with in this book is to understand the micropolitics of nationalism, tracking the local discourses and practices through which young Palestinian American Muslims got associated directly and indirectly with terrorism—continually cast as suspicious enemy aliens to be feared and disciplined. Although Arabs and Muslims have been configured as dangerous outsiders through a nationalist politics of belonging that takes place across social fields (e.g., the media and politics), public school, as I have shown here, is a key institution where ideas of national belonging (and not belonging) are produced, contested, and played out (see Abu El-Haj 2010; Benei 2008; García-Sánchez 2013; Ghaffar-Kucher 2014; Hall 2002; Jaffe-Walter 2013; Lee 2005; Olsen 1997; Ríos-Rojas 2014; Schiffauer et al. 2004). At Regional High, the nationalist politics of belonging unfolded through seemingly benign discourses of liberal multicultural nationalism, as well as through more explicitly racist expressions about Palestinians and Muslims that were consequences of the kind of "belligerent citizenship" (Ben-Porath 2006) that emerges in times of war, narrowing the scope of belonging and dissent. Moreover, I have argued there is a critical relationship between the discourses of liberal multicultural nationalism and the more obviously belligerent ones. Dominant discourses of liberal multicultural nationalism imagine the United States as the archetype for universal liberal values (individualism, liberty, diversity, and tolerance) while simultaneously imagining Arabs and Muslims as Others who belong to cultures and geographies that seem inimical to these values. It is this oppositional setup—one that was in place well before September 11, 2001—that made possible an immediate hardening of the boundaries of the US national imaginary, placing Arabs and Muslims on the "wrong" side of the border, subject to myriad exclusions, from the intimate interactions of everyday life to grand-scale government policies, including detention, deportation, and rendition.[2] Thus, the processes of racialization for Arab and Muslim communities are tied to contemporary circulating discourses of the American liberal multicultural imaginary that has been to a large extent constructed contrapuntally in relation to a hostile geopolitical imaginary of the "Muslim world" (Abu-Lughod 2013; Brown 2006; Das 2001; Gregory 2004; Grewal 2014; Mamdani 2004; Melamed 2006; Puar and Rai 2002; Rana 2011).

In focusing on the experiences of Palestinian American Muslim youth, and bringing attention to communities largely absent in educational research, I am, then, arguing for a need to develop a more complex understanding of the processes of racialization in our schools (as in our society). This understanding must account for *nationalism* as a key component of these processes of racialization. Nationalism creates a hierarchy of belonging to the national imaginary (Wemyss 2009) that positions groups in relation to an ideal national citizen—an ideal that is never fixed and stable for all times. I want to emphasize this flexible and relational aspect of the production of the national imaginary. For example, African Americans, Native Americans, Latino/as, and (East) Asian Americans have never been fully insiders to the US national imaginary, but after September 11, 2001, they were pulled a little more into the inner circle, as the border of national belonging was drawn more sharply to exclude those Others imagined to be Muslims (Volpp 2002). At the same time, even though they may have been positioned a little closer to the center after September 11, 2001, Latino/as and East Asian communities continually float at the borders of the national imaginary, occupying an ambiguous place between citizen and "foreigner" (Lowe 1996; Ngai 2004). Im/migrant youth are racialized through the discourses and practices of everyday nationalism,

2. Of course, these geographies of Otherness have even more dire and consequential outcomes for people in Iraq, Afghanistan, and the many countries in which the United States has engaged in drone wars.

and, unfortunately, contemporary educational research in the United States has, for the most part, failed to track the quotidian terms and traces of this nationalism in US schools (see Abu El-Haj 2010; Ghaffar-Kucher 2014; Lee 2005; Olsen 1997).

I am also arguing that we must pay careful attention to the ways that American nationalism is imperial in its scope. This fact was reflected both in the everyday discourse of Regional High's teachers and in the official curricular texts, which depicted the United States as a nation apart from the rest of the world, conceptualized as an island of democracy in a wider sea of despair. Despite the pride with which Regional High's educators hailed the school as a United Nations, for all intents and purposes the rest of the world was virtually invisible. The dominant beliefs that the Palestinian American youth encountered in so many interactions—from Samira Khateeb's teacher's hostile quip that "men in your country" treat women badly to Ms. Lawrence's gentler belief that cultural restrictions faced by Middle Eastern women were a result of men trying to protect women from unsafe societies—reflected lazy assumptions about the United States as a "haven in a heartless world" (see also Buck and Silver 2012; Ghaffar-Kucher 2014). At many moments, it seemed as if the rest of the world were merely a mirror through which the glory of America could be reflected.

The pervasive feeling expressed by so many of the educators at Regional High that im/migrants should be grateful for the lives they were able to lead in the United States and for the "beauty of America" in creating conditions of freedom and democracy depended on their ability to remain ignorant of, or indifferent to, the reasons that people have for migrating to this nation as well as the ways that US economic, military, and political policies are complicit in creating the conditions from which many people are fleeing. The responsibility that the United States shares in the ongoing Israeli occupation of Palestine (see R. Khalidi 2013) was never lost on the Palestinian American youth, but it seemed invisible to a majority of their teachers and peers. The United States' collaboration with and support for the many oppressive regimes in the Middle East—including, early on, that of Saddam Hussein (see Gregory 2004; R. Khalidi 2004; Mamdani 2004)—informed the Palestinian American students' views of the current conflicts; but most of their teachers and peers did not share this knowledge, leaving intact their sense that the United States was a "radically innocent" nation (Pease 2009), bent on supporting democratic values worldwide. This ignorance about the United States' role as an imperial power created a kind of "colonial amnesia" (Gregory 2004) that made critique and anger expressed against the United States illegible to many of

Regional High's educators (as well as to many Americans). Unable to "read" the contexts within which Palestinian American youth had developed their critical political stances, educators too often treated the Palestinian American students' viewpoints as irrational, unpatriotic, intolerant, and therefore illegitimate perspectives to be silenced rather than creating opportunities for learning and dialogue.

Nationalism worked its way into the everyday fabric of Regional High in multiple ways that affected the capacity of the Palestinian American Muslim youth to experience what I have called *substantive inclusion*—the capacity to participate fully in, and to contribute meaningfully to, all the activities of our schools and, by extension, our society (Abu El-Haj 2006). The contemporary nationalist politics of belonging positioned these young people as illiberal subjects who were outsiders to the national imaginary. They were often viewed as people in need of liberation from their putatively oppressive and violent "culture," or as threatening individuals to be contained and disciplined. At the same time, nationalist discourses produced a kind of imperial knowledge about the United States and its role in the world that denied and rejected the critical perspectives that many of the Palestinian American youth had developed and sought to express.

If we care about creating conditions for substantive inclusion in our schools, and by extension in multicultural democratic societies, it is imperative that educational researchers and practitioners pay careful attention to the production of everyday nationalism in our schools. As critical researchers and practitioners, we must widen our lens to build connections between the ways that young people are educated into the racialized landscape of this nation and the everyday production of nationalism that takes place in our schools and society.[3] This everyday nationalism simultaneously produces a sense of who belongs to the nation (and who does not) *and* a narrative about the nation and its role in the world—one that remains shrouded in an invisible mantle of imperial power. Both of these functions of nationalism are differentially consequential, not only for people living inside the national borders but also for many others across the world. Rather than taking nationalism for granted, as a necessary (if sometimes problematic) condition of any public education, I want us to consider the problem that nationalism poses to an ideal of just and equitable education—one in which all young people might find the conditions for substantive inclusion and participation in this society.

---

3. I find nationalism troubling across national imaginaries, but in order not to reach beyond the scope of this book, I want to stick here with the question of US nationalism.

Transnational Citizenship: Recognizing "Facts on the Ground"

My argument that we must understand how nationalism works as an exclusionary mechanism is, to a large extent, a normative one—a plea for decentering the educational imperative that makes the nation a primary site for identification and allegiance. It is, however, a normative argument grounded by the consequences that everyday nationalism had for the youth in this research. Moreover, it is a position sustained by the realities of contemporary life not only in the United States but across an increasingly diverse world. Palestinian American youths' everyday lives reflected the "facts on the ground" of modern processes of globalization. They lived and learned across transnational social fields; their experiences and perspectives inextricably braided together the landscapes and vocabularies of Palestine and the United States. These young people developed a multifaceted sense of belonging and citizenship, forged out of the everyday experiences of transnationalism, that was fluid, complex, and at times contradictory—one that, I argue, offers a hopeful vision of the creative ways that many young people craft active citizenship practices for social justice[4] across national borders (DeJaeghere and McCleary 2010; Dyrness 2012; Sánchez 2007; Maira 2009; Miller 2011; Nabulsi 2014; Seif 2011).

Most of the time, the Palestinian American youth spoke of themselves as first and foremost Palestinian. As described in part 1, their primary sense of belonging was tethered to a Palestinian national imaginary. This sense of belonging had multiple sources: long-term sojourns and short-term travel in Palestine and other Middle Eastern countries; daily life centered within a Palestinian American transnational community; linguistic, cultural, and religious practices; and engagement with Arab media. These young people had developed a strong sense of belonging to Palestine, its land, people, culture, and politics. At the same time, this sense of belonging was interlaced with their identifications with the United States, as Kamal Sha'ban put it, "flipping between these two [i.e., Palestinian and American] constantly." Many of the youth spoke of moments in which they became aware of their "Americanness." Some had been chided by Palestinians in the *bilād* for being too American. Others described moments when they identified strongly with aspects of the United States—for example, the educational opportunities available to them. They appreciated US citizenship and the rights they enjoyed in this nation

---

4. I want to sound a cautionary note about glossing transnational affiliations as inherently just. Certainly, transnational movements can also foster injustice, intolerance, and extremism. (See, for one example, Christou and Ioannidou 2014.)

that were denied their community elsewhere, and they felt a particular sense of identification with the ideals of equality and justice, espoused in dominant discourses about the United States. However, they were also critical that the United States often did not live up to its ideals, and they were particularly disenchanted with US foreign policy, especially in relation to Palestine, Iraq, and Afghanistan. Importantly, they were fully aware of the ways in which they were subject to processes of racialization, even as they remain an invisible group in discussions of the US racial regime, buried under their federal classification as white. They had no doubt about what to call the myriad forms of racism they experienced, from the wounding words of peers and teachers, to unfair disciplinary systems, to the constant fear that this nation's Secret Service might come knocking at their doors. They never forgot that civil and human rights had been circumscribed for many members of their communities, as well as for Arabs and Muslims in other parts of the world. However, they often drew on a sense of their rights as citizens, seeking, through words and action, to demand that the United States fulfill its promises of equality and justice for all. They also held political aspirations for an independent Palestinian state, and many engaged in civic activities and political action on behalf of that cause.

The particular political condition of Palestinians—as members of a nation without a state—is in many ways atypical of most im/migrant communities' experiences. Moreover, along with other Muslim communities living in the United States, these young Palestinians were also in the unusual position of being framed as enemy aliens. These conditions strengthened the young people's tenacious sense of belonging to a Palestinian nation; and it led them to engage in citizenship practices that were both local and global in orientation. However, Palestinian American youth are not alone in sustaining a sense of belonging to other national imaginaries, nor are they unique in understanding the necessity and value of juridical citizenship for guaranteeing their families access to basic social, political, and economic rights and opportunities. In so many ways, the Palestinian American youth represent the face of a modern, transnational form of citizenship in which modes of belonging, and the spaces for participation, are not bounded by one nation-state. Similar to young people from many transnational and racially minoritized communities, Palestinian Americans drew on collective experiences with injustice to articulate critical bids for citizenship, of which I say more below (DeJaeghere and McCleary 2010; Herrera and Sakr 2014; Sánchez 2007; Maira 2009, 2013; Miller 2011; Nabulsi 2014; Seif 2011).

Unfortunately, these young people faced a huge disjuncture between their experiences of belonging and citizenship, and the dominant expectations encountered in their schools and in the broader society. This disjuncture is symbolized in the question Khalida Saba's teacher posed: "Are you or are you not American?" This question may have made perfect sense to this teacher who demanded that Khalida express a clear sense of loyalty to the United States, but for Khalida and her peers, this question was anything but simple. Caught between a strong and positive affective sense of Palestinian belonging, and the exclusionary and hostile climate that they often faced in their US schools and in the society at large, this forced choice pushed many of the young people much more definitively to the "not American" side of the equation.

This teacher's question reflected dominant models of citizenship that continue to focus on the nation-state as the accepted boundary for belonging and civic and political engagement. From this dominant perspective on citizenship, the Palestinian American youths' affiliations to Palestine were seen, at best, as an unfortunate residue of recent immigration or, at worst, as a sign of disloyalty and danger. This model of citizenship frames dominant educational policies and practices aimed at im/migrant youth. From federal language policies that demand English-only education within two years of immigration to local expectations (expressed by so many Regional High teachers) that im/migrant students should adopt "American" ways, most models of education are premised on the ideal that newcomer communities should and will eventually become "Americans," transferring their primary sense of belonging and locus of activity to this nation-state. As a rule, civic education is also oriented to civic and political participation *within* local and national contexts. Critical perspectives on im/migrant and citizenship education suggest that pathways to inclusion are difficult for many newcomer communities, demonstrating that youth from these communities face enormous institutional barriers that limit their capacity for high academic achievement and substantive social incorporation in their new schools and society (see, for example, Lee 2005; Lopez 2003; Olsen 1997; C. Suárez-Orozco, M. M. Suárez-Orozco, and I. Todorova 2008; Valenzuela 1999). However, until very recently, there has been little focus on the normative assumption that one nation-state should be the primary focus for belonging and citizenship (Abowitz and Harnish 2006; Abu El-Haj 2007, 2010; Dyrness 2012; Lukose 2007; Sánchez 2007; Sánchez and Kasun 2012; Maira 2009).

The facts of modern globalization, embodied, as I have shown in this book, in the lives of the young Palestinian Americans with whom I worked, pose serious challenges to dominant models of citizenship education that are assimilative and focused around one nation-state. As I noted in the introduction to this book, I take a broad, anthropological view of citizenship education, which extends well beyond formal curriculum (particularly in history, government, and civics) to include all the implicit and explicit lessons young people learn about belonging to, norms for, and modes of participation in, their societies. These lessons saturate the fabric of everyday life inside schools as well as in communities and public discourses. Unfortunately, as I have shown in this book, too often these citizenship education lessons left the Palestinian American youth with a clear sense of exclusion from this society. There are plenty of communities similar to the Palestinian American one described here that live in transnational social fields for whom the demands to line up with notions of citizenship based around one nation-state do not work. As modes of economic, cultural, and political life have become deterritorialized through globalization, it may no longer make sense to expect one nation-state to serve as the locus for people's primary sense of belonging or their citizenship practices.

Bids for Transnational Citizenship

Recognizing transnational citizenship as a condition of modern life calls upon us to fundamentally reconceptualize citizenship education in ways that might support substantive inclusion in multinational democratic states. It might be difficult to imagine how to educate for citizenship in ways that are not, at the core, oriented to only one nation-state. However, I am optimistic that efforts to do so can be guided by thinking about the complex, fluid ways that many young people today construct belonging and citizenship across national borders. The work of challenging nationalist frameworks in our schools (and in our public discourse) is a daunting one, but I take courage from the Palestinian American youth with whom I worked. They, along with young people from many other communities, are paving the way to envision alternatives (DeJaeghere and McCleary 2010; Herrera and Sakr 2014; Knight 2011; Sánchez 2007; Maira 2009, 2013; Miller 2011; Nabulsi 2014; Seif 2011). In order to imagine how we might engage in this work, I want to turn attention to some of the ways that the Palestinian American youth expressed transnational bids for citizenship—the ways they made claims for belonging and participation across transnational fields and engaged in citizenship practices that sought equality, justice, and inclusion for communities near and far.

SEEDS OF PEACE: CHALLENGING DISCOURSES OF EXCLUSION

In the spring of 2005, the community arts organization that cosponsored Regional High's Arab American after-school club brought a media educator to work with students to make films that would speak back to key images that the group had identified as particularly damaging and problematic for their community. Bassam's film addressed the image of Palestinian males as dangerous terrorists. Bassam, who had spent much of his childhood and early adolescence in Palestine, narrates a story of being a peacemaker, mediating a fictional fight between two boys, one of whom has taken a bicycle from the other. Bassam's film describes a traditional process for settling disputes in his Palestinian village in which families in conflict approach a village elder for mediation. The film begins with a bucolic scene of an elderly Palestinian farmer walking on his land. A caption identifies a West Bank town "where village elders typically negotiate disagreements and keep the peace among families and friends." The film then moves to a US city where the rest of the action takes place. The images paint a picture of the cultural and political crossroads at which these young men live their lives. The protagonist of the argument carries a baseball bat, and sports a baseball cap and a jersey that reads "West Bank" on its back, inviting the viewer to see him as quintessentially American (a baseball player) but equally as a Palestinian (playing for a team named "West Bank"). Bassam, the peacemaker, arrives. The T-shirt he is wearing, which depicts the Palestinian flag and the Dome of the Rock mosque, and the black-and-white kafiyyeh that he sports across his shoulder signal his unambiguous affiliation with the Palestinian nationalist movement. Narrated in (subtitled) Arabic with a few English sentences peppered throughout, Bassam brokers an accord between the adversaries. Bassam discusses with the boys the differences between Palestinian culture[5] (where taking another's bicycle might be seen as simply an act of familial sharing) and American culture (where this act is read as theft). The film ends with a reconciliation, signified by a handshake, followed by a friendly game of cards the boys play around a picnic table.

The film's narrative and visual images offer a snapshot of the complex and interwoven themes about belonging, citizenship, and nationalism that have been central to this book. From one perspective, this is a story of the multifaceted and flexible cultural productions through which the Palestinian American youth forge a sense of belonging and citizenship between and across Palestine and the United States—within transnational fields. The youth signal Palestine as a place to which they belong, depicting the landscape and its people (represented by the fellah, peasant farmer), wearing its symbols, and speaking in Arabic; but they also adopt baseball, a key symbol

5. This whole notion of a singular Palestinian "culture" is, of course, untenable and related to the politics of culture with its construction of notions of authenticity, discussed in chapter 1.

that marks them as members of the United States through its "national pas-time." Bassam explicitly schools the boys in the cultural differences between Palestine and the United States, encouraging them to adapt appropriately to the place in which they are residing. And, although Bassam talks about dif-ferences between American and Palestinian ways of doing things, the film's images portray the interwoven, blended manner in which "culture" is lived and produced. In part, then, this film illustrates one key theme demonstrated throughout this book: the complex ways that Palestinian American youth navigate across worlds, adopting, adapting, and producing cultural forms, as they figure out how to belong to, and act within and upon, these various na-tional landscapes.

From another perspective, the film implicitly represents a second key theme: the contested politics of national belonging that shaped the lives of Bassam and his peers. Through the various symbols described above (the flag, the mosque, the kafiyyeh, and the "West Bank" team name), these young men implicate, without naming, their ongoing and central connection to a political landscape that extends far beyond the borders of the United States. Even as they sometimes couch this connection to a Palestinian national imaginary within the language of culture—the only legible language in the American multicultural register—these young people continually signaled their sense of belonging to the Palestinian nationalist movement.

At the same time, this film was also a deliberate and critical response to the US nationalist politics of belonging that Bassam and his peers encountered in their everyday life in the United States, particularly in their school. Dogged by dominant US discourses that framed Palestinian, Arab, and Muslim males as terrorists and enemy aliens dangerous to this nation, Bassam decided to leverage *cultural* images and practices to create an alternative narrative about Palestine and Palestinians. Highlighting a traditional process for mediating conflict, the film explicitly disassociates Palestine and its people from its pu-tative culture of violence (and implicitly signals the reality that Palestinian resistance includes a tradition of nonviolent forms). Constructing a response to the exclusionary nationalist politics of belonging they encountered in their post-9/11 schools, these young people decided to leave the political dimen-sions of belonging to the Palestinian national imaginary unvoiced, marked only in the visual dimension of this film. However, in a climate in which Bas-sam, and his peers, constantly had to face down the presumption that vio-lence and intolerance were key features of Palestinian culture, particularly of Palestinian masculinity, their film made a critical intervention that simulta-neously created an idyllic picture of "back home" (as a rural, peaceable place where disputes are mediated by village elders) and made a bid for citizenship in the United States—claiming a place for these young men in the American landscape. Bassam's film is a tableau that mobilizes visual "rhetoric" to illustrate the ways that young Palestinian Americans are constructing complex, flexible, critical perspectives on belonging and citizenship.

MARCHING FOR GAZA: ADVOCATING FOR THE LIVES OF OTHERS

Many of the Palestinian Americans were also engaged in more traditional forms of active citizenship practices—forms that were explicitly political. Many were involved in direct political action demanding that the US government change its policy of unbridled support for Israel, calling for justice for Palestinians. In the winter of 2009 during the Israeli invasion of Gaza, a group of Palestinian women decided to organize a women's peace march calling on the US government to push for an end to the hostilities. In preparation for this march, we met in the basement of a mosque that also houses the local Arab American community development organization. The purpose of the evening's event was to make banners and other props for the demonstration the following day. The room was a bustle of activity, and among the most active members of the evening's activities were several of the young women I knew from Regional High: Samira Khateeb, Khalida Saba, and Zena Khalili. I had not seen the three of them for some time, and we caught up while painting signs and building props—stretchers with wrapped "corpses" to represent the bodies of the mostly invisible casualties of that war. All three of the young women were currently attending the local community college, although Zena was planning to take a break because she was soon to be married and wanted to prepare for the wedding. Khalida and Samira were both pursuing degrees that would lead to certification as elementary school teachers. In the midst of studying and preparing for weddings, however, all three had been galvanized by the political crisis in Gaza. These young adults were feeling energized to speak out as Palestinians and as US citizens, trying against what they recognized as overwhelming odds to get the US government to put pressure on the Israelis to end the invasion. Two evenings later in the midst of rush hour, on one of the most frigid nights of that winter, we reassembled and, joined with around fifty other women, marched in silent vigil to the local Israeli consulate carrying the mock corpses in protest against the rising death toll from the Israeli invasion. These women, young and old, were symbolically calling upon the public to see the lives (and deaths) of Others too often hidden from view under the fiction that these wars have no costs, only the lives of "terrorists," which are not worth mentioning.

As I learned, even prior to the invasion, Samira had, along with a Jewish peer, cofounded a student group at the community college they both attended to educate about and advocate for an end to the Israeli occupation of Palestine. The trip she took to Palestine the summer after her senior year in high school (described in chapter 2) had spurred Samira to become more explicitly politically active on behalf of Palestinian independence. Samira described her goals for initiating the community college student organization:

> My main goal is to get people to be aware of what's going on there because not a lot of people do know. Everybody can hear stories about what's going on but they really don't know you know the full story. And really my main focus is on Americans, you know whether you're white or black.[6] Some people might not just care. Some people would like to listen to it for you know two minutes, think about it for a day and then get on with their lives, like you know, what can I do? Some people really do care and do want to help. I'm planning to work on you know, getting, grabbing people's attention and have them focus on this in their everyday lives. I want them to really think about it—think about what the kids are going through, think about what the mothers are going through. Just forget the fact that they're Arabs, just you know they're people and this is what they're going through every day and hopefully when we do get a lot of people to think about it and the boycotting starts and we have good feedback or whatever from the boycotting and from informing a lot, as many people as we can, hopefully the [US] government is able to do something. Hopefully once the government sees that so many people really want change over there, they would do something about it.

Samira felt that having experienced firsthand the struggles of the occupation, she was in a good position to make those stories come alive for Americans who had few means to understand the impact the occupation had on the lives of ordinary Palestinians—people she identifies here as "kids" and "mothers."[7] Samira believed that if she could make those stories visible, more and more Americans might be drawn to pressure the US government to push for an end to the Israeli occupation of Palestine.

Her words illustrate two moves important for realizing the political actions she desires. She hopes that the stories of ordinary women and children will

6. Samira's construction of "Americans" as white and black intimates a national imaginary in which Asians and Latinos are construed as "alien citizens" while indigenous populations remain invisible.

7. It is worth thinking about the ways that "innocence" is constructed in relation to women and children and not men—a distinction that reinforces dominant narratives and Israeli government policies that treat as suspicious all men from adolescence through midlife (see also Mikdashi 2014).

push Americans to think outside of the categorical boundaries—transforming Palestinians from "Arabs" into "people." Samira's perspective, born out of her experiences in transnational social fields, calls upon humanist, universal values to make a case for breaking down nationalist affiliations and recognizing all humans as equal. Perhaps just as important, if not more critical, she speaks of the need to get Americans to care about justice in Palestine in their everyday lives—rather than moving on quickly and getting reimmersed in their local lives. Samira aspired to make visible the lives of Palestinians in ways that highlight the interconnectivity of US policies in the region and the ongoing brutality of the Israeli occupation, in hopes that more and more Americans might come to understand how deeply and inextricably injustices occurring elsewhere are interwoven with policies made in this country.

Reorienting Citizenship Education beyond the National

Bassam's film and the young women's direct political action represent different kinds of transnational citizenship practices—everyday practices through which these young people were forging belonging and actively participating in transnational social, cultural, and political spheres. Samira and her peers were involved in easily identifiable democratic political action. Bassam was engaged in another kind of citizenship practice—one that illustrates the powerful role that the arts can play in the ongoing struggle to realize substantive inclusion in democratic societies (Abu El-Haj 2009b; Maira 2013; Young 2000). Each of these citizenship practices, however, shares an orientation that transcends the boundaries of any one nation-state while also spurring participants to act within their local setting—to be civically engaged citizens of the United States (see also Miller 2011; Seif 2011).

None of these citizenship practices was facilitated by these young people's formal educational curriculum. As I have shown, many of the young people I worked with were actively engaged in cultural and political activities in extra-curricular contexts, including community organizations. Despite their energetic efforts as cultural and political actors outside of school, many—including the four focal students in this study—drifted through their years at Regional High, putting in their time and getting by without any real connection to or sense of engagement with their studies. Between a school community that refused to address the racial discrimination they faced and a curriculum that failed to draw on their knowledge and interests, many of the Palestinian American students found little reason to be deeply committed to their high school education. Formal schooling left most of the youth in this research with an "education in citizenship" that modeled exclusion, disengagement, and disempowerment.

Fortunately, school was not the only site at which these young Palestinian Americans got an education in citizenship. Similar to many young people from transnational (and/or racially minoritized) communities, the Palestinian Americans drew on both the collective experiences of their community with dispossession and injustice, and rich cultural, linguistic, and religious resources to fashion a sense of belonging and citizenship that was complex and critical (Dyrness 2012; García-Sánchez 2013; M. Levinson 2012; Jaffe-Walter 2013; Maira 2009; Rubin 2007; Sánchez 2007). Out of their everyday citizenship education, these young Palestinian Americans crafted active citizenship practices that challenged inequitable and oppressive conditions in the United States and elsewhere. What lessons can we take from these two illustrations above, as well as from the many stories of the youth in this study, to help us imagine citizenship education that would lead to substantive inclusion (Abu El-Haj 2006) rather than marginalization for young people such as the Palestinian Americans? I offer two orienting principles for designing this kind of citizenship education.

SHIFTING FROM (MULTI)CULTURAL TO TRANSNATIONAL CITIZENSHIP

Young people such as Khalida, Samira, Adam, Zayd, and their peers deserve an education that acknowledges transnational citizenship as a grounded and legitimate way to forge a sense of belonging to, and engagement with, the multiple social, cultural, economic, and political fields that shape many young people's lives today. Transnational citizenship is a mode of everyday practice through which people create and sustain affective relationships to multiple people, places, and politics (Abu El-Haj 2007; Dyrness 2012; Maira 2009; Sánchez 2007).

As discussed above, this lived form of citizenship is significantly different from the dominant conceptualizations of citizenship that young people from im/migrant communities encounter in their schools—conceptualizations that are assimilative, and individualist, expressed in educators' assumptions that Palestinians, like other im/migrant youth, should and would eventually adopt "American" norms and values. However, transnational citizenship is also different from the ideas of cultural citizenship that have guided contemporary critiques of these assimilative frameworks.

In recent decades, calls for cultural recognition and cultural citizenship[8]

8. These terms are not coterminous, but they both reference similar claims for justice in multicultural democratic states.

have challenged these models, suggesting that group affiliations and cultural resources are essential to people's capacity to participate fully in democratic society (Flores and Benmayor 1997; Kymlicka 1995; Rosaldo 1994; Taylor 1992). The call for cultural citizenship offers a critical corrective to assimilative models of citizenship. As Rosaldo writes:

> Cultural citizenship refers to the right to be different and to belong in a participatory democratic sense. It claims that, in a democracy, social justice calls for equity among all citizens, even when such differences as race, religion, class, gender, or sexual orientation potentially could be used to make certain people less equal or inferior to others. (1994, 402)

Cultural citizenship acknowledges the institutional structures that make substantive participation and inclusion difficult, even impossible, for groups of people who are positioned as different from the ideal citizen. Cultural citizenship and cultural recognition are not abstract ideals debated in the academy. They grew out of activist movements in countries across the world working to expand the scope and practices of democratic citizenship.

In educational institutions, this demand for cultural citizenship has had the most impact in reshaping the canon to be inclusive of marginalized groups in society. Ethnic studies, women's and gender studies, queer studies, can all be read as outcomes of the movement for cultural citizenship. In the K–12 setting, multicultural curriculum can be seen as an attempt, albeit a tepid one, to acknowledge these demands for cultural (rather than straight-line assimilative) citizenship. Critiques of the ways these demands for cultural citizenship have typically translated in schools are long-standing (for a few examples, see Abu El-Haj 2006; McCarthy 1990, 1993; McLaren 1994; Mohanty 1989–90), and this book offers one more illustration of the deeply problematic ways that cultural diversity is invoked (and displayed) in dominant educational models, doing little to challenge the institutional structures of exclusion and oppression in our schools. Nevertheless, cultural citizenship as an ideal aims to transform not only educational institutions but also democratic society to challenge structural inequalities and become truly inclusive of its members.

Transnational citizenship extends the scope of critique that cultural citizenship has offered to dominant norms for citizenship. Acknowledging transnational citizenship as a legitimate way to orient to the world focuses attention on the ways that people construct cultural, economic, and political ties across the borders of nation-states. If schools recognized transnational citizenship as a legitimate form of *belonging*, Palestinian American students would not have been challenged to explain, or required to hide, their perspectives on and affiliations with Palestine and its independence movement.

Rather than being asked to choose between being American and being Palestinian, or being asked to subsume their political aspirations under the rubric of flavorful cultural diversity, these young people would have been able to speak about, express, and act upon the cultural and political commitments they had developed in relation to Palestine, the United States, and for some, other countries. Their knowledge about and perspectives on, for example, Palestine, Islam, and the Middle East would have been seen as valuable resources for learning from (and with) this community of young people. Transnational perspectives decenter the nation as the primary site for developing social, cultural, and political knowledge, or for challenging inequality and injustice (of which I will say more below).

A transnational framework would also encourage young people such as the Palestinian Americans in this study to develop more complex perspectives on the politics of culture rather than falling into dichotomous and essentialized views that drive many im/migrant communities' search for "authenticity" (Grewal 2014; Ghaffar-Kucher 2014; Hall 2004; Naber 2012; Sarroub 2005) and also frame most practices of multicultural education. As Bassam's film makes visible, even as the protagonist explains the difference between "American" and "Palestinian" norms, the young men are illustrating the complex, multifaceted, and inextricably interwoven ways that youth produce cultural forms that are anything but dichotomous or essentialized. Moreover, the film highlights the political nature of culture, and the young men wear their politics on their shoulders, and leverage culture to combat racist images of their community. However, without developing a critical assessment of the politics of culture, bids for citizenship based on some notion of cultural authenticity risk reinforcing other kinds of inequalities, including sexism and heteronormativity (Naber 2012). Citizenship education oriented to transnationalism could explicitly teach young people (and their teachers) to think critically about the messy nature of "culture" and belonging, in ways that might help them further embrace the complexity rather than risk producing dichotomizing and essentialist perspectives (Ghaffar-Kucher 2014; Grewal 2014; Hall 2002).

CITIZENSHIP EDUCATION FOR LOCAL AND GLOBAL JUSTICE

A second orienting principle puts questions of inequality and justice at the heart of citizenship education. To a large extent, the sense of alienation that many of the young Palestinian Americans felt from their school communities grew out of the gap they saw between the professed American ideals of democracy, freedom, and equality, and the ways that these ideals were belied both by the everyday encounters they had with racism in their schools and communities and by the broader government policies that failed to uphold those principles. These young people found many ways to express and act upon their critiques of inequality, but few of the venues they found were in the formal educational curriculum. Again and again, as I and my colleagues at the Arab American community organization engaged youth in critical analyses of their experiences, young people asked us, "Why can't school be like this?" Why indeed? What if Regional High had been like that for the young people with whom I worked?

Fortunately, in recent years, citizenship education projects that focus on social justice have been gaining momentum in both school and community contexts, encouraging young people to define and investigate issues in their schools and communities, and advocate for change (for a few examples, see Abu El-Haj 2009b; Cammarota 2008; Dyrness 2012; Flores-Gonzalez, Rodriguez, and Rodriguez-Muniz 2006; Guajardo and Guajardo 2008; Kwon 2008; M. Levinson 2012; Rubin and Hayes 2010). These educational efforts focus attention on young people's experiences with "civic disjuncture" (Rubin 2007)—the gap between the promises of equality and the lived realities of inequality and oppression. Focusing on educating for activist citizenship (Yuval-Davis 2011), these types of educational projects teach young people practices through which they can struggle against the inequalities they face in their schools and communities, and imagine themselves as powerful participants in democratic life. It was precisely this kind of project in which our after-school club engaged, creating a space for Palestinian American youth to analyze and respond to the ways they and members of their community were being positioned as racialized Others.

The experiences of young people from transnational communities suggest, however, the need to expand this model of citizenship education to *purposefully* orient to both local *and* global contexts of inequality. This means paying attention to the ways that the disjunctures they recognize are as much about experiences of inequality and oppression outside the country as they are within it. Palestinian American students were deeply concerned about, and compelled to work for justice in, Palestine. They also had a heightened sense of how important it was to do this work from their position in the United States, since they recognized the ways that the intransigence of the Israeli occupation was bolstered by US government economic and military aid. Education that supports young people in understanding inequality and oppression, and in working for justice and equity, must expand the scale for such work to include global contexts of injustice—contexts that for many young people are experienced in the intimacies of everyday life. Because so many young people and their communities live "glocal" lives, engaging these youth in education that feels relevant and important requires fundamentally decentering the local (and the national) as the primary locus for attention and action, and building a more robust orientation outward toward the world.[9]

Creating a world-centered citizenship education, however, requires not only denaturalizing the United States as the primary locus for attention and concern but also challenging the narrative of this nation's "radical innocence" both at home and abroad. Supporting young people in developing perspectives on, and actions on behalf of, local and global injustices must hold a mirror up to the United States and its role as an imperial power in today's world. As the stories of the Palestinian American students have illustrated, it was often their knowledge and critiques of the role this country plays on the world stage that led to conflict, silencing, and exclusion in their school. Uncritical perspectives on this country leave intact a willful blindness to the role the United States continues to play[10] in contributing to devastating economic and political conditions in too many countries—conditions that are often intimately interwoven with the reasons that people migrated to this country in the first place. This reality was never lost on the Palestinian American youth.

Citizenship education that supports young people, such as the Palestinian Americans, in developing a powerful sense of belonging to and inclusion in the multiple communities with which they affiliate must help them to challenge local and global inequality and injustice. If Palestinian American youth and others like them are to have any hope of experiencing *substantive* inclusion—of being full and equal participants—in our schools and society, we will need to figure out how to create educational spaces that encourage the development of activist citizenship practices that truly embrace transnational modes of belonging.

However, it is not only Palestinian American youth—or other youth from transnational communities—who need a radically reconfigured citizenship education. Global inequalities and conflicts spill across all borders and affect all nations. The risk is that we greet this spillage without compassion—by

9. Calls for global education have been gaining traction in recent years, even leading the US Department of Education to issue a comprehensive "International Strategy." This increased attention on global education is an important development, especially in the US educational context, in which most schools remain remarkably limited in their efforts to educate children and youth about the rest of the world. Unfortunately, current efforts too often reinforce, rather than decenter, nationalist/imperialist perspectives. This critique is, however, beyond the scope of this book.

10. I do not intend to suggest that the United States bears sole responsibility for the conditions of many other countries.

sending children back across the US-Mexican border to the gang violence tearing apart communities in Central America; calling for quarantines on entire foreign populations who "threaten" us with disease; or refusing to worry about casualties of our foreign wars if we perceive any risk to a single "American" person—and without understanding that "our" lives are inextricably linked with the lives of Others. Treating Other people as if they were invisible unless and until they have a direct impact on our national community is a dangerous game. Developing models of citizenship education that support all young people in actively engaging in citizenship practices that fight inequality and oppression both within and across the artificial borders of nation-states must be a central goal for any justice-oriented citizenship education.

Acknowledgments

I have been working on this project for over a decade now, and many, many people have accompanied me along various parts of this journey. First and foremost, I am deeply grateful for the trust and generosity shown me by the young Palestinian Americans whose wisdom and stories ground this book. Their tenacious commitment to stating their truths even in the face of a dangerous political climate gives me much hope for this world. Many adults worked with me at Regional High to create spaces within which these young people could examine, and speak back to, the dominant discourses that framed their community in a negative light. My thanks to Laureen Griffin, Sonia Rosen, Hazami Sayed, and Ahlam Yassin, and the two sponsors of the after-school program who must remain nameless here for reasons of confidentiality but without whose support none of this work would have been possible. Teachers and administrators at Regional High are due thanks for their willingness to participate in this research, which was, by its very nature, contentious. For their generosity in talking openly about difficult topics, I am grateful. Many years of conversation with Hazami Sayed about how to leverage artistic media in the service of civic education have deepened my understanding of this relationship. Dahna Abourahme has been an intellectual and activist partner in thinking about how to support young people in "speaking truth to power."

I have been blessed with a number of fabulous research assistants along the way: Sally Bonet, Nehad Khader, Sonia Rosen, Shelley Wu, and Ahlam Yassin. Mara Hughes provided detailed copyediting of the first version of this manuscript. Thanks also to Susan J. Cohan for her attention to detail and stylistic advice on the final version of the book.

Without the support of a National Academy of Education / Spencer Foundation Postdoctoral Fellowship, I would never have been able to do this research. A 2013–14 fellowship from the Institute for Research on Women (IRW) at Rutgers University offered both the needed course release and the intellectual community that supported me in finishing this manuscript. Thanks also to *Harvard Educational Review* for permission to reprint, with revisions, selections that first appeared in the journal.

Many individuals read and commented on conference papers and journal articles that have found their way into this book in some form: Patricia Buck, Rosalie Rolón-Dow, Michelle Fine, Ameena Ghaffar-Kucher, Kathy Hall, Bradley Levinson, Meira Levinson, Ray McDermott, Patricia Mascias, Catherine Raissiguier, Robyn Rodriguez, Zakia Salime, Carla Shalaby, Doris Warriner, and members of the 2008 Columbia University Women and Society Seminar. Thanks also to Yana Rogers for her thoughtful discussant comments, and to members of the 2013–14 Rutgers University IRW seminar for their generous reading of chapter 4. Sa'ed Atshan is due thanks for commenting on my "lay" history of Palestine. Brahim El Guabli helped me with the Arabic transliterations.

Lesley Bartlett, Andrea Dyrness, Bradley Levinson, and one anonymous reviewer offered generous and critical readings of the book manuscript in its entirety, pushing me to read new literatures and clarify further aspects of my arguments. I know how much of a commitment it takes to read an entire manuscript so carefully, and to each of you, I am truly grateful. Elizabeth Branch Dyson, my editor, talked through my ideas for this book over more years, and more lunches, than I can count. For having the faith, even without having read a single page, that I would one day hand you a complete manuscript, I thank you. This is a much better book for your wise editorial advice and your deep knowledge of what makes a person want to read a book.

Writing is often characterized as a lonely profession, and yet many people have written alongside me for much of this journey in coffee shops, libraries, and on retreat in Vermont. I consider this my adult version of parallel play. Until our teaching schedules became incompatible, Rosalie Rolón-Dow offered consistent companionship and intellectual conversation. Ariana Mangual Figueroa brought new energy to my thinking about citizenship when she joined me as a colleague and friend at Rutgers. Samira Haj and Jane Huber have each spent time writing with me in Vermont. For knowing how to balance intense work with deep conversation, good cooking, and play, I thank you both. Because I write at the High Point coffee shop, the center of my local community, I had the great fortune to meet Lorrin Thomas along this journey. Thank you, Lorrin, for writing and knitting alongside me, thinking with me about citizenship, laughing and crying about the joys and struggles of being a mother and a professor, and holding a historian's perspective on how long it actually takes to write a book. Kathy Schultz wrote with me once a week for over a decade until she moved to California. I think you know, Kathy, how much I miss you constantly and how you remain a part of all of my work. For being a steadfast friend and colleague, true intellectual partner, sharer of great literature, and model of a life committed to making schools everywhere more loving places for children and teachers, I am grateful. Beth Rubin has offered deep friendship and the kind of intellectual and professional collaboration that makes me look forward to going to work. You cannot possibly know how much the development of my thinking about youth citizenship education has been so fundamentally connected to your own work. Thanks for this intellectual companionship, and for your generous and numerous reads of different parts of this text, as well as for growing with me these past eleven years, for writing with and next to me, for sharing your time in Guatemala, for "retreating" in New York and Vermont, and for making it work for our families to be friends together even though we are separated by a state. Ellen Skilton and I have written side by side once a week for at least fifteen years now, and she has read more drafts of various pieces of this book than I can remember. Her thinking about what it means to craft an education that truly *sees* other people has shaped my own profoundly. There is so much to thank you for: constant, unfaltering love and friendship; taking time to play as hard as we work; figuring out how to laugh in moments when that seems impossible; reminding me that this is the only job you and I would ever be suited for; knitting, knitting, knitting; and always, always being on the other end of the perceiver hotline.

Two people are due special thanks for having been my writing partners. Reva Jaffe-Walter has read every chapter of this book, often with lightning speed. Her own brilliant work about Muslim im/migrant youth in Danish schools, her knowledge of our mutual field, and careful readings of my work have pushed my thinking in many directions. I could not have written this book without Jennifer Riggan. We formed our writing group at a moment when I was losing faith in my project. These past two years of sharing every piece of this book made it possible for me to continue, and reading and re-reading her own amazing book about Eritrean teachers, state schools, and nationalism opened up many new lines of thinking in my own. Jen, I cannot thank you enough for your faith in this project, and your incredible attention to both argument and detail. Your unrelenting support made me finish.

Many friends have supported me in emotional and material ways, and they have not given up on me when I put them off because I had to work on this book. Thanks especially to Karen and Alan Zaur, Cheryl Stayton, Janelle Junkin, and Fadwa Kashkash for all your support.

My family has been amazing, providing the love and care necessary to undertake this kind of project. Thanks to my sisters, Nadia and Tabatha Abu El-Haj, for emotional support and intellectual conversation throughout this journey. Mildred Rosenzweig has been the best of mothers to me for many, many years now. My daughters have not only patiently shared me with yet another book project; they have also encouraged me at every point of the journey. Both writers and artists, they know the ups and downs of the creative process, and they have reminded me to keep going even through the tough places. Once again, I could not have done this project without my life partner, Steve Rosenzweig, who supports my work in all the emotional and material ways necessary. For your steadfast belief that this work is worth doing, and for your love, companionship, integrity, and partnership on this life's journey, I am truly blessed.

References

Abourahme, D. 2010. *The Kingdom of Women: Ein El Hilweh* (documentary, 54 min., Lebanon, 2010). Produced by ARCPA/Al-Jana.

Abowitz, K. K., and J. Harnish. 2006. "Contemporary Discourses of Citizenship." *Review of Educational Research* 76 (4): 653–90.

Abu El-Haj, T. R. 2002. "Contesting the Politics of Culture, Rewriting the Boundaries of Inclusion: Working for Social Justice with Muslim and Arab Communities." *Anthropology and Education Quarterly* 33 (3): 308–16.

———. 2005. "Global Politics, Dissent and Palestinian-American Identities: Engaging Conflict to Re-invigorate Democratic Education." In *Beyond Silenced Voices: Class, Race and Gender in United States Schools*, rev. ed., edited by L. Weis and M. Fine, 119–215. Albany: SUNY Press.

———. 2006. *Elusive Justice: Wrestling with Difference and Educational Equity in Everyday Practice*. New York: Routledge.

———. 2007. "'I Was Born Here but My Home It's Not Here': Educating for Democratic Citizenship in an Era of Transnational Migration and Global Conflict." *Harvard Educational Review* 77 (3): 285–316.

———. 2009a. "Becoming Citizens in an Era of Globalization and Transnational Migration: Re-imagining Citizenship as Critical Practice." *Theory into Practice* 48 (4): 274–82.

———. 2009b. "Imagining Postnationalism: Arts, Citizenship Education and Arab American Youth." *Anthropology and Education Quarterly* 40 (1): 1–19.

———. 2010. "'The Beauty of America': Nationalism, Education and the 'War on Terror.'" *Harvard Educational Review* 80 (2): 242–74.

Abu El-Haj, T. R., and S. W. Bonet. 2011. "Education, Citizenship, and the Politics of Belonging: Muslim Youth from Transnational Communities and the 'War on Terror.'" Invited article for *Youth Cultures, Language and Literacy*, 29–59. Review of Research in Education, vol. 34. Thousand Oaks, CA: SAGE Publications.

Abu-Lughod, L. 2002. "Do Muslim Women Really Need Saving? Anthropological Reflections on Cultural Relativism and Its Others." *American Anthropologist* 104 (3): 783–90.

———. 2007. "Return to Half-Ruins: Memory, Post-memory, and Living History in Palestine." In *Nakba: Palestine, 1948, and the Claims of Memory*, edited by A. H. Sa'di and L. Abu-Lughod, 77–106. New York: Columbia University Press.

———. 2013. *Do Muslim Women Need Saving?* Cambridge, MA: Harvard University Press.

Abu-Lughod, L., and A. H. Saʿdi. 2007. "Introduction: The Claims of Memory." In *Nakba: Palestine, 1948, and the Claims of Memory,* edited by A. H. Saʿdi and L. Abu-Lughod, 1–26. New York: Columbia University Press.

Adeeb, P., and P. Smith. 1995. "The Arab Americans." In *Educating for Diversity: An Anthology of Voices,* edited by C. Grant, 191–207. Boston: Allyn and Bacon.

Ahmad, M. 2002. "Homeland Insecurities: Racial Violence the Day after September 11." *Social Text* 72 (3): 101–15.

Ajrouch, K. J. 2004. "Gender, Race, and Symbolic Boundaries: Contested Spaces of Identity among Arab American Adolescents." *Sociological Perspectives* 47 (4): 371–91.

Akram, S. M., and K. R. Johnson. 2004. "Race and Civil Rights Pre–September 11, 2001: The Targeting of Arabs and Muslims." In *Civil Rights in Peril: The Targeting of Arabs and Muslims,* edited by E. C. Hagopian, 9–25. Chicago: Haymarket Books.

The American Vision. 2005. Columbus, OH: Glencoe/McGraw-Hill.

Anderson, B. (1983) 1991. *Imagined Communities: Reflections on the Origin and Spread of Nationalism.* New York: Verso. First published 1983.

Appadurai, A. 1996. *Modernity at Large: Cultural Dimensions of Globalization.* Minneapolis: University of Minnesota Press.

Arab American Institute. 2012. "The American Divide: How We View Arabs and Muslims," August 23. http://www.aaiusa.org/reports/the-american-divide-how-we-view-arabs-and-muslims/.

Arab American Institute Foundation. 2011. PDF showing an analysis of Pennsylvania's Arab American population. http://b.3cdn.net/aai/72af9f877452484227_pbm6iilih.pdf.

Aronson, G. 2013. "Settlement Monitor." *Journal of Palestine Studies* 42 (2, Winter): 143–58.

Arzubiaga, A. E., S. C. Nogeuron, and A. L. Sullivan. 2009. "Education of Children in Im/migrant families." *Review of Research in Education* 33: 246–71.

Asad, T. 2003. *Formations of the Secular: Christianity, Islam, and Modernity.* Stanford, CA: Stanford University Press.

———. 2007. *On Suicide Bombing.* New York: Columbia University Press.

Bakalian, A., and M. Bozorgmehr. 2009. *Backlash 9/11: Middle Eastern and Muslim Americans Respond.* Berkeley: University of California Press.

Balibar, E. 1991. "Is There a 'Neo-racism'?" In *Race, Nation, Class: Ambiguous Identities,* edited by E. Balibar and I. Wallerstein, 17–28. London: Verso.

Banks, J. A. 1997. *Teaching Strategies for Ethnic Studies.* 6th ed. Boston: Allyn and Bacon.

———. 2004. "Introduction: Democratic Citizenship Education in Multicultural Societies." In *Diversity and Citizenship Education: Global Perspectives,* edited by J. A. Banks, 3–17. San Francisco: Jossey-Bass.

———. 2008. "Diversity, Group Identity and Citizenship Education in a Global Age." *Educational Researcher* 37 (3): 129–39.

Basch, L., N. Glick Shiller, and C. Szanton Blanc. 1994. *Nations Unbound: Transnational Projects, Postcolonial Predicaments, and Deterritorialized Nation-States.* Amsterdam: Gordon and Breach Science Publishers.

Baumann, G. 2004. "Introduction: Nation-State and Civil Enculturation." In *Civil Enculturation: Nation-State, School and Ethnic Difference in The Netherlands, Britain, Germany, and France,* edited by W. Schiffauer, G. Baumann, R. Kastoryano, and S. Vertovec, 1–20. New York: Berhahn Books.

Bayoumi, M. 2008. *How Does It Feel to Be a Problem? Being Young and Arab in America*. New York: Penguin Books.

Benei, V. 2008. *Schooling Passions: Nation, History, and Language in Contemporary Western India*. Stanford, CA: Stanford University Press.

Ben-Porath, S. 2006. *Citizenship under Fire: Democratic Education in Times of Conflict*. Princeton, NJ: Princeton University Press.

Bhabha, H. K. 1990. "Introduction: Narrating the Nation." In *Nation and Narration*, edited by H. K. Bhabha, 1–7. London: Routledge.

Bhatia, S. 2002. "Acculturation, Dialogical Voices, and the Construction of the Diasporic Self." *Theory and Psychology* 12 (1): 55–77.

Billig, M. 1995. *Banal Nationalism*. London: SAGE Publications.

Boggs, C. 2003. "Introduction: Empire and Globalization." In *Masters of War: Militarism and Blowback in the Era of American Empire*, edited by C. Boggs, 1–16. New York: Routledge.

Bonet, S. W. 2011. "Educating Muslim American Youth in a Post-9/11 Era: A Critical Review of Policy and Practice." *High School Journal* 95 (1): 46–55.

Bonilla-Silva, E. 2006. *Racism without Racists: Colorblind Racism and the Persistence of Racial Inequality in the United States*. Lanham, MD: Rowman and Littlefield.

Bosniak, L. 2006. *The Citizen and the Alien: Dilemmas of Contemporary Membership*. Princeton, NJ: Princeton University Press.

Brown, W. 2006. *Regulating Aversion: Tolerance in the Age of Identity and Empire*. Princeton, NJ: Princeton University Press.

Buck, P., and R. Silver. 2012. *Educated for Change: Muslim Refugee Women in the West*. Charlotte, NC: Information Age Publishing.

Cainkar, L. A. 2008. "Thinking outside the Box: Arabs and Race in the United States." In *Race and Arab Americans before and after 9/11: From Invisible Citizens to Visible Subjects*, edited by A. Jamal and N. Naber, 46–80. Syracuse, NY: Syracuse University Press.

———. 2009. *Homeland Insecurity: The Arab American and Muslim American Experience after 9/11*. New York: Russell Sage Foundation.

Calhoun, C. 2007. *Nations Matter: Culture, History and the Cosmopolitan Dream*. New York: Routledge.

Cammarota, J. 2008. "The Cultural Organizing of Youth Ethnographers: Formalizing a Praxis-Based Pedagogy." *Anthropology and Education Quarterly* 39 (1): 45–58.

Castles, S., and A. Davidson. 2000. *Citizenship and Migration: Globalization and the Politics of Belonging*. New York: Routledge.

Christou, M., and E. Ioannidou. 2014. "Opening Networks, Sealing Borders: Youth and Racist Discourse on the Internet." In *Wired Citizenship: Youth Learning and Activism in the Middle East*, edited by L. Herrera with R. Sakr, 121–38. New York: Routledge.

Chun, E. W. 2013. "Styles of Pledging Allegiance: Practicing Youth Citizenship in the United States." *Language and Communication* 33 (4): 500–514.

Cole, D. 2003. *Enemy Aliens: Double Standards and Constitutional Freedoms in the War on Terror*. New York: New Press.

Darwish, M. 1964. "Identity Card." http://www.barghouti.com/poets/darwish/bitaqa.asp.

Das, V. 2001. "Violence and Translation." *Anthropology Quarterly* 75 (1, Winter): 105–12.

Davis, R. A. 2007. "Mapping the Past, Re-creating the Homeland: Memories of Village Places in Pre-1948 Palestine." In *Nakba: Palestine, 1948, and the Claims of Memory*, edited by A. H. Saʾdi and L. Abu-Lughod, 53–76. New York: Columbia University Press.

———. 2011. *Palestinian Village Histories: Geographies of the Displaced*. Stanford, CA: Stanford University Press.

DeJaeghere, J. G., and K. S. McCleary. 2010. "The Making of Mexican Migrant Youth Civic Identities: Transnational Spaces and Imaginaries." *Anthropology and Education Quarterly* 41 (3): 228–44.

Delgado, R. 2003. *Justice at War: Civil Liberties and Civil Rights during Times of Crisis*. New York: New York University Press.

Dick, H. 2010. "Imagined Lives and Modern Chronotypes in Mexican Nonmigrant Discourse." *American Ethnologist* 37 (2): 275–90.

Dyrness, A. 2012. "*Contra Viento y Marea* (Against Wind and Tide): Building Civic Identity among Children of Emigration in El Salvador." *Anthropology and Education Quarterly* 43 (1): 41–60.

Ewing, K. P. 2008. *Stolen Honor: Stigmatizing Muslim Men in Berlin*. Stanford, CA: Stanford University Press.

Ewing, K. P., and M. Hoyler. 2008. "Being Muslim and American: South Asian Muslim Youth and the War on Terror." In *Being and Belonging: Muslims in the United States since 9/11*, edited by K. P. Ewing, 80–103. New York: Russell Sage.

Fass, P. 1989. *Outside In: Minorities and the Transformation of American Education*. New York: Oxford University Press.

Fine, M. 2004. "Witnessing Whiteness / Gathering Intelligence." In *Off White: Readings on Race, Power and Society*, 2nd ed., edited by M. Fine, L. Weis, L. C. Powell, and L. M. Wong, 245–56. New York: Routledge.

Flapan, S. 1987. *The Birth of Israel: Myths and Realities*. New York: Pantheon.

Flores, W. V., and R. Benmayor. 1997. *Latino Cultural Citizenship: Claiming Identity, Space and Rights*. Boston: Beacon Press.

Flores-Gonzalez, N., M. Rodriguez, and M. Rodriguez-Muniz. 2006. "From Hip-Hop to Humanization: Batey Urbano as a Space for Latino Youth Culture and Community Action." In *Beyond Resistance: Youth Activism and Community Change*, edited by Shawn Ginwright, Pedro Noguera, and Julio Cammarota, 175–96. New York: Routledge.

Foley, D., B. Levinson, and J. Hurtig. 2001. "Anthropology Goes Inside: The New Educational Ethnography of Ethnicity and Gender." In *Review of Research in Education*, edited by W. Secada, 37–99. Washington, DC: American Educational Research Association.

Foley, D., and A. Valenzuela. 2005. "Critical Ethnography: The Politics of Collaboration." In *The Sage Handbook of Qualitative Research*, 3rd ed., edited by N. K. Denzin and Y. S. Lincoln, 217–34. Thousand Oaks, CA: SAGE.

Fouron, G. E., and N. Glick-Schiller. 2002. "The Generation of Identity: Redefining the Second Generation within a Transnational Social Field." In *The Changing Face of Home: The Transnational Lives of the Second Generation*, edited by P. Levitt and M. C. Waters, 168–210. New York: Russell Sage Foundation.

Gallup. 2014. "Islamophobia: Understanding Anti-Muslim Sentiment in the West." http://www.gallup.com/poll/157082/islamophobia-understanding-anti-muslim-sentiment-west.aspx#3.

García-Sánchez, I. M. 2013. "The Everyday Politics of 'Cultural Citizenship' among North African School Children in Spain." *Language and Communication* 33 (4): 481–99.

Gerges, F. 2003. "Islam and Muslims in the Mind of America." *Annals of the American Academy of Political and Social Science* (July): 73–89.

Gerstle, G. 2001. *American Crucible: Race and Nation in the 20th Century*. Princeton, NJ: Princeton University Press.

Ghaffar-Kucher, A. 2009. "Citizenship and Belonging in an Age of Insecurity: Pakistani Immigrant Youth in New York City." In *Critical Approaches to Comparative Education: Vertical Case Studies from Africa, Europe, the Middle East and the Americas*, edited by F. Vavrus and L. Bartlett, 163–80. New York: Palgrave.

———. 2012. "The Religification of Pakistani-American Youth." *American Educational Research Journal* 49 (1): 30–52.

———. 2014. "'Narrow-Minded and Oppressive' or a 'Superior Culture'? Implications of Divergent Views of Islam for Pakistani American Youth." *Race, Ethnicity, and Education.* doi: 10.1080/13613324.2014.889111.

Gibson, M. A. 1988. *Accommodation without Assimilation: Sikh Immigrants in an American High School.* Ithaca, NY: Cornell University Press.

Gibson, M. A., and J. P. Koyama. 2011. "Immigrants and Education." In *A Companion to the Anthropology of Education*, edited by B. A. U. Levinson and M. Pollock, 391–406. Malden, MA: Wiley Blackwell.

Goodstein, L. 2013. "Members of Jewish Student Group Test Permissible Discussion on Israel." *New York Times*, December 29, 21.

Gregory, D. 2004. *The Colonial Present.* Malden, MA: Blackwell Publishing.

Grewal, Z. 2014. *Islam Is a Foreign Country: American Muslims and the Global Crisis of Authority.* New York: New York University Press.

Guajardo, M., and F. Guajardo with C. Casperalta. 2008. "Transformative Education: Chronicling a Pedagogy for Social Change." *Anthropology and Education Quarterly* 39 (1): 3–22.

Gutmann, A. 1987. *Democratic Education.* Princeton, NJ: Princeton University Press.

Haddad, Y. Y., J. I. Smith, and K. M. Moore. 2006. *Muslim Women in America.* New York: Oxford University Press.

Hall, K. D. 2002. *Lives in Translation: Sikh Youth as British Citizens.* Philadelphia: University of Pennsylvania Press.

———. 2004. "The Ethnography of Imagined Communities: The Cultural Production of Sikh Ethnicity in Britain." *Annals of the American Academy of Political and Social Science* 59: 108–21.

Hammer, J. 2005. *Palestinians Born in Exile: Diaspora and the Search for a Homeland.* Austin: University of Texas Press.

Harvey, D. 2003. *The New Imperialism.* Oxford: Oxford University Press.

Herrera, L., and R. Sakr. 2014. "Introduction: Wired and Revolutionary in the Middle East." In *Wired Citizenship: Youth Learning and Activism in the Middle East*, edited by L. Herrera with R. Sakr, 1–16. New York: Routledge.

Hess, D. 2009. *Controversy in the Classroom: The Democratic Power of Discussion.* New York: Routledge.

Hirshman, N. 2003. *The Subject of Liberty: Toward a Feminist Theory of Freedom.* Princeton, NJ: Princeton University Press.

Hirst, D. 1977. *The Gun and the Olive Branch.* London: Faber and Faber.

Huntington, S. 1996. *The Clash of Civilizations and the Remaking of the World.* New York: Simon and Schuster.

Ibish, H. 2003. *Report on Hate Crimes and Discrimination against Arab-Americans: The Post–September 11 Backlash.* Washington, DC: Arab American Anti-discrimination Committee.

———. 2008. *Report on Hate Crimes and Discrimination against Arab-Americans: 2003–2007.* Washington, DC: Arab American Anti-discrimination Committee.

Jaffe-Walter, R. 2013. "'Who Would They Talk About If We Weren't Here?' Muslim Youth, Liberal Schooling, and the Politics of Concern." *Harvard Educational Review* 83 (4): 613–35.

Jamal, A. 2008. "Civil Liberties and the Otherization of Arab and Muslim Americans." In *Race and Arab Americans before and after 9/11: From Invisible Citizens to Visible Subjects*, edited by A. Jamal and N. Naber, 114–30. Syracuse, NY: Syracuse University Press.

Jarmakani, A. 2008. *Imagining Arab Womanhood: The Cultural Mythology of Veils, Harems, and Belly Dancers in the U.S.* New York: Palgrave-Macmillan.

Jiryis, S. 1976. *The Arabs in Israel.* New York: Monthly Review Press.

Joseph, S. 1999. "Against the Grain of the Nation: The Arab." In *Arabs in America: Building a New Future*, edited by M. Suleiman, 257–71. Philadelphia: Temple University Press.

Joseph, S., and B. D'Harlingue with A. K. H. Wong. 2008. "Arab Americans and Muslim Americans in the *New York Times* before and after 9/11." In *Race and Arab Americans before and after 9/11: From Invisible Citizens to Visible Subjects*, edited by A. Jamal and N. Naber, 229–75. Syracuse, NY: Syracuse University Press.

Kaestle, C. 1983. *Pillars of the Republic: Common Schools and American Society, 1780–1860.* New York: Hill and Wang.

Kasinitz, P., M. C. Waters, J. H. Mollenkopf, and M. Anil. 2002. "Transnationalism and the Children of Immigrants in Contemporary New York." In *The Changing Face of Home: The Transnational Lives of the Second Generation*, edited by P. Levitt and M. C. Waters, 96–122. New York: Russell Sage Foundation.

Khalidi, R. 1997. *Palestinian Identity: The Construction of Modern National Consciousness.* New York: Columbia University Press.

———. 2004. *Resurrecting Empire: Western Footprints and America's Perilous Path in the Middle East.* Boston: Beacon Press.

———. 2006. *The Iron Cage: The Story of the Palestinian Struggle for Statehood.* Boston: Beacon Press.

———. 2013. *Brokers of Deceit: How the U.S. Has Undermined Peace in the Middle East.* Boston: Beacon Press.

Khalidi, W., ed. 2006. *All That Remains: The Palestinian Villages Occupied and Depopulated by Israel in 1948.* Beirut: Institute for Palestine Studies.

Kibria, N. 2002. "Of Blood, Belonging, and Homeland Trips: Transnationalism and Identity among Second-Generation Chinese and Korean Americans." In *The Changing Face of Home: The Transnational Lives of the Second Generation*, edited by P. Levitt and M. C. Waters, 295–311. New York: Russell Sage Foundation.

———. 2007. "The 'New Islam' and Bangladeshi Youth in Britain and the US." *Ethnic and Racial Studies* 31 (2): 243–66.

Kimmerling, B., and J. S. Migdal. 2003. *The Palestinian People: A History.* Cambridge, MA: Harvard University Press.

Kinsella, H. M. 2007. "Understanding a War That Is Not a War: A Review Essay." *Signs* 33 (1): 209–31.

Knight, M. 2011. "'It's Already Happening': Learning from Civically Engaged Transnational Immigrant Youth." *Teachers College Record* 113 (6): 1275–92.

Kramer, G. 2008. *A History of Palestine: From the Ottoman Conquest to the Founding of the State of Israel.* Princeton, NJ: Princeton University Press.

Kull, S. 2003. "Misperceptions, the Media, and the Iraq War." PIPA / Knowledge Networks

Poll, October 2. University of Maryland. Accessed March 17, 2014. http://www.worldpublic opinion.org/pipa/pdf/oct03/IraqMedia_Oct03_rpt.pdf.

Kwon, Soo Ah. 2008. "Moving from Complaints to Action: Oppositional Consciousness and Collective Action in Political Community." *Anthropology and Education Quarterly* 39 (1): 59–76.

Kymlicka, W. 1995. *Multicultural Citizenship: A Liberal Theory of Minority Rights*. New York: Oxford University Press.

Lee, S. J. 1996. *Unraveling the "Model Minority" Stereotype: Listening to Asian-American Youth*. New York: Teachers College Press.

———. 2005. *Up against Whiteness: Race, School and Immigrant Youth*. New York: Teachers College Press.

Levinson, B. A. U. 2001. *We Are All Equal: Student Culture and Identity at a Mexican Secondary School*. Durham, NC: Duke University Press.

———. 2005. "Citizenship, Identity, Democracy: Engaging the Political in the Anthropology of Education." *Anthropology and Education Quarterly* 36 (4): 329–40.

———. 2011a. "Symbolic Domination and the Reproduction of Inequality: Pierre Bourdieu and Practice Theory." In *Beyond Critique: Exploring Critical Social Theories and Education*, edited by B. A. U. Levinson, 113–38. Boulder, CO: Paradigm.

———. 2011b. "Toward an Anthropology of (Democratic) Citizenship Education." In *A Companion to the Anthropology of Education*, edited by B. A. U. Levinson and M. Pollock, 279–98. Malden, MA: Wiley Blackwell.

Levinson, B. A. U., and D. Holland. 1996. "The Cultural Production of the Educated Person: An Introduction." In *The Cultural Production of the Educated Person*, edited by B. Levinson, D. E. Foley, and D. C. Holland, 1–54. Albany: SUNY Press.

Levinson, M. 2012. *No Citizen Left Behind*. Cambridge, MA: Harvard University Press.

Levitt, P. 2002. "The Ties That Change: Relations to the Ancestral Home over the Life Cycle." In *The Changing Face of Home: The Transnational Lives of the Second Generation*, edited by P. Levitt and M. C. Waters, 123–44. New York: Russell Sage Foundation.

Levitt, P., and N. Glick Schiller. 2004. "Conceptualizing Simultaneity: A Transnational Social Field Perspective on Society." *International Migration Review* 38 (3): 1002–39.

Levitt, P., and M. C. Waters. 2002. Introduction to *The Changing Face of Home: The Transnational Lives of the Second Generation*, edited by P. Levitt and M. C. Waters, 1–30. New York: Russell Sage Foundation.

Lewis, A. E. 2005. *Race in the Schoolyard: Negotiating the Color Line in Classrooms and Communities*. New Brunswick, NJ: Rutgers University Press.

Lewis, B. 2002. *What Went Wrong? Western Impact and Middle Eastern Response*. London: Oxford University Press.

Lopez, N. 2003. *Hopeful Girls, Troubled Boys*. New York: Teachers College Press.

Louie, A. 2002. "Creating Histories for the Present: Second-Generation (Re)definitions of Chinese American Culture." In *The Changing Face of Home: The Transnational Lives of the Second Generation*, edited by P. Levitt and M. C. Waters, 312–40. New York: Russell Sage Foundation.

Lowe, L. 1996. *Immigrant Acts: On Asian-American Cultural Politics*. Durham, NC: Duke University Press.

Lukose, R. A. 2007. "The Difference That Diaspora Makes: Thinking Through the Anthropology of Immigrant Education in the United States." *Anthropology and Education Quarterly* 38 (4): 405–13.

———. 2009. *Liberalization's Children: Gender, Youth and Consumer Citizenship in Globalizing India*. Chapel Hill, NC: Duke University Press.

Mahmood, S. 2005. *Politics of Piety: The Islamic Revival and the Feminist Subject*. Princeton, NJ: Princeton University Press.

Maira, S. M. 2002. *Desis in the House: Indian American Youth Culture in New York*. Philadelphia: Temple University Press.

———. 2009. *Missing: Youth, Citizenship and Empire after 9/11*. Durham, NC: Duke University Press.

———. 2013. *Jil Oslo: Palestinian Hip Hop, Youth Culture, and the Youth Movement*. Washington, DC: Tadween Publishing.

Makdisi, S. 2008. *Palestine Inside Out: An Everyday Occupation*. New York: Norton.

Mamdani, M. 2004. *Good Muslim, Bad Muslim: America, the Cold War and the Roots of Terror*. New York: Pantheon.

Mangual Figueroa, A. 2011. "Citizenship and Education in the Homework Completion Routine." *Anthropology and Education Quarterly* 42 (3): 263–80.

Mannitz, S. 2004a. "The Place of Religion in Four Civil Societies." In *Civil Enculturation: Nation-State, School and Ethnic Difference in The Netherlands, Britain, Germany, and France*, edited by W. Schiffauer, G. Baumann, R. Kastoryano, and S. Vertovec, 88–118. New York: Berhahn Books.

———. 2004b. "Pupils' Negotiations of Cultural Difference: Identity Management and Discursive Assimilation." In *Civil Enculturation: Nation-State, School and Ethnic Difference in The Netherlands, Britain, Germany, and France*, edited by W. Schiffauer, G. Baumann, R. Kastoryano, and S. Vertovec, 242–303. New York: Berhahn Books.

———. 2004c. "Regimes of Discipline and Civil Conduct in Berlin and Paris." In *Civil Enculturation: Nation-State, School and Ethnic Difference in The Netherlands, Britain, Germany, and France*, edited by W. Schiffauer, G. Baumann, R. Kastoryano, and S. Vertovec, 164–209. New York: Berhahn Books.

Mannitz, S., and W. Schiffauer. 2004. "Taxonomies of Cultural Difference: Constructions of Otherness." In *Civil Enculturation: Nation-State, School and Ethnic Difference in The Netherlands, Britain, Germany, and France*, edited by W. Schiffauer, G. Baumann, R. Kastoryano, and S. Vertovec, 60–87. New York: Berhahn Books.

Marshall, T. H. 1964. *Class, Citizenship, and Social Development: Essays of T. H. Marshall*. Westport, CT: Greenwood.

Massad, J. A. 2006. *The Persistence of the Palestinian Question: Essays on Zionism and the Palestinians*. New York: Routledge.

McCarthy, C. 1990. *Race and Curriculum: Social Inequality and the Theories and Politics of Difference in Contemporary Research on Schooling*. London: Falmer Press.

———. 1993. "Multicultural Approaches to Racial Inequality in the United States." In *Understanding Curriculum as Racial Text: Representations of Identity and Difference in Education*, edited by L. A. Castenell Jr. and W. F. Pinar, 225–46. Albany: SUNY Press.

McLaren, P. 1994. "White Terror and Oppositional Agency: Toward a Critical Multiculturalism." In *Multiculturalism: A Critical Reader*, edited by D. T. Goldberg, 45–74. Cambridge, MA: Basil Blackwell.

Melamed, J. 2006. "The Spirit of Neoliberalism: From Racial Liberalism to Neoliberal Multiculturalism." *Social Text* 89, 24 (4): 1–24.

Mikdashi, M. 2014. "Can Palestinian Men Be Victims? Gendering Israel's War on Gaza." *Jadaliyya*, July 23. Accessed October 20, 2014. http://www.jadaliyya.com/pages/index/18644/can-palestinian-men-be-victims-gendering-israels-w.

Miller, A. 2011. "'Doing' Transnationalism: The Integrative Impact of Salvadoran Cross-Border Activism." *Journal of Ethnic and Migration Studies* 37 (1): 43–60.

Mir, S. 2014. *Muslim American Women on Campus: Undergraduate Social Life and Identity.* Chapel Hill: University of North Carolina Press.

Moallem, M., and I. A. Boal. 1999. "Multicultural Nationalism and the Poetics of Inauguration." In *Between Woman and Nation: Nationalisms, Transnational Feminism, and the State*, edited by C. Kaplan, N. Alarcon, and M. Moallem, 243–63. Durham, NC: Duke University Press.

Mohanty, C. T. 1989–90. "On Race and Voice: Challenges for Liberal Education in the 1990s." *Cultural Critique* (Winter): 179–208.

Mondal, A. A. 2008. *Young British Muslim Voices.* Oxford: Greenwood World.

Moore, K. M. 1999. "A Closer Look at Anti-terrorism Law: *American-Arab Antidiscrimination Committee v. Reno* and the Constructs of Aliens' Rights." In *Arabs in America: Building a New Future*, edited by M. Suleiman, 84–99. Philadelphia: Temple University Press.

Morris, B. 2004. *The Birth of the Palestinian Refugee Problem Revisited.* Cambridge: Cambridge University Press.

Murray, N. 2004. "Profiled: Arabs, Muslims and the Post-9/11 Hunt for the 'Enemy Within.'" In *Civil Rights in Peril: The Targeting of Arabs and Muslims*, edited by E. C. Hagopian, 27–68. Chicago: Haymarket Books.

Naber, N. 2000. "Ambiguous Insiders: An Investigation of Arab American Invisibility." *Journal of Ethnic and Racial Studies* 23 (1): 37–61.

———. 2008. "'Look, Mohammed the Terrorist Is Coming': Cultural Racism, Nation-Based Racism, and the Intersectionality of Oppressions after 9/11." In *Race and Arab Americans before and after 9/11: From Invisible Citizens to Visible Subjects*, edited by A. Jamal and N. Naber, 276–304. Syracuse, NY: Syracuse University Press.

———. 2012. *Arab America: Gender, Cultural Politics, and Activism.* New York: New York University Press.

Nabulsi, M. 2014. "'Hungry for Freedom': Palestinian Youth Activism in an Era of Social Media." In *Wired Citizenship: Youth Learning and Activism in the Middle East*, edited by L. Herrera with R. Sakr, 105–20. New York: Routledge.

Ngai, M. 2004. *Impossible Subjects: Illegal Aliens and the Making of Modern America.* Princeton, NJ: Princeton University Press.

Nussbaum, M., and J. Cohen, eds. 1996. *For Love of Country?* Boston: Beacon Press.

Ogbu, J. 1987. "Variability in Minority School Performance: A Problem in Search of an Explanation." *Anthropology and Education Quarterly* 18 (4): 312–34.

Ogbu, J., and H. Simons. 1998. "Voluntary and Involuntary Minorities: A Cultural-Ecological Theory of School Performance with Some Implications for Education." *Anthropology and Education Quarterly* 29 (2): 155–88.

O'Leary, C. 1999. *To Die For: The Paradox of American Patriotism.* Princeton, NJ: Princeton University Press.

Olneck, M. 1989. "Americanization and the Education of Immigrants: An Analysis of Symbolic Action." *American Journal of Education* 97 (4): 398–423.

———. 2001. "Immigrants and Education." In *Handbook of Research on Multicultural Education*, edited by J. A. Banks and C. A. McGee Banks, 310–27. San Francisco: Jossey-Bass.

Olsen, L. 1997. *Made in America: Immigrant Students in Our Public Schools*. New York: New Press.

Omi, M., and H. Winant. 1986. *Racial Formation in the United States: From the 1960s to the 1980s*. New York: Routledge.

Ong, A. 1999. *Flexible Citizenship: The Cultural Logics of Transnationality*. Durham, NC: Duke University Press.

Pappe, I. 2006. *The Ethnic Cleansing of Palestine*. Oxford: One World Publications.

Parker, W. C. 2006. "Public Discourses in Schools: Purposes, Problems and Possibilities." *Educational Researcher* 35 (8): 11–18.

Parker, W. C., and D. Hess. 2001. "Teaching with and for Discussion." *Teaching and Teacher Education* 17: 273–89.

Pease, D. 2009. *The New American Exceptionalism*. Minneapolis: University of Minnesota Press.

Pollock, M. 2004. *Colormute: Race Talk Dilemmas in an American School*. Princeton, NJ: Princeton University Press.

Portes, A., L. Guarnizo, and P. Landolt. 1999. "The Study of Transnationalism: Promises and Pitfalls of an Emergent Research Field." *Ethnic and Racial Studies* 22 (2): 217–37.

Portes, A., and R. G. Rumbaut. 2001. *Legacies: The Story of the Immigrant Second Generation*. Berkeley: University of California Press.

———. 2014. *Immigrant America: A Portrait*. 4th ed. Berkeley: University of California Press.

Portes, A., and M. Zhou. 1993. "The New Second Generation: Segmented Assimilation and Its Variants." *Annals of the American Academy of Political and Social Science* 530: 74–96.

Puar, J. K., and A. S. Rai. 2002. "Monster, Terrorist, Fag: The War on Terror and the Production of Docile Patriots." *Social Text* 72, 20 (3, Fall): 118–48.

Ramos-Zayas, A. Y. 1998. "Nationalist Ideologies, Neighborhood-Based Activism, and Educational Spaces in Puerto Rican Chicago." *Harvard Educational Review* 68 (2): 164–92.

Rana, J. 2011. *Terrifying Muslims: Race and Labor in the South Asian Diaspora*, chap. 1. Durham, NC: Duke University Press.

Ríos-Rojas, A. 2014. "Managing and Disciplining Diversity: The Politics of Conditional Belonging in a Catalonian Institute." *Anthropology and Education Quarterly* 45 (1): 2–22.

Robbins, B. 2012. *Perpetual War: Cosmopolitanism from the Viewpoint of Violence*. Durham, NC: Duke University Press.

Rosaldo, R. 1994. "Cultural Citizenship and Educational Democracy." *Cultural Anthropology* 9: 402–11.

Rubin, B. C. 2007. "'There's Still No Justice': Youth Civic Identity Development amid Distinct School and Community Contexts." *Teachers College Record* 109 (2): 449–81.

———. 2012. *Making Citizens: Transforming Civic Learning for Diverse Social Studies Classrooms*. New York: Routledge.

Rubin, B. C., and B. Hayes. 2010. "No Backpacks versus 'Drugs and Murder': The Promise and Complexity of Youth Civic Action Research." *Harvard Educational Review* 30 (3): 352–78.

Rumbaut, R. G. 2002. "Severed or Sustained Attachments? Language, Identity, and Imagined Communities in the Post-immigrant Generation." In *The Changing Face of Home: The Transnational Lives of the Second Generation*, edited by P. Levitt and M. C. Waters, 43–95. New York: Russell Sage Foundation.

Sa'di, A. H., and L. Abu-Lughod, eds. 2007. *Nakba: Palestine, 1948, and the Claims of Memory*. New York: Columbia University Press.

Said, E. W. 1978. *Orientalism*. New York: Vintage Books.

———. 1979. *The Question of Palestine*. New York: Vintage Books.

———. 1994. *The Politics of Dispossession: The Struggle for Palestinian Self-Determination, 1969–1994*. New York: Vintage Books.

———. 2001. "The Clash of Ignorance." *Nation* 273 (12): 11–13.

Samhan, H. H. 1999. "Not Quite White: Race Classification and the Arab American Experience." In *Arabs in America: Building a New Future*, edited by M. Suleiman, 209–26. Philadelphia: Temple University Press.

Sánchez, P. 2007. "Urban Immigrant Students: How Transnationalism Shapes Their World Learning." *Urban Review* 39 (5): 489–517.

Sánchez, P., and G. S. Kasun. 2012. "Connecting Transnationalism to the Classroom and to Theories of Immigrant Student Adaptation." *Berkeley Review of Education* 3 (1): 71–93.

Sarroub, L. K. 2001. "The Sojourner Experience of Yemeni American High School Students: An Ethnographic Portrait." *Harvard Educational Review* 71 (3): 390–412.

———. 2005. *All American Yemeni Girls: Being Muslim in Public Schools*. Philadelphia: University of Pennsylvania Press.

Sarroub, L., T. Pernicek, and T. Sweeney. 2007. "'I Was Bitten by a Scorpion': Reading in and out of School in a Refugee's Life." *Journal of Adolescent and Adult Literacy* 8 (50): 668–79.

Schiffauer, W., G. Baumann, R. Kastoryano, and S. Vertovec, eds. 2004. *Civil Enculturation: Nation-State, School and Ethnic Difference in The Netherlands, Britain, Germany, and France*. New York: Berhahn Books.

Schiffauer, W., and T. Sunier. 2004. "Representing the Nation in History Textbooks." In *Civil Enculturation: Nation-State, School and Ethnic Difference in The Netherlands, Britain, Germany, and France*, edited by W. Schiffauer, G. Baumann, R. Kastoryano, and S. Vertovec, 33–59. New York: Berhahn Books.

Schulz, H. L., with J. Hammer. 2003. *The Palestinian Diaspora: Formation of Identities and Politics of Homeland*. London: Routledge.

Scott, J. 2007. *Politics of the Veil*. Princeton, NJ: Princeton University Press.

Seif, H. 2011. "'Unapologetic and Unafraid': Immigrant Youth Come Out from the Shadows." In *Youth Civic Development: Work at the Cutting Edge*, edited by C. A. Flanagan and B. D. Christens. *New Directions for Child and Adolescent Development*, no. 134: 59–75.

Shryock, A. 2008. "The Moral Analogies of Race: Arab American Identity, Color Politics, and the Limits of Racialized Citizenship." In *Race and Arab Americans before and after 9/11: From Invisible Citizens to Visible Subjects*, edited by A. Jamal and N. Naber, 81–112. Syracuse, NY: Syracuse University Press.

Sirin, S., and M. Fine. 2008. *Muslim American Youth: Understanding Hyphenated Identities through Multiple Methods*. New York: New York University Press.

Smith, R. 1988. "The 'American Creed' and American Identity: The Limits of Liberal Citizenship in the United States." *Western Political Quarterly* 41 (2): 225–51.

Somers, M. 2008. *Genealogies of Citizenship: Markets, Statelessness, and the Right to Have Rights*. Cambridge: Cambridge University Press.

Soysal, Y. N. 1994. *Limits of Citizenship: Migrants and Postnational Membership in Europe*. Chicago: University of Chicago Press.

Stockton, R. R. 2009. "Civil Liberties and Foreign Policy." In Detroit Arab American Study Team, *Citizenship and Crisis: Arab Detroit after 9/11*, 193–262. New York: Russell Sage.

Stoler, A. L. 2006. "Intimations of Empire: Predicaments of the Tactile and Unseen." In *Haunted by Empire: Geographies of Intimacy in North American History*, edited by A. L. Stoler, 1–22. Durham, NC: Duke University Press.

Suárez-Orozco, M. M. 1987. "'Becoming Somebody': Central American Immigrants in U.S. Inner-City Schools." *Anthropology and Education Quarterly* 18 (4): 287–99.

———. 2001. "Globalization, Immigration, and Education: The Research Agenda." *Harvard Educational Review* 71 (3): 345–65.

Suárez-Orozco, C., H. J. Bang, and H. Y. Kim. 2011. "'I Felt Like My Heart Was Staying Behind': Psychological Implications of Family Separations and Reunifications for Immigrant Youth." *Journal of Adolescent Research* 26 (2): 222–57.

Suárez-Orozco, C., M. M. Suárez-Orozco, and I. Todorova. 2008. *Learning a New Land: Immigrant Students in American Society.* Cambridge, MA: Harvard University Press.

Suleiman, M. 2002. "Stereotypes, Public Opinion, and Foreign Policy: The Impact on Arab-American Relations." *Journal of Arab Affairs* (April): 147–66.

Sunier, T. 2004. "Argumentative Strategies." In *Civil Enculturation: Nation-State, School and Ethnic Difference in The Netherlands, Britain, Germany, and France,* edited by W. Schiffauer, G. Baumann, R. Kastoryano, and S. Vertovec, 147–63. New York: Berhahn Books.

Tamari, S. 1999. *Who Are the Arabs? The Arab World in the Classroom,* 1–12. Washington, DC: Center for Contemporary Arab Studies, Georgetown University.

Tamir, Y. 1993. *Liberal Nationalism.* Princeton, NJ: Princeton University Press.

Taylor, C. 1992. *Multiculturalism and the "Politics of Recognition."* Princeton, NJ: Princeton University Press.

———. 2002. "Modern Social Imaginaries." *Public Culture* 14 (1): 91–124.

Tetrault, C. 2013. "Cultural Citizenship in France and le Bled among Teens of Pan-southern Heritage." *Language and Communication* 33 (4): 532–43.

Tocci, Nathalie. 2010. "The EU and the Palestinian-Arab Minority in Israel." Brussels: Euro-Mediterranean Human Rights Network. http://adalah.org/Public/files/English/International_Advocacy/EUArabMinorityReport.pdf.

Valenzuela, A. 1999. *Subtractive Schooling: U.S.-Mexican Youth and the Politics of Caring.* Albany: State University of New York Press.

Vertovec, S. 1999. "Conceiving and Researching Transnationalism." *Ethnic and Racial Studies* 22 (2): 447–62.

Volpp, L. 2002. "The Citizen and the Terrorist." *UCLA Law Review* 49 (June): 1575–1600.

Waldinger, R. 2008. "Between 'Here' and 'There': Immigrants' Cross-Border Activities and Loyalties." *International Migration Review* 42 (1): 3–29.

———. Forthcoming. "Beyond Transnationalism: An Alternate Perspective on Immigrants' Homeland Connections." In *Oxford Handbook of International Relations,* edited by M. Rosenblum and D. Tichenor.

Waldinger, R., and D. Fitzgerald. 2004. "Transnationalism in Question." *American Journal of Sociology* 109 (5): 1177–95.

Wemyss, G. 2009. *The Invisible Empire: White Discourse, Tolerance, and Belonging.* Surrey, England: Ashgate.

Winant, H. 2004. *The New Politics of Race: Globalism, Difference, Justice.* Minneapolis: University of Minnesota Press.

Wolf, D. L. 2002. "There's No Place Like 'Home': Emotional Transnationalism and the Struggles of Second-Generation Filipinos." In *The Changing Face of Home: The Transnational Lives of the Second Generation,* edited by P. Levitt and M. C. Waters, 255–94. New York: Russell Sage Foundation.

Wray-Lake, L., A. K. Syversten, and C. A. Flanagan. 2008. "Contested Citizenship and Social

Exclusion: Adolescent Arab American Immigrants' Views of the Social Contract." *Applied Developmental Science* 12 (2): 84–92.

Young, I. M. 2000. *Inclusion and Democracy.* Oxford: Oxford University Press.

Yuval-Davis, N. 2011. *The Politics of Belonging: Intersectional Contestations.* London: SAGE.

Yuval-Davis, N., F. Anthias, and E. Kofman. 2005. "Secure Borders and Safe Haven and the Gendered Politics of Belonging: Beyond Social Cohesion." *Ethnic and Racial Studies* 28 (3): 513–35.

Zhou, M. 1997. "Growing Up American: The Challenge Confronting Immigrant Children and the Children of Immigrants." *Annual Review of Sociology* 23: 63–95.

Zine, J. 2001. "Muslim Youth in Canadian Schools: Education and the Politics of Religious Identity." *Anthropology and Education Quarterly* 32 (4): 399–423.

———. 2006. "Unveiled Sentiments: Gendered Islamophobia and Experiences of Veiling among Muslim Girls in a Canadian Islamic School." *Equity and Excellence in Education* 39: 239–52.

Zuñiga, V., and E. T. Hamann. 2009. "Sojourners in Mexico with U.S. School Experience: A New Taxonomy for Transnational Students." *Comparative Education Review* 53 (3): 329–53.

Index

nationalist iconography, 54
nation building, immigrant education and, 6n7
neoliberalism, 115n8
neutrality, politics of, 168–69
Ngai, M., 3n4, 6, 77, 104, 207
Nogeuron, S. C., 3n5
Nussbaum, M., 104

Obama, Barack, Cairo speech of, 136
Occupied Palestinian Territories, 24–25, 26; Israeli
     settlement of, 53; living in, 70–71, 74–76, 87–96;
     permission to return to, 48–49
Ogbu, J., 72, 98
O'Leary, C., 105
Olneck, M., 6n7
Olsen, L., 6, 9, 21, 41, 61, 66
Olympic athletes, dissent of, 195–96
Omi, M., 114, 144
Ong, A., 4, 43, 52n5, 53, 78, 97
Orientalism, 11, 110, 172
Oslo Accords, 13–14, 26–27, 182n4; return to
     homeland with, 48–49
Other, 6; advocating for, 216–18; dangerous, 5;
     illiberality of, 151–52; imaginary of, 150–58;
     imagining lives of, 193; Palestinian youth as,
     194–96; problematic, 11–13; racialized, 32–34,
     150, 178, 205–6, 222; US nationalism and, 8–9
Othering discourses, 205–6
Otherness, discursive constructions of, 179–80
Other places: belonging to, 172–73, 196–202; as
     illiberal and violent, 140, 144, 204–5; imaginary
     of, 150–58
Ottoman Empire, 22
outsider/insider categories, creation of, 33
outsiders, 33, 192; Muslims and Arabs as, 206–7.
     See also boundaries: insider/outsider; exclusion

Pahlavi, Mohammad Reza (Shah of Iran), 122
Palestine: association with terrorism, 124, 132–
     33; banning symbols of, 185–87; cultures of,
     214–15; desire to return to, 53–54; existence of,
     179–87; film about, 221; history of, 21–28; as
     idyllic land, 58–60; as intimate, moral space,
     53–60; sense of belonging to, 210–12; suffering,
     struggle, and sacrifice in, 67–72; United Na-
     tions and, 22–23; village life in, 50–51, 56–58.
     See also Occupied Palestinian Territories
Palestine Liberation Organization (PLO), 25–26
Palestinian American youth: American identity
     of, 40–41; as enemy aliens, 173–79; exclusion of,
     198–99; geopolitical conflicts affecting, 162–63;
     as "impossible subjects," 3, 6, 104–7, 202; intoler-
     ance of, 148–49; as outsiders, 187–88, 194–96;
     Palestinian identity of, 45–47; racializing of, 3–9,
     11–14, 32–34, 72–73, 94, 106–7, 205–7, 222; social

identities of, 3; struggle for national identity of,
     39–73; transnational experience of, 96–100
Palestinian Authority, 26
Palestinian community, belonging to, 3–4
Palestinian diaspora, 27, 43–44, 67
Palestinian flag: banning of, 185–87; dancing with,
     200–201
Palestinian-Israeli conflict, 13–14; expressing
     political perspectives on, 185–86; lack of edu-
     cation about, 180–81; politics of, 182–83; in US
     curriculum, 128–31; US policy in, 193
Palestinian Muslim transnational community,
     17–19
Palestinian national identity: ancestral descent
     in, 54; building, 48–53; cultural authenticity
     in, 60–67; folk arts and, 54–55; maintaining,
     44; meaning of, 45–47; religious practices in,
     62–65; rooted in memories, 56–58; symbols
     of, 54; through family stories, 55–56; through
     language, 58n9; through religious identity, 61
Palestinian national imaginary, 10, 19, 45–47, 53–
     56, 73, 97–98, 104, 210–11. *See also* belonging:
     being Palestinian and
Palestinian nationalist movement, 67–72
Palestinian resistance, 25–26. *See also* intifada
Palestinians: dispossession of, 24–25; exclusion
     of, 6–7; film about, 213–16; as illiberal subjects,
     140; racialization of, 6–7, 171–72; refugee status
     of, 3n5, 23–24; self-determination struggle
     of, 40
Pappe, I., 23n21
Parker, W. C., 166–67
passions, taming, 165–67
PATRIOT Act, Titles I and II, 77–78
patriotism, 104–5
peace, advocating for, 213–16
Pease, D., 7, 111, 112, 119, 133–34, 135, 149, 208
Pledge of Allegiance: as banal nationalism, 170,
     172–73, 189–90; legislation requiring recitation
     of, 172; question of, 188–93; refusing to stand
     for, 170–3, 174, 199
PLO acronym, banning of, 182, 190
political consciousness, 70–71, 74–76
political rights, 97
Pollock, M., 142
Portes, A., 10, 72
post-Cold War era: ideology of, 5; Muslim world
     in, 8
Puar, J. K., 111, 207

race, as transnational phenomenon, 12–13
racial/ethnic tensions, failure to address, 188–90
racial exclusion, 144
racial formations: global, 10–14, 137, 140–41, 179;
     US, 10–14

Speaker Questions

1. What are aspects of curriculum that need change or improvements to embrace identity & belonging?
2. After school club — too inclusive w/ own community?
3.

~~~~~~

Abu-El Haj Interview

- immigrants form transnational ties through their communities across the nation
- across multiple groups, youth are forging solidarity among causes
- Salad Bowl vs. Melting Pot

A political — MP - assimilation & losing cultural identities; blend in
    — SB - multi-culturalism
    — Neither model has reckoning for different political landscapes
- We are growing up in war time yet youth generally do NOT recognize this.
    — It would help build understanding for why people immigrate or leave country.
    — Issue is global so solution needs to be global.
- Us vs. Them
    - Not in human nature
    - Racialized community has prejudice against
    - Lack opportunity to engage in diversity (ex-segregated schools; not present in curriculum)

How do im/migrant youth develop perform, & negotiate identities across transnational social fields?
    - transnational - being Palestinian in US.
    - search for opportunities to learn about culture (ex-take class)

Pt. II Discussion - Politics of Belonging

- Everyday bids for citizenship
    - Pledge of Allegiance ...?

Made in the USA
Middletown, DE
03 September 2021